CHAUCER IN CONTEXT

MANCHESTER MEDIEVAL STUDIES

SERIES EDITOR Dr S. H. Rigby

SERIES ADVISORS Professor J. H. Denton
Professor R. B. Dobson Professor L. K. Little

The study of medieval Europe is being transformed as old orthodoxies
are challenged, new methods embraced and fresh fields of inquiry
opened up. The adoption of inter-disciplinary perspectives and the
challenge of economic, social and cultural theory are forcing medievalists
to ask new questions and to see familiar topics in a fresh light.

    The aim of this series is to combine the scholarship traditionally
associated with medieval studies with an awareness of more recent
issues and approaches in a form accessible to the non-specialist reader.

FORTHCOMING TITLES IN THE SERIES

English society and the Hundred Years War
Ann Curry

The reign of King Stephen
Paul Dalton

*Between God and the devil: picturing women
in late medieval and Renaissance art*
Christa Grossinger

Political society in fifteenth-century England
M. A. Hicks

The twelfth-century Renaissance
Robert Swanson

How Christian was medieval Europe?
Norman Tanner

*The commercialisation of
English society, 1000-1500*
(revised edition) R. H. Britnell

Money in the medieval economy
J. L. Bolton

MANCHESTER MEDIEVAL STUDIES

CHAUCER IN CONTEXT

SOCIETY, ALLEGORY AND GENDER

S. H. Rigby

Manchester University Press

Manchester and New York

distributed exclusively in the USA by St. Martin's Press

Published by Manchester University Press
Oxford Road, Manchester M13 9NR, UK
and Room 400, 175 Fifth Avenue, New York, NY 10010, USA

Distributed exclusively in the USA
by St. Martin's Press, Inc., 175 Fifth Avenue, New York, NY 10010, USA

British Library Cataloguing-in-Publication Data
A catalogue record is available from the British Library

Library of Congress Cataloging-in-Publication Data
Rigby, S. H. (Stephen Henry), 1955–
    Chaucer in context — (Manchester medieval studies)
        Includes bibliographical references.
    ISBN 0-7190-4235-6. — ISBN 0-7190-4236-4 (pbk)
        1. Chaucer, Geoffrey, d. 1400—Political and social views.
2. Chaucer, Geoffrey, d. 1400—Contemporary England. 3. Chaucer,
Geoffrey, d. 1400—Canterbury tales. 4. Literature and society—England—
History. 5. Civilization, Medieval—14th century. 6. England—Civilization
—1066-1485. 7. Social problems in literature. 8. Sex role in literature.
9. Allegory. I. Title. II. Series.
PR1933.S59R54   1966
82T'.1—dc20   96-20883

ISBN 0 7190 4235 6 *hardback*
     0 7190 4236 4 *paperback*

First published 1996
00 99 98 97 96   10 9 8 7 6 5 4 3 2 1

Typset in Monotype Bulmer
by Koinonia Limited, Manchester
Printed in Great Britain
by Bell & Bain Limited, Glasgow

CONTENTS

ABBREVIATIONS

All references to Chaucer's works are from L. D. Benson, ed., *The Riverside Chaucer* (Oxford, 1989) and are cited in the text by an abbreviated form of the title with a page or line reference. All other works are cited by its author or editor and date, with page numbers where appropriate. A full bibliography of references appears at the end of this volume. All biblical quotations are taken from Bishop Challoner's Douay–Rheims translation.

ABBREVIATIONS USED IN TEXT AND NOTES

ABC	*An ABC*
Bo	*Boece*
BS	*Biblia Sacra cum Glossa Ordinaria* (Antwerp, 1634)
CA	John Gower, *Confessio Amantis*, in G. C. Macaulay, ed., *The English Works of John Gower*, vols I and II (EETS, Extra Series, vols 81 (1900) and 82 (1902)).
CL	*A Complaint to his Lady*
CM	*The Complaint of Mars*
CP	*The Complaint of Chaucer to his Purse*
CT	*The Canterbury Tales*
DC	J. D. Sinclair, ed., *The Divine Comedy of Dante Alighieri, vol. I: Inferno* (New York, 1961).
EETS	Early English Text Society
Fo	*Fortune*
HF	*The House of Fame*
IPP	John Gower, 'In Praise of Peace', in G. C. Macaulay, ed., *The English Works of John Gower*, vol. II (EETS, Extra Series, vol. 82 (1902))
LB	*Lenvoy de Chaucer a Bukton*
LGW	*The Legend of Good Women*
MO	*Mirour de l'Omme*, in G. C. Macaulay, ed., *The Complete Works of John Gower: the French Works* (Oxford, 1899)
PF	*The Parliament of Fowls*
PL	*Patrologia Latina*, ed. J. P. Migne, 221 volumes, Paris 1841–1905
PPB	William Langland, *The Vision of Piers the Plowman: A Compete Edition of the B-Text*, ed. A. V. C. Schmidt (London, 1989)

QR   *La Querelle de la Rose: Letters and Documents* (*North Carolina Studies in the Romance Languages and Literature,* 199 (1978), eds J. L. Baird and J. R. Kane

ST   *Lydgate's Siege of Thebes,* ed. A. Erdmann, Parts I and II (EETS, Extra Series, vols 108 (1911) and 125 (1930)

TC   *Troilus and Criseyde*

VC   John Gower, *Vox Clamantis* in G. C. Macaulay, ed., *The Complete Works of John Gower, vol. IV: the Latin Works* (Oxford, 1902)

PREFACE

As an historian, my primary purpose in writing this book has not been that of most works of literary criticism, i.e., to generate new interpretations of Chaucer's works: we already have an excess of readings of Chaucer available to us. Rather, my aim has been to survey competing approaches to understanding medieval literature in its historical context; to put the case for each of them in as persuasive a fashion as possible; to assess the relative merits of these approaches; and to discuss how we can reconcile or decide between the wildly divergent interpretations of Chaucer's work which they produce. Although as an historian I am primarily concerned with the social meaning of Chaucer's work, the approach adopted here is by no means intended to transform the brilliant and complex poetry of the *Canterbury Tales* into a mere political tract. After all, we do not primarily read Chaucer today because of his theology, social theory or political beliefs but rather because of his ability to bring together an unparalleled range of inherited genres, from the epic and the saint's life to the *fabliau* and the animal-fable, and, in the process, to rework and transform them into new and more sophisticated forms. Any historical criticism will be damned if it ignores this achievement and simply reduces the bricks of great literature to the straw of sociological analysis.[1] But what an historical perspective *can* provide is an awareness that the bricks of Chaucer's literature were intended to construct an edifice with purposes which were often very different from those which we today expect of works of art. It emphasises that the concepts of society and of 'human nature' contained in works of literature, and even the very notion of literature itself, are never natural or eternal but are always specific according to time and place and thus capable of being analysed in historical terms.

Certainly, in the late fourteenth century itself, poetry was not seen simply as a vehicle for expressing personal feelings (although, of course, personal and emotional experiences are themselves always shot through with socially and historically specific values and assumptions). Instead, poetry was used to discuss a wide range of contemporary questions, such as the nature of good kingship, the failings of the Church or the conduct of the war in France, the kind of problems which we today might explore in various forms of non-literary prose such as newspaper articles or polemical pamphlets. More generally, medieval literary theory, as we shall see below (Chapter 3), regarded poetry as a branch of ethics and thus saw it as intimately connected with political, social and gender issues since medieval writers themselves saw such issues as questions of personal morality. It is not just modern critics who wish to look at the social significance of literature: the medieval period itself blurred the distinction between literature, ethics, politics and social theory. More specifically, in the case of the *Canterbury Tales*, a work which opens with a panoramic survey of contemporary social types, we do not have to decide between analysing literary form on the one hand and looking at social meaning on the other. On the contrary, what is at issue is the question of how Chaucer's choice of literary form, such as his adoption of a multiplicity of different voices, his use of first-person monologues and his use of particular generic conventions, generates specific social meanings. Thus, whilst I have every sympathy with Walker's rejection of modern attempts to psychoanalyse Chaucer's fictional characters as though they were real people, it does *not* follow that the academic study of medieval literature must confine itself to the study of a work's 'textual devices' and 'verbal constructs'. We cannot restrict an analysis of Chaucer's texts to how he achieved particular literary effects (suspense, comedy, a sense of character etc.) but will also be interested in how his use of specific textual devices is related to the overall meaning and social significance of his work, including its view of human nature, its social and political assumptions, and its religious attitudes.[2]

Anyone who seeks an understanding of the social meaning of the *Canterbury Tales* is struck immediately by the contradictory and mutually exclusive interpretations of Chaucer's work which modern literary critics have put forward. One the one hand, Chaucer's work is seen as providing a mirror of his age, one which reflects the social reality of late medieval England. On the other, his social vision is portrayed as the product of traditional, even centuries-old, concepts and conventions (see Chapter 1, below). For some critics, Chaucer was a defender of contemporary social inequalities; for others, he unmasked contemporary justifications of inequality as social ideology (Chapter 2). Many of those who see Chaucer as a social conservative argue that his work depends upon the traditional methods of Augustinian allegory; by constrast, those who oppose them claim that Chaucer himself parodied the techniques of such allegorization (Chapter 3). This debate extends to Chaucer's views on society's gender relations and inequalities, with some critics asserting that Chaucer reproduced the misogyny common to his age whilst others characterise him as a proto-feminist in his sexual politics (Chapter 4).

In order to choose between such mutually exclusive interpretations of a particular work, critics often call for an historically informed reading of it. Locating a text within the broader context of contemporary social relations, religious beliefs, notions of gender and so on might allow us to arrive at a consensus about what would constitute a plausible interpretation of the author's

meaning: 'our reading needs to be informed by a serious attempt to recon-
struct the text's moment of production, its own contexts of discourse and
social practices within and for which it achieved meaning'. Seeing Chaucer in
the context of the social conflicts, political strife, religious controversies,
thought-structures, literary conventions and iconographic traditions of his
own day seems, to many critics, to provide at least the possibility of deciding
which interpretations of his work are to be preferred. Reading Chaucer historically might allow us to reach 'some degree of certainty in literary interpretation' even if it cannot generate an 'authoritative, never-to-be-disputed
reading of Chaucer's text'.[3] Yet, immediately, we are faced with the problem
that there are a number of rival and mutually incompatible historical
approaches on offer to us: historical context provides no easy court of interpretive appeal, not least because the provision of a context in which to understand
any work is itself the result of a process of interpretation. The main purpose of
this book is to use the works of Chaucer, particularly the *Canterbury Tales*, to
illustrate the range of contextual approaches to medieval literature which are
now available to us and to provide an assessment of such competing perspectives. I have thus approached Chaucer's work on the assumption that, as
Pearsall puts it, 'no writer can withdraw himself from the social and cultural
practices in which his existence as an individual and the language that he uses
are embedded'.[4] However, in turn, this claim applies as much to historians
and to literary critics as it does to the authors whom they study. My own political and religious prejudices will doubtless soon become apparent to the reader
but, nevertheless, I have tried here to avoid either demonstrating that Chaucer
was lucky enough to have anticipated the wisdom of my own views by six
centuries or berating him for having failed to do so: 'the historian is not a
judge, still less a hanging judge'.[5] As George Eliot once said, 'we cannot
reform our forefathers'; my aim here is to understand Chaucer, not to reform
him.

I would like to express my gratitude to a number of scholars for their willingness to comment on earlier versions of this book: Alastair Minnis provided
reassurance about the argument set out in Chapter 2 when it was particularly
needed; David Shepherd and Carole Weinberg also helped to clarify the
structure of this chapter; Jeff Denton offered extremely useful advice on Chapter 3; and Lesley Johnson was kind enough to read and to comment on the
whole book even though she can scarcely have agreed with a word of it.
Richard Davies is owed particular thanks for his exacting criticisms of both my
logic and prose style. Finally, above all, I would like to thank Rosalind Brown-
Grant who read many versions of the book in draft and suggested innumerable
improvements to both its content and the presentation of its case. Naturally, all
of those named above are absolved of any responsibility for what follows.

Notes

1 Wood, 1995.
2 Walker, 1985.
3 Minnis, 1982: v; Aers, 1986a: 1-2, 6-7; Aers, 1988a: 3-4; Knight, 1986: 3, 5-6; Pearsall, 1986: 123-4; Knapp, 1990: 1-2.
4 Patterson, 1987: 43-4, 150-2; Pearsall, 1992: 244; Pearsall, 1986.
5 Carr, 1970: 77 quoting D. Knowles.

Chaucer: real-life observation versus literary convention

> 'And out of olde bokes, in good feyth,
> Cometh al this newe science that men lere'. (*PF*, 24-5)

CHAUCER'S lifetime, from his birth early in the 1340s to his death in 1400, encompasses one of the most dramatic periods of English history.[1] Economically, this was a period of disruption and change, as the Black Death (1348-9) and later outbreaks of plague reduced England's population by almost a half between 1348 and 1377. Socially, this was a time of intense conflict. At a local level, peasants and workers attempted to take advantage of the new shortage of tenants and labourers to obtain better terms of tenure and higher wages. At a national level, during the Peasants' Revolt of 1381, peasant rebels seized the capital, killed the Treasurer and Chancellor and demanded the end of serfdom. Politically, this was an age of dissension with, from the 1370s, virulent criticism of the conduct of the war with France, of the administration of the royal household and of the policies pursued by Edward III (1327-77), Richard II (1377-99) and their ministers. In religion too, this was a time of controversy and strife. The European Church as a whole was riven by the papal schism of 1378-1417 in which western Christendom was confronted with two popes, one at Avignon and one at Rome, and eventually even with three papal claimants. Within England itself, anti-clerical sentiment was at its pre-Reformation peak and received its most extreme expression in the heretical doctrines of John Wyclif and his Lollard followers, doctrines which provided an all-out attack on the wealth, power and status enjoyed by the clerical estate and which were to find a sympathetic audience even amongst some members of the royal court.

As the son of a London vintner, a member of royal and aristocratic households, a civil servant and a diplomat, Geoffrey Chaucer enjoyed a privileged vantage-point at the intersection of a number of social worlds:

London and its merchants, the English nobility and county gentry, the court of Richard II, and the European courts.[2] Indeed, the political affairs, military and diplomatic problems, social conflicts and religious divisions of the time were an immediate force in Chaucer's own life. The Essex peasants burst into London in June 1381 through the Aldgate where he was then living. He fought and was captured in the Hundred Years War and was present in Calais in 1360 for the ratification of the Treaty of Brétigny with France. He attracted rewards from Richard II, John of Gaunt and Henry Bolingbroke. His fortunes may have received a set-back after 1386 because of his status as one of the fringe-members of the court party but then revived in 1389 when Richard II reasserted his power. His diplomatic mission to Milan in 1378 may have involved discussions of the effects of the papal schism. He was the friend of 'Lollard knights' at court, such as Lewis Clifford, John Montagu, and John Clanvowe.

What was the relationship between Chaucer's poetry and the change and conflict characteristic of his day? How can we locate the work of Chaucer in its contemporary context? A common approach to answering such questions is to see literature as a 'mirror' which passively 'reflects' the reality of its age, the assumption being that the mirror has 'no tendency of its own'. Chaucer's 'positive depictions of merchants and master-craftsmen' cannot, it has been argued, 'simply be taken as stereotypes' but were 'a genuine reflection of reality'.[3] The problem with this view of literature as the mirror of contemporary experience is that, as anyone who has ever been to a fairground hall of mirrors knows, what we see in the mirror is as much the product of the mirror's own properties as it is of the object reflected. In other words, no experience is self-interpreting but is always actively interpreted and formulated according to particular theories, prejudices, categories, conventions and concepts.[4] Certainly, Chaucer himself was not only the observer of a number of social worlds but was also well-read in the works of classical authors, (although he would frequently have read Latin works such as those of Ovid and Boethius in French translation or in *florilegia* such as John of Wales's *Communiloquium*),[5] in the Bible and the Church Fathers, in medieval science, theology and philosophy, and in the literature of contemporary France and Italy. When Chaucer presents himself to us, it is usually as a 'fanatic bibliophile' and as 'conspicuously bookish'.[6] How useful is it to see Chaucer's works as holding up a mirror to life (section i)? What sorts of literary and non-literary conventions were at his disposal for making sense of the society around him (section ii)?

(i) 'Real-life' Chaucer

Traditionally, much historically inclined Chaucer criticism has been concerned to supply the background information necessary for the modern reader to grasp the connotations of words, figures and allusions which Chaucer could take for granted on the part of his readers. A classic instance is Bowden's indispensable work which provides a knowledge of many of the ideas, customs and institutions of Chaucer's England needed to make sense of the 'General Prologue' to the *Canterbury Tales*.[7] However, this concern to see Chaucer's work in its contemporary context can sometimes lead to a view of his poetry as implicitly or explicitly dealing with actual historical episodes or real-life characters. Since Chaucer does, on occasion, explicitly allude to actual historical events, as in the long list of battle honours in his description of the Knight, critics have even been tempted into interpreting the *Canterbury Tales* as political *romans à clef* which allude to contemporary political occurrences. The search for actual events underlying Chaucer's poetry certainly has a long history behind it. In a infamous example from 1924, Hotson claimed that the description of Russell the fox as a 'colfox' and Chauntecleer's repeated insistence that 'murder will out' in the 'Nun's Priest's Tale' were intended as references to a Nicholas Colfox who, along with his master, Thomas Mowbray, Duke of Norfolk, was involved in the murder of the Duke of Gloucester in 1397. The descriptions of Chauntecleer and Russell are then seen as referring to the colours borne by Mowbray and Bolingbroke in their trial by combat of 1398, which means that the 'Nun's Priest's Tale' must have been written shortly after these events, perhaps in October or November 1398.[8] This approach continues to be adopted by some modern critics, whether in seeing specific references within the tales as allusions to contemporary events, such as Hamel's identification of Jankyn's remark in the 'Wife of Bath's Prologue' about adulterous wives who kill their husbands in their own beds as a reference to a notorious murder of 1387-8,[9] or as a key to the broader meaning of the tales. Thus, in *The Age of Saturn*, a fascinating and all-too-rare example of collaboration between an historian and a literary scholar, Brown and Butcher suggest that 'at every stage of the narrative of the "Merchant's Tale" (in which the elderly January is deceived by his young wife, May), 'there is the thinly veiled presence' of the relationship between the elderly Edward III and his mistress, Alice Perrers, a relationship which the late fourteenth century took as emblematic of contemporary social and political crisis. Similarly, they see the events of the 'Knight's Tale' as 'framed' by key events in Richard II's reign, in particular those of the period 1386 to 1397. The tale begins with the return of Theseus to Athens, an allusion to John of Gaunt's return from Spain and Portugal in 1389; continues with the conflict of Palamon and Arcite, identified respectively as Richard II and Thomas, Duke of Gloucester; and concludes with the marriage of Palamon to Emily, which can be seen as the marriage of Richard II and Isabella of France in 1396.[10]

More specifically, the search for a historical Chaucer has led critics to look for the 'real-life models' of the pilgrims described by Chaucer in the *Canterbury Tales*. This approach is traditionally associated with J. M. Manly, whose work, in its day, offered a welcome emphasis on the need to see Chaucer in a historical context. Perhaps the most famous example of this identification of one of Chaucer's pilgrims with a real-life model is Harry Bailly, the 'Host' who greets the pilgrims when they gather at the Tabard Inn in Southwark and then leads them to Canterbury (*CT*, I: 20, 747-57, 4358). In fact, a 'Henry Bailly' was one of the burgesses for Southwark summoned to the parliaments of 1376 and 1378 and a man of that name was listed as an 'ostyler' (keeper of a hostelry) in the Southwark poll-tax return of 1380-1. For at least some of the pilgrims, Chaucer seemed to Manly to be offering naturalistic 'portraits drawn from living models'. Some of Manly's identifications of the pilgrims continue to be adopted by modern critics, as when Kolve accepts that the claim made about the Sergeant of Law in the 'General Prologue' that 'Ther koude no wight pynche at his writyng' (*CT*, I: 326) is a punning allusion to Thomas Pynchbek, a real-life Sergeant of the Law known to Chaucer.[11]

Nevertheless, even though medieval writers such as Dante could include contemporaries as characters in fictional works, attempts to identify historical events or real-life individuals in the narratives of the *Canterbury Tales* face a number of difficulties. Firstly, even if we assess the search for historical allusions on its own ground, we immediately come up against the problem of the dating of the tales, an issue about which we have very little evidence. For instance, since Brown and Butcher see the 'Knight's Tale' as including references to the parliament of 1397, they therefore have to defend a dating of the tale to the '1390s'.[12] Yet Chaucer had written a 'book' of 'the love of Palamon and Arcite' (which is now lost) by the time of *The Legend of Good Women* (*LGW*, F: 417-21; G: 405-9), which probably dates Chaucer's earliest version of the work to before 1386, with a likely date of the early 1380s. Moreover, there are a number of indications that this original version of the tale underwent little revision for its inclusion in the *Canterbury Tales*, as when the Knight refers to himself as 'writing' or 'endyting' the tale he is narrating (*CT*, I: 1201, 1209, 1380, 2741).[13] That the

'Knight's Tale' originally had a different narrator may also explain why the Knight as narrator of the tale himself claims to have seen ('Ther saugh I') the Temples of Mars and of Diana built by Theseus, a claim which otherwise seems an example of his 'tendency towards self-advertisement' (*CT*, I: 1995, 2005, 2011, 2073).[14] In other words, it is difficult to accept that the 'Knight's Tale' can refer to events of the 1390s if the tale was basically completed by 1386. An even more fundamental problem is why we should assume that the narrative of the 'Knight's Tale' was based on contemporary political events in the first place. After all, Palamon and Emily are not married in the 'Knight's Tale' because Richard II and Isabella married in 1396. They marry because Chaucer is following here the events of his major source, Boccaccio's *Il Teseida delle nozze d'Emelia* ('The Story of Theseus concerning the nuptials of Emily'),[15] written *c.* 1340, which, in turn, was based on Statius's *Thebaid*. It is certainly likely that readers of the late 1390s might have found resonances in the marriage of Palamon and Emily, which cemented the alliance between Thebes and Athens, with the marriage of Richard and Isabella, just as fifteenth-century readers might have seen it as a parallel for the marriage of Henry V to Princess Katherine of France arranged in the Treaty of Troyes (1420). But this is rather different from saying that the 'Knight's Tale' is a direct political satire in which the marriage of Emily and Palamon should be 'seen as' Richard's marriage to Isabella.[16]

If we do want to continue to relate Chaucer's work to specific historical events and characters, it may be most fruitful to examine the occasion which produced them or the patron by whom they were commissioned. For instance, the *Legend of Good Women*, which, we are told, was to be presented to Queen Anne (*LGW*, F: 496-7), has been seen as a eulogy of the bravery of Richard II's queen in her efforts to save Simon Burley from the anger of the Appellants, although it is not clear whether or not the poem was ever actually given to the queen. Nevertheless, only for the *Book of the Duchess*, which was probably written to commemorate the death of Blanche, Duchess of Lancaster and wife of John of Gaunt, is there any unanimity amongst critics on the occasion for which Chaucer was writing and it is even more difficult to link the *Canterbury Tales*, which were written over the period of the dozen years before Chaucer's death, with any particular patron or event.[17] It has been suggested that some of the works which Chaucer wrote as individual pieces but later included in the *Canterbury Tales* may originally have been intended for specific state occasions. For instance, the 'Prioress's Tale', with its reference to Little St Hugh of Lincoln (*CT*, VII: 684), has been associated with the visit of Richard II and Queen Anne to Lincoln in 1387 where they were enrolled amongst the members of the cathedral fraternity.[18] Yet, even if this were the case, the significance of a miracle of the Virgin read aloud by Chaucer at Lincoln would become very different once it was put into the mouth of the Prioress and placed in the fictional context of the tales told by the other pilgrims.

There are similar problems in attempts to see the pilgrims of the *Canterbury Tales* as based on real-life models. Firstly, since most of the pilgrims described in the 'General Prologue' are not named or given a place of origin, identifications of them with real-life individuals are necessarily speculative. Rickert and Bowden, for instance, suggested Gilbert Maghfeld of London, who was one of Chaucer's creditors, as the 'living prototype' for Chaucer's Merchant, although one suspects that the popularity of this identification rests on little more than the fact that the unique survival of one of Maghfeld's account books means we are particularly well informed about him.[19] Secondly, even if we accept that Chaucer's 'portraits' of the pilgrims were painted 'from life',[20] the pictures that resulted were at least as much the result of the descriptive conventions and forms of classification available to him as of the reality of the individuals concerned, just as portraits by Leonardo or Van Gogh produce rather different impressions of their real-life models according to the historically specific conventions of representation which they employ.

The temptation to interpret Chaucer's works as an immediate description of the world around him can be seen at the opening of the *Legend of Good Women*, which seems to shift us from the dusty world of the study to the richness of real life when Chaucer describes how, in May, he deserts his books to go out into the meadow where he seeks his favourite flower, the daisy (*LGW*, F: 36-57). Yet the cult of the daisy, the marguerite, was itself a well-established literary tradition, one Chaucer drew from French writers such as Machaut, Deschamps and Froissart: Chaucer's debt to literary convention is, ironically, nowhere more apparent than when he seems to be leaving the world of books behind, a world which he himself had then to return to in order to find 'adequate means to praise it artfully'.[21] Similarly, in the *Canterbury Tales*, Chaucer's descriptions of both the pilgrims and the characters within their tales are a number of steps removed from 'real life'. His achievement seems to result 'less from the sympathetic observation of personality than from a magisterial dispassionate deployment of inherited literary forms' and of a series of extra-literary conventions and concepts. In Chaucer's work, reading comes to have a priority over experience as literature provides the categories and concepts which allow us to recognise, shape and order our perceptions of life.

Chaucer's originality lies in bringing together his sources in specific combinations and, in particular, in the ways in which he developed and played with inherited conventions, rather than simply reproducing them in their traditional form.[22]

(ii) Scientific, literary and social stereotypes

What are the literary conventions and intellectual traditions which inform the presentation of the pilgrims and characters of the *Canterbury Tales*? Firstly, Chaucer's accounts of the pilgrims are often couched in terms of the stock 'scientific' stereotypes of his day and thus describe individuals in terms of the attributes thought appropriate to their age, astrological character and physiological make-up. Medieval scientific thought, the essentials of which are conveniently set out for us in Book VII of Gower's *Confessio Amantis*, believed that all matter was comprised of four basic elements: earth, water, fire and air, invisible essences or spirits which imparted attributes such as heat, weight and moistness to specific material substances. Within the human body, four humours correspond to the attributes of these four basic elements: 'black bile' or 'melancholy', corresponding to the coldness and dryness of the earth; phlegm, corresponding to the moistness and coldness of water; choler, corresponding to the dryness and heat of fire; and blood, corresponding to the warmth and moistness of the air. Each of these humours had its seat in a particular organ, giving rise to a particular 'complexion': the melancholic, phlegmatic, choleric and sanguine respectively. 'Complexion' in this context refers both to physical appearance *and* to temperament and character as determined by the individual's particular balance of humours.[23]

In turn, the balance of humours within the individual was held to be determined astrologically by the position of the seven 'planets' (the Moon, Mercury, Venus, the Sun, Mars, Jupiter and Saturn) as they moved around the earth through the twelve houses of the zodiac. The Moon, the watery planet, was associated with those of phlegmatic complexion; Mercury was associated with the melancholic, making people studious and bookish; Venus, the 'Planete of love', was associated with blood and those of sanguine complexion; the followers of the Sun are of good will and 'liberal' in character; the warlike Mars, 'the Planete bataillous' as Gower put it, was linked with the choleric; Jupiter, by contrast, was the planet of 'pes and no debat', those under its sway being soft, sweet, meek and patient; cold Saturn, the most distant of the planets, causes 'malice and crualte' to those under its influence. However, the influence of the planets was also determined by their position as they moved through the twelve houses of the zodiac. Each of these twelve houses was ruled by a particular planet, each planet having a specific house or houses as its 'home'. The Sun was at home in Leo, the Moon in Cancer, Mercury in Gemini and Virgo, Venus in Libra and Taurus, Mars in Aries and Scorpio, Saturn in Capricorn and Aquarius and Jupiter in Pisces and Sagittarius. In addition, each of the signs of the zodiac was itself associated with one of the four elements. The zodiacal year begins with Aries in March, followed by Taurus, Gemini, Cancer, Leo, Virgo, Libra, Scorpio, Sagittarius, Capricorn, Aquarius and Pisces, the qualities of fire, earth, air and water being ascribed to each of the signs in succession (thus fire applies to the first, fifth and ninth signs of the zodiac: Aries, Leo and Sagittarius). At any one time, six houses of the zodiac are visible passing across the sky, three rising over the eastern horizon and three declining towards the west. Whilst the houses of the zodiac complete their circuit annually, the orbits of the planets vary in length, that of Mars taking two years, that of Jupiter twelve. The position of the planets and stars at a person's birth, in particular the sign which is 'ascendant' (just rising over the eastern horizon) and the planet within it, are thus crucial for determining a person's character and fortunes. Finally, each planet was also associated with two further signs, one which was its 'exaltation', which particularly magnified its influence and one which was its 'depression' in which its influence was at its weakest.[24]

These stock physiological and astrological types can be seen at work in the pilgrims who gather at the Tabard. We are explicitly told, for instance, that the Franklin is 'sangwyn' in his complexion (*CT*, I: 333), which means that he was not just red-faced but also healthy, vigorous and confident. The Reeve, by contrast, is a 'colerik man' (*CT*, I: 587), which determines not only his physiognomy (he is 'sclendre') but also makes him sharp-witted, cunning, crafty, vengeful and lecherous.[25] In addition, the influence of the humours on an individual's complexion was also believed to be related to his or her age. Young people were believed to feel the influence of the blood, associated with the planet Venus and the houses of Libra and Taurus, whose moist and heat encourages the amorousness found in the Squire. By contrast, the bitter, aged Reeve, who terrifies those beneath him yet himself takes affront at the 'Miller's Tale', is presumably ruled by Saturn, which makes him easily offended and hard to please.[26]

One of the most detailed of the physiological descriptions in the 'General Prologue' is that of the Summoner, who has a fire-red face, swollen eyelids, black eyebrows, a beard with its hair falling out, a face covered in pustules and swellings of which children were afraid, and who loves garlic, onions, leeks and red wine (*CT*, I: 624-35). The Summoner's appearance and character have been interpreted as the product of a choleric complexion which tends to produce, as it has in his case, black hair and a red face along with personal qualities such as slyness, lasciviousness and a quickness to anger, as can be seen when the Summoner takes offence at the tale told by the Friar about a summoner taken off by a devil (*CT*, III: 1665-7). His swollen 'saucefleem' face is also physiological in origin, resulting from a mixture of choler with phlegm. His characteristics are linked to the influence of Mars, the planet which governs the choleric and whose influence, like that of the Summoner's diet, exacerbates the dryness and heat of his dominant humour. In addition to humoural physiognomy, in which the individual's character follows changes in the physical make-up of the body, medieval science also analysed character in terms of an affective physiognomy in which changes in the body result from the affections of the soul such as love, fear, grief and pleasure. Friedman argues that Chaucer tended to explain his lower-class characters in terms of humoural physiognomy, as in the case of the adulterous Alison in the 'Miller's Tale' whose arched black eyebrows are a classic sign of a lecherous temperament (*CT*, I: 3245-6). He reserved analysis in terms of affective physiognomy for his more noble characters, such as Criseyde in *Troilus and Criseyde*, whose inner lives are described in more detail and whose personalities, unlike the stock, lower-class characters of the *fabliau*, are revealed gradually, evolving in the course of the narrative.[27]

In addition to the influence of medieval physiognomy, many of the Canterbury pilgrims have been seen as astrological stereotypes. Chaucer's refusal to present the characters of the 'General Prologue' in hierarchial social order (*CT*, I: 743-4) has often been interpreted as reproducing the disorder of real life but, in fact, the pilgrims may be described in the order of the zodiacal year. Thus, just as the entry of the Sun into Aries signals the beginning of the astrological year, so the first pilgrim to be described is the Knight, who, having devoted his life to crusading warfare, seems the perfect embodiment of the influence of the 'colerik hotte signe' (*CT*, V: 51) of Aries, in which the warlike Mars, 'that is of knyghthood welle' (*CM*: 75), has its home. Next comes the Squire, who, as a lover and skilled musician, has the traditional Venusian attributes of the sign of Taurus, followed by the Knight's Yeoman, who, as a servant, was associated with Mercury whose home is Gemini, and so on.[28] Perhaps the best-known example of astrological characterisation in the *Canterbury Tales* is the Wife of Bath's explanation of – or rather her excuse for – her character in terms of the position of the planets at the time of her birth. The Wife is a Taurean, the 'ascendant' house at her time of birth, and thus a 'child of Venus', who loves 'ryot and dispence'. Her lustful, sanguine character, hot and moist, thus pits her in opposition to those cold, dry, 'melancholic' clerks, the children of Mercury, to whose criticisms of women the Wife takes such exception. As she says, 'Mercurie is desolat / In Pisces, wher Venus is exaltat', in other words, Pisces is the 'depression' of Mercury and the 'exaltation' of Venus. Furthermore, the Wife tells us that at her birth, Mars was within the sign of Taurus. Thus whilst the 'Venerian' influence of Taurus produces her 'likerousnesse', Mars created her 'hardynesse' and her ability to subdue her husbands. As a gloss to the Ellesmere Manuscript of the *Canterbury Tales* explains, if at a woman's birth her ascendant house is Taurus or Libra (the two houses of Venus) and Mars is within it, 'the woman will be unchaste' and will have 'an unseemly mark upon the face', just like the Wife herself. Thus, in her inability to withhold her 'chambre of Venus from a good felawe', the Wife claims to be simply following her 'constellation' (*CT*, III: 604-20, 697-710).[29]

Secondly, in addition to such 'scientific' stereotypes, Chaucer draws upon traditions of character-description which are more specifically literary in origin. This is most obviously so in the case of the characters within the tales told by the pilgrims. The *Canterbury Tales* are, after all, an encyclopedia of medieval literary forms, ranging from the historical epic told by the Knight to the bawdy *fabliau* recounted by the Miller, the romance attempted by the Squire, the allegorical animal-fable of the Nun's Priest, the Clerk's moral *exemplum*, the saint's life told by the Second Nun and the 'Tale of Melibee', the moral treatise in prose delivered by Chaucer the pilgrim.[30] The characters within each tale are appropriate to its genre: Theseus, the wise ruler in the 'Knight's Tale'; John, the deceived husband, and Nicholas, the lustful young clerk, in the 'Miller's Tale'; the personified virtue of Prudence in the 'Tale of Melibee'. However, the characters of the pilgrims themselves as they are depicted in the frame-narrative of the tales are heavily indebted to stock literary stereotypes. Thus, the terms in which the crusading Knight is described, his valour, courtesy, honour, generosity and loyalty (*CT*, I: 43-50, 68-72), are the commonplaces of chivalric literature, such as Watriquet de Couvin's praise of Gautier de Chatillon in his *Dit du Conestable de France*. Modern readers might find surprising the description of Chaucer's Knight as 'meeke as is a mayde' but Watriquet praises his hero for never saying anything boorish and having a sweet manner 'gentler than that of a lady or a maid'. Similarly, an early fourteenth-century English poem, 'The Simonie', praises those knights who fulfil the duties of their order by fighting for

Christ in the Holy Land and criticises those who speak villainously and in whom 'meekness is driven down and pride is risen on high'.[31] The description of the Squire, with his fashionable clothes, his ability to ride, sing, draw and dance and his inability to sleep because of love (*CT*, I: 79-100) owes much to the stock conventions of courtly love (see below, pp. 132-7). In the *Roman de la Rose*, the God of Love commands the Lover to wear beautiful clothes and to be skilled in agreeable and diverting entertainments such as riding and singing, and tells him of the lack of sleep which afflicts the lover.[32] Even Chaucer's characterisation of the Squire as a 'bacheler' (*CT*, I: 80) has a distinctive sense in a literary context, where it is used to mean a young, unmarried man of the knightly class, as opposed to its sense in the records of noble households where it is used to refer to a retainer who, irrespective of age or marital status, is one of the lord's most trusted companions.[33]

The descriptions of the pilgrims set out in the 'General Prologue' owe a particular debt to one specific medieval literary genre, that of the estates satire, a genre which, in turn, incorporated a range of contemporary moral, social and religious discourses. Such estates satires were popular in medieval European literature from the twelfth to the seventeenth centuries, whether as works in themselves, or inserted as passages in larger works; they were written in Latin and in the vernacular, in verse and in prose. They took the form of a survey of the 'estates' or ranks of society, sometimes of the classic three estates of those who fight, those who work and those who pray or sometimes a longer catalogue of occupations, each of which is denounced for its failure to live up to the socially necessary duties which it should perform. Virtue and vice are thus defined in terms appropriate to one's estate or occupation: knights should fight to defend the Church and society, not for their own private gain; the clergy should pray for society, not treat the church as a private treasure-house; the poor should labour to feed society, and so on.[34] Within such estates satires, the failings of the clergy often receive particular attention. Gower's *Confessio Amantis*, for instance, bemoans the decline of the clergy from the standards of (unspecified) 'daies olde', when clerics sought wisdom and virtue and lived a life of patience and simplicity instead of seeking rich prebends and worldly honour (*CA*, Prologue: 193-498). His *Vox Clamantis* denounces clerical abuses at every level of the ecclesiastical hierarchy: the pope usurps temporal power and the *Curia Romana* is ruled by bribes; the prelates live lives of luxury, gluttony and lust; rectors neglect the care of souls, preferring the pleasures of hunting and lechery; stipendiary priests spend their money on harlots and drink. The regulars too have abandoned their ideals: amongst the monks and canons, asceticism, poverty, chastity and patience have given way to gluttony, drunkenness, lust and pride, nuns are corrupted by priests whilst the friars no longer obey the rules of their orders or practice what they preach (*VC*, III–IV).

The 'General Prologue' to the *Canterbury Tales* has many parallels with the estates satires found in Gower's works but Chaucer seems particularly to have drawn upon Langland's *Piers Plowman* for his selection of pilgrims.[35] The Canterbury pilgrims are classic estate types who are defined in terms of their social rank and occupation. Indeed, we are frequently told that the pilgrims excel in their particular profession, like the Shipman whose knowledge of his crafts excels that of anyone 'from Hulle to Cartage' or the Doctor of Physic of whom 'In al this worlde ne was ther noon hym lik, / To speke of phisik and surgerye' (*CT*, I: 401-4, 412-13). The pilgrims' vices and virtues are similarly defined in terms of whether or not they match up to their estate ideal. The crusading Knight, pious Parson and patient Ploughman have often been seen as the ideal embodiments of the three traditional estates of the *bellatores*, *laboratores* and *oratores*, those who fight, those who work and those who pray, although other pilgrims may also be included amongst those who fulfil the duties of their estate.[36] The pilgrims' failings are also defined in social rather than individual terms. This is most apparent in the portraits of the clerical pilgrims who evoke the traditional anti-clericalism of the estates satire which in every century bemoaned the decline of the clergy from the standards of some previous age. Thus, riding out to hunt is not sinful *per se*, but it becomes so in the case of the Monk who has supposedly withdrawn from the world to devote himself to a life of poverty and humility yet who actually regards the rule of St Benedict as far too strict and old-fashioned and prefers hunting to a life of study or of labour (*CT*, I: 173-6, 184-92). This definition of vice in terms of social estate is also found in the case of the lay pilgrims. The Miller, for instance, has the proverbial dishonesty of his profession ('Wel koude he stelen corne and tollen thries; And yet he hadde a thombe of golde') whilst even his red beard (see below, p. 31), his delight in telling dirty stories and his ability to play the bagpipes are amongst the customary disreputable attributes of his craft (*CT*, I: 552, 560-5; *PPB*, II: 111; X: 43-4). As a 'janglere', Robin the Miller has an inability to remain silent, as is demonstrated at the end of the 'Knight's Tale' when he refuses to allow the Monk to speak and insists on telling his own tale with which to 'quite' the Knight (*CT*, I: 3118-31). Traditionally, mills seem often to have been associated with wagging tongues, as in the *Ancrene Riwle* which says that 'a chattering woman is one who is grinding chaff' and describes the mouth as like the flood-gates which are opened at a mill. Indeed, Chaucer's Parson tells us that 'Janglynge is whan a man speketh to muche biforn folk, and clappeth as a mille, and taketh no keep what he seith' (*CT*, X: 405).[37]

In short, what often appear to the modern reader to be individual traits or naturalistic details in portraits of the pilgrims provided by the 'General Prologue' are, in fact, often traditional or stereotypical characteristics of their estates. Friar Huberd, for instance, may seem to be strongly individualised with his merry songs and his affected lisp (*CT*, I: 264-6). Yet, in fact, many of his seeming idiosyncrasies are, like Chaucer's description of Friar John in the 'Summoner's Tale', linked to an anti-fraternal tradition which can be traced back to the mid thirteenth century and, in particular, to William of Saint-Amour's attack on the mendicants in the 1250s. Such anti-mendicant literature flourished in fourteenth-century England in the works of writers such as Richard FitzRalph and Richard de Bury as well as in poems such as 'The Simonie', Langland's *Piers Plowman* and John Gower's estate satires. From the 1240s onwards, the friars had been attacked for abandoning the ideals of their founders, for cultivating the rich and the powerful, for captivating weak, conscience-stricken women with their preaching, for their anti-apostolic begging, hypocrisy and worldly wealth, for their tendency to pride and anger instead of humility and forgiveness, for their willingness to encroach on the pastoral rights of the secular clergy, for their excessive rhetoric and ingenious glossing of texts, and for their lechery and scandalous contacts with women. The friars were thus frequently compared to the proud and hypocritical Pharisees of Matthew 23, a key text for anti-mendicant writers. Alternatively, they were likened to the '*pseudoapostoli*' or false preachers denounced by St Paul (2 Corinthians 11: 13) or seen as a fulfilment of his prophecy concerning the '*antichristi*' who would appear in the Last Days (2 Timothy 3: 1-9). As a result, they were described as lacking peace and affection, being puffed up with pride, loving earthly pleasures more than God, having only an outer appearance of godliness, creeping into houses where they lead captive 'silly women laded with sin' and, though ever learning, never attaining a knowledge of genuine truth.[38]

In line with this tradition, Chaucer's Friar Huberd is portrayed as 'an esy man to yeve penaunce' to those from whom he will receive silver. His persuasive tongue allows him to wheedle a farthing from the poorest widow although, in general, he favours the company of franklins and 'worthy women' and prefers to frequent taverns to attending the sick. His dress, a 'semycope' of expensive 'double worstede', more like that of 'a maister or a pope' than the 'thredbare cope' of a poor scholar, is familiar from the sermons of anti-mendicant preachers, such as John Ashwardby, who urged their audiences to withhold alms from friars who wore fine copes. Even Huberd's ability in singing and harp- playing were traditional associations of the friars, their defenders describing them as 'God's minstrels', their opponents seeing them as rivals to wandering 'jongleurs' (*CT*, I: 208-70).

Friar John in the 'Summoner's Tale' also has many of the failings traditionally attributed to the mendicants in anti-fraternal satire including a love of 'glosynge' texts to his own advantage and a facility in verbal trickery, as when he pretends to have seen a child's death in a vision – once he has been told of it by the child's mother. In particular, he is guilty of hypocrisy, taking delight in fine food despite his claims to lead an apostolic life of poverty and abstinence, and, despite having earlier preached against the sin of wrath, falling into a rage when Thomas tricks him into receiving a fart in his hand. He ignores the scriptures, travelling 'with scrippe and tipped staf', contrary to Christ's injunction to his apostles to take nothing for their journeys, 'neither staff nor scrip' (Luke 9: 3), and neglects the example of St Francis, devoting himself to begging to finance a fine stone church for his order despite St Francis's preference for small, wooden friaries. Christ criticised the pride of the scribes and the Pharisees saying 'Neither be ye called masters; for one is your master, Christ' (Matthew 23: 7, 10), Friar John by contrast allows himself to be called master three times by Thomas and his wife, even though he later proclaims his humility to Thomas's lord. Like the Biblical false prophets who criticised St Paul for working with his hands rather than being supported by those to whom he preached and who themselves preached for gain, Friar John lives by begging and by delivering sermons designed to raise cash from his audience. Like St Paul's *antichristi* and the friar who appears at the end of Langland's *Piers Plowman*, Friar John he is a *penetrans domus* (2 Timothy 3: 6; *PPB*, XX: 341): 'in every hous he gan to poure and prye', and is particularly able to ingratiate himself with the wife of the household. More specifically, the tale's many allusions to St Thomas of India emphasise the contrasts between Friar John's activities and those of the apostle whose church-building was subordinated to preaching and acts of charity to the poor (*CT*, III: 1737-7, 1781, 1793-4, 1800, 1802-9, 1836, 1839-41, 1854-60, 1873, 2005, 2106, 2149, 2158, 2166, 2184-6).

Far from allowing us an insight into the historical reality of the English Church in the late fourteenth century, the satire of the friar in the 'Summoner's Tale' reproduces the stock charges which had been made against the friars for the previous century and a half, charges which owed more to theological tradition and conventional symbolism than to a concern for empirical truth. Naturally, we need to appreciate the way in which medieval stereotypes evolved over time and how specific authors could use particular aspects of such traditions. For instance, in common with other late fourteenth-century works, the 'Summoner's Tale' does not not accuse its friar of lechery even though this was a sin traditionally ascribed to the mendicants by theologians and by writers such as Boccaccio. (Chaucer may however hint at Friar Huberd's immorality in the 'General Prologue' when he says that Huberd had 'maad ful many a mariage / Of yonge wommen at his owene cost', perhaps suggesting he has had to find husbands and dowries for women he has seduced, and that his hood was stuffed 'ful of knyves / And pynnes, for to yeven faire wyves' (*CT*, I: 212-13, 233-4).) Instead, Chaucer emphasises Friar John's tendency to wrath, a characteristic which writers such as FitzRalph saw as incompatible with the friars' supposed poverty and renunciation of lordship. Furthermore, even traditional anti-fraternal accusations, such as the desire for ostentatious buildings for which Friar John is criticised and which the friars had been charged for since the time of Mathew Paris, could acquire new connotations when seen in the context of the rise of new theories of dominion and poverty which came to be used to attack the mendicants. The important point for our purposes is that even though stereotypes could evolve and take on new meanings, stereotypes they remained, stereotypes based on Biblical and theological traditions and generated with particular aims and vested interests in mind rather than being based on a direct observation of social reality.[39]

(iii) Conclusion

In general, rather than seeing the *Canterbury Tales* as an immediate or passive reflection of contemporary society, the pilgrims and the characters within their tales are best seen as active reinterpretations of reality in terms of the literary conventions, scientific doctrines and stock social satires of the day. Given this distance from social reality, we should not expect Chaucer's works to offer us direct evidence about late fourteenth-century society. Nevertheless, this does not mean that we have to abandon the quest for an historical Chaucer. Firstly, even if we accept that Chaucer was making use of accepted conventions and traditions, we still need to examine the way that Chaucer combines and adapts them and, in particular, to consider their meaning for the specific period and audience which

Chaucer was addressing.[40] The Knight forms a classic case in point. He is
not simply portrayed in abstract terms, like the ideal knight of Gower's *Vox
Clamantis*, as someone ready to defend the Church and the community,
the widowed and the orphaned (*VC*, V, 1: 7). Instead, we are provided with
a detailed list of specific battles and fields of combat in which the Knight
has been involved (*CT*, I: 51 -66). This lengthy catalogue is not just there
as exotica or even just to show his extreme skill in his own professional
function. Rather these battles refer the reader to specific policy issues and
discussions at the court of Richard II.[41] Secondly, even when, as is more
typically the case, Chaucer does not directly discuss historical events, his
works still confront the broader social, political and religious questions
raised by the events of his day: how can society can be arranged so as to
maximise the common profit? What distinguishes true kingship from illegitimate tyranny? How can the unity of Christendom be achieved? How
can the individual achieve salvation? What is the ideal relationship between the sexes? What is the relationship between individual morality and
the wider social order? As we shall see, contending schools of literary critics have very different views about how Chaucer answered these questions. It is to these debates that we now turn.

Notes

1 For reading on the historical backround to Chaucer's literature, see the Select
   Bibliography.
2 For the life of Chaucer, see Pearsall, 1992.
3 Hadow, 1914: 156; Hilton, 1992: 107.
4 Callinicos, 1987: 223-4. On the notion of 'reflection' in literature, see Pearsall,
   1986: 126-31 .
5 Pearsall, 1992: 32, 243-4; Pratt, 1966.
6 Boyd, 1973: 1; Boitani, 1986: 40; Blamires, 1987: 6.
7 Bowden, 1954.
8 Hotson, 1924: 98-116.
9 Hamel, 1979: 133, 139 n.3.
10 Brown and Butcher, 1991: 157-20 4, 20 6-11, 224-6, 237-9, 247, 249.
11 Manly, 1926b: 70, 73, 77-83, 147-57, 226, 293; Williams, 1965: 9-10 , 152-66; Kolve
   1984: 290 -1.
12 Brown and Butcher, 1991: 20 6, 238.
13 Pearsall, 1985: 3, 117; Cooper, 1989: 61-2; Kolve, 1984: 219; Benson, 1989: 826;
   Pearsall, 1992: 152-3.
14 Jones, 1980: 164-6.
15 McCoy, 1974: 312-27.
16 Brown and Butcher, 1991: 210 .

17 Allen, 1982: 263-6; Pearsall, 1992: 189, 191; Payne, 1973: 118; Palmer, 1974.

18 Ferris, 1981. See also Giffin, 1956: chapters 2 and 4.

19 Rickert, 1926-7; James, 1955-6; Rigby, 1983: 426-8; Specht, 1981: 134-41, 181.

20 Bowden, 1954: 283.

21 Braddy, 1979: 148; Allen, 1982: 269; Pearsall, 1992: 192, 194; Payne, 1973: 93-5. Blamires argues that Chaucer the poet is critical of the literalness and empiricism of Chaucer the narrator in this Prologue. See Blamires, 1989: 37-42.

22 Patterson, 1983: 658; Phillips, 1993; Mann, 1973: 188-9; Mann, 1991b: 4, 8.

23 CA, VII: 223-520 . For an extremely useful introduction, see Winny, 1968: 159-62.

24 CA, VII: 692-946; Winny, 1968: 162-4, 170 -2; Spencer, 1970 .

25 Curry, 1960: 72-3.

26 Burrow, 1986: 38, 162-7.

27 Braswell-Means, 1991; Friedman, 1981.

28 Spencer, 1970; North, 1988: 50 6-13.

29 Winny, 1968: 172; Spencer, 1970: 162-3; Curry, 1960: 93-118, 172-80; Knowles, 1972: 179-80; see also Hamlin, 1974.

30 Payne, 1973: 156; Cooper, 1983: 52, 84.

31 Bowden, 1954: 46-50; Wright, 1839: 334-5; Mann, 1973: 10 8; Cooper, 1983: 79.

32 Dahlberg, 1983: 2125-535.

33 Bean, 1972: 118, 122, 126.

34 Mohl, 1933.

35 Mann, 1973: 20 7-8.

36 Mehl, 1986: 137-8, 143-7; Donaldson, 1977: 8; Hilton, 1985: 247; Josipovici, 1979: 89; Pearsall, 1992: 250; see also below, pp. 29-33.

37 Jones, 1955; Mann, 1973: 160-1; Salu, 1990: 31-2, 39; see also CT, IV: 1200.

38 Williams, 1953; Fleming, 1966; Taitt, 1975: 4-11, 17-22; Miller, 1977: 245-63; Havely, 1985: 258-64; Szittya, 1986; Wright, 1839: 331; Wright, 1859: 263-70 .

39 Bowden, 1954, 139, 141; Mann, 1973; 37-54; Blamires, 1987: 19; Williams, 1956-7: 117-18; Fleming, 1966: 692, 696; Clark, 1976: 166-8; Szittya, 1977; Szittya, 1986: esp. ch. 6; Scase, 1989: 147-8; Haveley, 1979: 339; Havely, 1985: 258, 260; Scase, 1989: 3, 7, 21, 34-5, 55-6.

40 Scase, 1989: 3-4.

41 Hatton, 1968; Olson, 1986, 10-11, 19-20; see below, pp. 31-3.

2

Monologic versus dialogic Chaucer

All things are necessarily connected and arranged for the best ... Private misfortunes contribute to the general good, so that the more private misfortunes there are, the more we find that all is well.

Candide and Dr Pangloss in *Candide* (Voltaire, 1972: 26-7, 31).

I F Chaucer's descriptions of the pilgrims and characters of the *Canterbury Tales* are constructed in terms of inherited stereotypes and literary conventions (Chapter 1), the question which primarily concerns us here is how Chaucer adapted such conventions to the needs and issues of his own time and what their significance was for his contemporary audience. In general, critics who consider the social meaning of Chaucer's *Canterbury Tales* fall into two main schools. Firstly, there are those who interpret Chaucer as essentially 'conservative' in his social outlook, whether or not they themselves approve of this outlook, and who present his social thought as an expression of the dominant spirit or ideology of his day (section ii). Secondly, there are those who see Chaucer as possessing a more heterodox voice, one which in some sense questions or challenges the official world-view of his age and which reveals, as perhaps does all 'authentic' art, the processes by which ideology attempts to pass itself off as the expression of eternal truths or as self-evident common sense.[1] This second approach tends to be adopted only by those who approve of such questioning (section iii). This chapter attempts to put the case for each of these views as persuasively as possible, examining them in terms of Mikhail Bakhtin's distinction between the conservative monologic work and the more subversive, dialogic text (a distinction set out in section i), before going on to offer an assessment of their relative merits (section iv). Chapters 3 and 4 then show how this controversy spills over into debates about Chaucer's relationship to medieval literary theory and his representation of women.

(i) Literature: monologic and dialogic

An extremely useful starting point for an analysis of Chaucer's social outlook is provided by the work of the Russian literary theorist, Mikhail
Bakhtin (1895-1975) since Bakhtin was, above all else, concerned with language and literature as social acts. For Bakhtin, the social nature of
language means that it is inherently 'dialogic', i.e., it pertains to the situation of dialogue inherent in the roles of speaker and listener. For instance,
it may seem when I give a lecture that I am engaged in an individual monologue. In fact, my lecture must, inevitably, use inherited words and concepts, it will adopt, revise and refute previous arguments, and it will
attempt to anticipate my audience's reactions, questions and objections,
i.e., it is necessarily located in an on going dialogue with both past and
future. For Bakhtin, the human situation is itself dialogic: to be human is to
be involved in a dialogue in which there is no final word since humanity is
in a permanently unfinalised condition. However, those engaged in
specific dialogues do not simply occupy the roles of abstract speakers and
listeners; instead they come to the roles with differing degrees of social
authority, depending on their age, class, gender, occupation and so on.
The specific languages or 'speech-genres' which we use in such dialogues
express definite ways of seeing the world; they are, in effect, distinct social
ideologies. Literary genres are characterised by particular 'chronotopes',
formal constructions which manifest particular and linked conceptions of
time and space.[2]

Although *all* language is dialogic, some literary texts attempt to suppress this fact; they pass themselves off as authoritative and claim, in effect,
to have the final word. Such monologic works are often thought of as conservative in their content, as in the case of John Gower's defence of the
traditional hierarchies beloved of medieval ideology (see below, pp. 21-2).
In fact, it is perfectly possible for monologic works to have a radical political content, as in the case of Voltaire's *Candide*, a text which, for all its
challenge to traditional outlooks, still insistently advocates a particular
outlook and presents its author's view as Truth.[3] Bakhtin contrasted such
'monologic' texts, whether conservative or radical, with more dialogic
works, in particular with the 'novel'. By 'novelistic' works, Bakhtin did not
simply mean the prose narratives of writers such as Balzac and Dickens.
The 'novel' is the term Bakhtin uses to refer to 'whatever force is at work
within a given literary system to reveal the limits, the artificial constraints
of that system', thus undermining the claims to authority of any single
dominant discourse. In particular, 'parodic stylisations of canonised

genres and styles occupy an essential place in the novel'. Bakhtin saw the novel as dialogic in nature, i.e., it is characterised by a multiplicity of voices or languages which engage with each other. This variety can take two forms: stylistic and ideological. Stylistically, a novelistic work can have three different levels of speech. Firstly, there is narrational speech, whether that of an external narrator, or a first-person reporter. Secondly, there is the reported speech of a variety of characters, each of whom may possess a distinctive style of their own. Thirdly, the 'novel' can employ 'double-voiced' speech, double-voiced in the sense that it does not only refer to some object but also alludes to other forms of language. Parody, for instance, is a classic form of double-voiced speech whereby some linguistic form is alluded to or used so as to undermine or to ridicule the original.[4]

In addition to such stylistic or formal variety, a work of literature can also be dialogic in the sense that it participates in the 'larger polyphony of social and discursive forces' which Bakhtin calls 'heteroglossia', i.e. a situation in which the world is seen as a 'roiling mass of languages, each of which has its own distinct formal markers' and is associated with 'a set of distinctive values and oppositions'. However, there is no reason why the degree of a novel's ideological variety and openness should necessarily correspond with the extent of its linguistic variety. Indeed, according to Bakhtin, the works of Tolstoy have *more* linguistic variety than those of Dostoevsky yet they are actually *less* dialogic in character. Whilst Tolstoy's works provide us with an authoritative narrator or author whose all-embracing superior vision ranks the novel's conflicting discourses according to a hierarchy of truth, Dostoevsky's 'polyphonic' works have less authorial resolution of the competing viewpoints they present to us and leave readers to make up their own minds. Such dialogic works place their readers in a dialogue with them rather than telling them what to think, as does a more monologic text. As a result, they require us to revise and reassess our viewpoint as we go along and refuse to offer any fixed truth or set of values.[5]

According to Bakhtin, the high literary culture of the Middle Ages was characterised by a number of monologic literary genres which were particularly well suited to convey the socially-dominant religious and social ideologies of the day. He saw the epic which celebrated the heroism of the past, as did the Arthurian literature which was so popular in medieval England, as the most monologic of genres: 'completed, conclusive, immutable as a fact, an idea and a value'. Nevertheless, such monologic characteristics were, according to Bakhtin, shared to a greater or lesser extent by all the high genres of medieval literature.[6] In late fourteenth-century England, the hierarchical seriousness of official ideology nowhere received a clearer expression than in the works of Chaucer's friend John Gower, such as the *Mirour de l'Omme*, the *Vox Clamantis* and the *Confessio Amantis* (although it should be stressed that Bakhtin himself did not discuss Gower's work). The monologic character of Gower's outlook was based on the fundamental idea of division and disunity as the source of all ills, from the individual and the physical to the social and the political. Thus, if man were made out of only one material his body would never be corrupted; it is the division and the disunity of the elements of which he is composed which mean that he must age and die (see above, p. 7). Similarly, it was the disunity and conflict between the body and the soul which originally let sin into the world and caused our expulsion from Paradise. Ever since, division has been the cause of decline within the state and in society. Division is the 'moder of confusion' which means that 'no worldes thing mai laste' and has led to the decline of the great empires, including that of Rome. It is 'thurgh lacke of love' that lands are divided and thus 'fare amis'. (*MO*: 26605-940; *CA*, Prologue: 576-7, 830-52, 892-3, 975-1010; VII: 223-448, *VC*, VII: 8). For Gower, the ideal of social unity can be achieved only when society is an ordered, hierarchical whole in which everyone performs their proper function, contributing to and sharing in the health of the whole. He therefore rehearses the traditional ideal of society as comprised of three functionally interdependent estates: the clergy, the knighthood and the peasants: those who pray on society's behalf, those who fight to defend the Church and the community, and those who work to provide sustenance for humanity, each estate being indispensable for the welfare of the others (*VC*, III: 1; V: 1, 9). To question this divinely ordained structure is to be guilty of the sin of pride by pitting one's will against that of God.[7] For Gower, society is in decline because, instead of thinking of the social good, each man thinks only of his own advantage and each estate seeks to gain at the expense of the others. The churchmen use holy office for their own personal enrichment whilst the Church is divided from top, with the papal schism, to bottom, with the emergence of the 'newe secte of Lollardie / And also many an heresie / Amongst the clerkes in hemselve' (*CA*, Prologue, 303-9, 331-3, 348-51). Similarly, the knights fight for their own gain and personal honour rather than to defeat the enemies of Church and country (*VC*, V: 1, 58), whilst the third estate demands extortionate wages for little work and, in the rising of 1381, had sunk to the level of ravening, monstrous beasts (*VC*: I: 1-15; V, 9-10; VII: 23; *CA*, Prologue: 499-509). Finally, the judges and lawyers, whom Gower added to the traditional catalogue of the three estates, exploit the law for their own profit, taking bribes to pervert justice and oppressing the poor (*VC*, VI: 1-6).[8]

For Bakhtin, the power of monologic world-views such as Gower's was challenged within the medieval period by the dialogic force of 'carnival'. Medieval carnival found expression in three main forms: in ritual spectacles, pageants and comic shows; in comic verbal compositions and parodies; and in popular curses and oaths. A classic instance of carnival involving both spectacle and parody is the 'boy-bishop' ceremonies found all over medieval Europe, from abbeys and cathedrals (including Bury, Salisbury and York) to collegiate and parish churches. Here, the clerical hierarchy was temporarily turned upside down with the election on the feast of St Nicholas (6 December), the patron saint of scholars and youth, of a boy-chorister to act as a bishop until the Feast of the Innocents (28 December), assuming the episcopal authority, presiding at services, delivering a sermon and even going on a mock visitation. Bakhtin argued that carnival, in all of its forms, 'celebrated temporary liberation from the prevailing truth and from the established order; it marked the suspension of all hierarchical rank, privileges, norms and prohibitions. Carnival was the true feast of time, the feast of becoming, change and renewal. It was hostile to all that was immortalised and completed'. 'For a short time life came out of its usual, legalised consecrated furrows and entered the sphere of utopian freedom.' Carnival can be understood in terms of a series of oppositions with the official culture of the age. Whereas official culture was serious, popular carnival culture was universally comic, directing its humour even at its own participants. Against the dogmatic and gloomy single truth propounded by official culture, carnival asserts the 'gay relativity of prevailing truths and authorities', countering the eternal, the immovable, the absolute and the unchangeable with the unfinished, the open and a joy in change and renewal. Whilst official culture consecrates existing social inequalities, carnival is a time of equality or of inverted hierarchy, a utopian moment of community, freedom, equality and abundance. Whilst official culture justifies itself in terms of the spiritual and the heavenly, carnival employs a 'grotesque realism' in which the material bodily functions of sexuality, eating and excretion bring down to earth all that aspires to be spiritual and abstract. For Bakhtin, it was only in the late medieval period and the Renaissance, above all in the works of Rabelais, that the world of carnival humour entered 'great literature', where it formed the basis of a 'new free and critical historical consciousness'.[9]

In some respects, Bakhtin's presentation of carnival is rather ambivalent, and not merely in the sense that he saw carnival itself as a rejection of

polarised alternatives and certainties. On the one hand, he presented carnival as opposed to, and sharply distinguished from, the 'serious, official,
ecclesiastical, feudal and political cult forms and ceremonials of the middle
ages' which sanctioned and reinforced the existing social order. Carnival
in this perspective is outside and alien to the intolerant and 'icy petrified
seriousness' of official culture. It constructs its own Church and its own
state for itself, one which represents 'the defeat of power, of earthly kings,
of the earthly upper classes, of all that oppresses and restricts'. Only in the
Renaissance did the walls between official and non-official culture crumble
as folk humour of carnival broke through to fertilise high literature. On the
other hand, Bakhtin realised that the world of carnival could co-exist
alongside official culture and be tolerated, adopted and even encouraged
by it, as is emphasised by the boy-bishop ceremonies which were licensed,
encouraged and sponsored by the ecclesiastical authorities. As a result,
official culture came to have a semi-legalised carnival shadow. After all,
those who composed unbridled parodies of the scriptures and the
sacraments themselves 'sincerely accepted and served' the religion of the
day. Such men thus participated in two lives: the official and the carnival
and two aspects of the world, the serious and the comic, coexisted in their
consciousness. The carnival world was not simply the world of 'antifeudal,
popular truth', it was also 'a world in which all medieval people participated more or less'.[10] Perhaps Bakhtin's ambivalence arises from the dual
possibilities of carnival itself. On the one hand, carnival can be a time of
licensed excess, a social safety-valve, a period of release which precedes
and is subordinate to the penance and fasting of Lent. 'An everlasting
carnival does not work: an entire year of ritual observance is needed in
order to make the transgression enjoyable'. Thus, 'without a valid law to
break, carnival is impossible'. On the other hand, where social tensions
and conflicts are deepening, carnival can become a force which disrupts
the social order, challenging existing hierarchies and values and allowing
simmering antagonisms to come to the surface.[11]

Finally, if Bakhtin claimed that the realm of carnival entered high literature only in the late medieval and Renaissance periods, he believed that
there was a much earlier literary tradition which offered a dialogic counter
to the dominant monologic genres: the Menippean satire. The classical
serio-comic genre of Menippean satire includes the works of Lucian,
Seneca's *Apocolocyntos*, Petronius's *Satyricon* and Apuleius's *Golden Ass*,
along with later works known to Chaucer including Martianus Capella's
fifth-century *Marriage of Philology and Mercury* and Nigel Longchamps's
twelfth-century *Speculum Stultorum* ('The Mirror of Fools'). Bakhtin saw

the Menippean satire as a carnivalised genre which emphasised invention and fantasy and whose primary aim was not to embody some pre-given truth but rather to test all truths and philosophical positions. Its satire was directed not simply at those who fail to live up to some particular ideal but against *all* idealistic attempts to order the chaos of human experience in terms of universalising philosophical and moral systems. It stressed the inadequacies of all truths and, in its dialogue of characters and perspectives, focuses upon the ever-continuing search for truth rather than the reassuring certainty of a false conclusion. As a result, Menippean satire frequently involved the parody of other texts and genres, emphasising the multiplicity of world-views available to us and the inadequacy of each of them.[12]

How useful is Bakhtin's distinction between the monologic and the dialogic text for an understanding of *The Canterbury Tales*? Is there an authoritative, monologic voice present within Chaucer's work? To what extent do the tales involve a carnivalesque disruption or Menippean satire of the claims of the official world-view of late medieval England? Does Chaucer anticipate Rabelais in transferring the popular culture of carnival to the realm of high literature? At first sight, it would seem that Chaucer's humorous tolerance and irony present a marked contrast with Gower's apocalyptic seriousness and traditional denunciations of the failings of his age. Indeed, Lodge has suggested that it is precisely Chaucer's 'novelistic' qualities (in Bakhtinian terms) which make his work seem so 'startlingly modern and accessible' compared with other, more monologic Middle English texts which now seem 'either quaint or tedious'.[13] Nevertheless, a number of critics have attempted to present Chaucer in terms which make his social outlook rather closer in spirit to that of the monologic Gower than many modern readers would like to believe. Where then does the *Canterbury Tales* stand on the spectrum of dialogic–monologic works? Here we attempt to put the case both for the interpretation of the *Canterbury Tales* as a monologic work (section ii) and for that which sees it as dialogic text (section iii) before offering an assessment of the relative merits of these approaches (section iv).

(ii) The *Canterbury Tales* as monologic text

That the *Canterbury Tales* are dialogic in the sense of simply employing a variety of different voices, there can be no doubt. It is, after all, Chaucer's ability to adopt such a wide range of voices which gives the tales much of their enduring fascination. Firstly, Chaucer makes use both of external narrators, as in the 'Knight's Tale' ('Whilom, as olde stories tellen us, / Ther was a duc that highte Theseus', *CT*, I: 859-60), and of first-person reporters, as in the 'Wife of Bath's Prologue' ('For lordynges, sith I twelve yeer was of age ... Housbondes at chirche dore I have had five', *CT*, IV: 4, 6). Secondly, the tales include the reported speech of a variety of characters, each of whom has a distinctive style appropriate to his or her rank, occupation, gender and even region. There is, for instance, the contrast between the 'literary and bookish' discourse of Chaucer's Knight and the 'oral, colloquial' style of the Miller, or between the rhetorical inadequacy of the young Squire's prolix speech and the Franklin's more mature eloquence. The characters' speech is often spattered with the technical jargon of their occupation, as in the Canon's Yeoman's frequent use in his tale of the obscure technical vocabulary of alchemy. As Lydgate put it, in the *Canterbury Tales* each man speaks 'lik to his degre' (*ST*, Prologue: 21; *CT*, VIII: 751, 758-9, 790-800, 1394-8).[14] Thirdly, the tales also make use of 'double-voiced' forms of speech which allude to other forms of language. Thus the tale of 'Sir Thopas' told by Chaucer the pilgrim, which the Host attacks as 'rym dogerel' (*CT*, VII: 925), has been seen by Cooper as 'a brilliant parody of everything that can go wrong' with the tail-rhyme romances which were so common in Middle English.[15]

Yet, despite this *stylistic* plurality, it has been questioned whether Chaucer's outlook and values should be seen as fundamentally different from the monologic works of his friend John Gower. Scholars such as Huppé, Delany and P. A. Olson have all presented Chaucer as committed to a view of society as a divinely ordained hierarchy, a view which prefers order to equality, which sees 'love' as the glue binding the social orders together, and which criticises those members of the lower orders, such as Robin the Miller, who refuse to accept their place in society.[16] However, those who see Chaucer as 'conservative' in his outlook and as a defender of traditional medieval social hierarchies are themselves divided into two separate camps. Firstly, there are those who argue that although medieval society was profoundly unequal and hierarchical, it was relatively free from social conflict. Thus, in expressing a traditional vision of social harmony, Chaucer's social ideals reflect the reality of the organic social structure of his day. Certainly, a number of historians have argued that pre-industrial societies, including later medieval England, lacked the polarised classes familiar from Marxist social theory. Pre-industrial social hierarchies, it is claimed, were comprised not of economic classes, i.e., groups defined by their wealth or property rights, but of orders or estates defined by their functions (such as fighting, praying and labouring).

Social hierarchies were arranged in terms not of wealth but of social esteem based on the status ascribed to the functions of each estate. Unlike the modern western world, where all citizens enjoy a legal equality and in which classes are relatively fluid and open, the members of a particular order enjoyed specific legal rights and privileges: 'each member of society occupied a fixed place in the social structure and each knew his superiors and gave them his loyalty and obedience'. The emphasis here is not on polarised interests and the conflict of dichotomic economic classes but on the functional interdependence of the different orders, each of which had its own internal gradations of rank, and on the deference of social inferiors to their superiors on the basis of a consensus about the esteem which should be accorded to each social order. Social conflict between peasants and lords tends, therefore, to be explained in terms of specific, 'external' factors, such as a poor harvest, heavy state taxation or defeat in war, rather than to be seen as inherent in feudal social relations.[17]

The implications of this view of medieval society for an understanding of the literature of Chaucer can be seen in the work of D. W. Robertson (see also below, pp. 79-81). For Robertson, the modern world sees itself in terms of dynamic polarities, tensions and conflicts, whether within the individual (such as the ego versus the id) or within society (class struggle and economic change). Setting up a polarity of his own, Robertson argued that 'the medieval world with its quiet hierarchies knew nothing of these things'. Rather than seeing the world in terms of polarity, the medieval outlook was based on the inevitability of hierarchy, whether within nature as whole, within society, or even within the individual, where man's higher faculty of reason should rule over the lower desires of the flesh. This strong sense of hierarchy meant that 'medieval men' saw disturbances in society as violations of the divinely ordained order of things and 'failures to maintain the integrity demanded by one's estate or degree were thought to be productive of social chaos'. Robertson recognised that during Chaucer's lifetime 'rural society was undergoing astonishingly rapid changes' but, nevertheless, argued that Chaucer's fundamental assumptions remained 'fairly traditional'. As a result, Chaucer was not 'class-conscious' in any modern sense of the word. Rather, he judged people 'on the basis of their moral qualities and on their abilities to contribute to the coherence of community life with self-restraint and industry'. Thus, in the 'Knight's Tale', the actions of Duke Theseus of Athens, ruler of the city of Minerva, the goddess of wisdom, in subordinating the Amazons, the 'regne of Femenye', and Thebes, the city of Venus and Bacchus, are 'directed towards the establishment and maintenance of those traditional hierarchies which were dear to the medieval mind', reason and order overcoming discord and passion (*CT*, I: 866).[18]

In fact, far from being fundamentally harmonious, medieval social relations seem to have involved the inherent conflict of lord and peasant, a conflict which was becoming more intense in the late fourteenth century as the peasants attempted to take advantage of contemporary economic and demographic change to obtain personal freedom, low money rents and high wages.[19] But in that case, if social relations were dysfunctional, why did Chaucer continue to adhere to a traditional medieval vision of social harmony and functional interdependence? This brings us on to the second version of our 'conservative' Chaucer, one which sees his work not as an accurate depiction of a harmonious social reality but rather as a form of 'dominant ideology' which, in a society riven with social conflict, legitimated the wealth, power and status of specific social groups. Traditionally, this view of literature as bound up with the expression of particular social interests has been associated with Marxist literary criticism. For Marx, 'it is not the consciousness of men that determines their social existence but their social existence that determines their consciousness'. Crucial for the definition of man's social being are class and property relations which, for Marx, constitute the economic 'base' or 'foundation' of society 'to which correspond definite forms of consciousness' including politics, religion, philosophy and – of particular interest to us – art. These 'ideological forms' are said to 'express', 'reflect' or 'correspond to' the individual's class position and social interests. However, according to Marx, the dominant social groups have an interest in obscuring the true nature of the class relations of their society, concealing the fact that such relations are built on exploitation and the reality that, far from being eternal, they are a human product which can be changed by human agency. Such forms of social consciousness are 'ideological'; they do not simply 'reflect' the social reality but distort it in order to justify the existing order of society and the wealth, power and status enjoyed by particular social groups. Ideology attempts to suppress social conflicts and contradictions and to portray social relations as eternal, as the product of 'human nature' or, in the Middle Ages, of divine will.[20]

More recently, this emphasis on the connection between literature and the expression of specific social interests has been developed by American 'New Historicist' critics. Like Bakhtin, the New Historicists emphasise that literature, as is the case with all language, is a social act, one which is saturated with power and social interests. As a result, the New Historicists reject the 'close reading' of texts as organic, self-contained wholes which was favoured by the 'New Critics', the Romantic view of art or literature as a realm of spiritual transcendence or authentic being set against the alienating repressive realm of material and social reality, and the Formalist emphasis on what *distinguishes* literature from other forms of language.[21] Thus, despite its differences from Marxism, such as its stress on non-class forms of social inequality and its emphasis on the way that social discourses, such as those of gender, actively help to constitute social relations rather than simply passively reflecting them, New Historicism has much in common with Marxist literary theory. Like Marxism, New Historicism stresses the social context and significance of literary production, not least when literature is busy passing itself off as a sphere of life cut off from everyday social practices. Thus, despite its tendency to produce grand banalities ('There can be no motiveless creation' etc.), New Historicist criticism, like its more sober British 'cultural materialist' cousin, performs a useful function in reminding us of the ways in which literature is tied in with the consolidation of social order, the subversion of such order, and the attempted containment of subversion.[22]

What is the significance of such theories for the study of Chaucer? For the New Historicists, as for Marxist literary critics, those medieval discourses which presented society as an ordered, harmonious hierarchy, such as the theory of the three estates, were not the expression of some abstract world-view possessed by 'medieval man' in general or of some universal 'spirit of the age'. Rather they were the product of particular social groups who were in conflict with other groups.[23] For many critics, Chaucer's works, with their ideal of 'mesure' based on 'the sober acceptance of things as they are' and their stress on the need for 'perfection within the specified roles required for the functioning of the three estates', are a classic instance of such monologic feudal ideology. When seen against the background of contemporary economic change, social conflict, political turmoil and religious strife, they thus constitute, at least when judged by modern standards, 'a brilliant and dangerous superstructure legitimising unacceptable social practice'.[24]

In general, those critics who see Chaucer in monologic and conservative terms make two main assumptions. The first is that the 'General Prologue' to the *Canterbury Tales* sets out Chaucer's social vision, one which is consistent with the views found in his earlier works, and that it supplies us with the information with which to judge the character and morality of the pilgrims, predisposing us to accept or reject their particular perspective by depicting them as ideal or perverted embodiments of their estates. The second key assumption underlying conservative interpretations of

Chaucer is that the voice of specific pilgrims can be equated with the views of Chaucer the author himself. In particular, those who see Chaucer as conservative in outlook regard the Knight and the Parson as the mouth-pieces for Chaucer's own views, an assumption made explicit by Huppé when he said that the Knight, 'which, of course, means Chaucer', sub-scribed to a particular social outlook.[25] This reading of Chaucer as con-servative in his outlook has been developed with particular clarity by P. A. Olson. For Olson, Chaucer was not simply a tolerant and detached observer of humanity who was lukewarm or indifferent in matters of poli-tics and religion. Chaucer was a poet engaging with the public issues of his day, particularly the relationship between the 'Two Swords' of temporal and spiritual power and, above all, with the relationship between the three estates of medieval social theory. It is thus futile to argue over the correct order in which the pilgrims tell their tales. What is important is that all the tales take up the issues set out in the 'General Prologue': 'the tales are all elaborations of the prologue regardless of order'. Once more the emphasis is on the consistency and uniformity, on the monologic quality, of Chaucer's social theory.[26]

For Olson, Chaucer's adherence to the traditional morality of the three-estates model of society can be seen from the ideal figures of the 'General Prologue', the ones who fulfil the roles required of their own estate and who live in harmony with their fellows rather than creating social tension and conflict by usurping the roles and prerogatives of other social ranks. Certainly, many critics have seen the Knight, the Parson and the Plough-man as the ideal embodiments of the three traditional estates of those who fight, those who pray, and those who work. Thus Chaucer's Knight is not one of those condemned by Gower for having fought merely for personal glory, for the love of a lady or for the spoils of war (VC, V: 1-8). Instead, the Knight has every traditional chivalric virtue: prowess, courtesy, honour, liberality, loyalty, bravery and wisdom. Nor, in contrast with the knights satirised by the preacher Bromyard, has he feared to travel to the Holy Land to fight God's enemies but has devoted his entire life to 'his lordes werre' (CT, I: 47), fighting against the infidel in Spain and northern Africa, alongside King Peter of Cyprus at Alexandria and elsewhere in the Middle East, and with the Teutonic knights in northern Europe.[27] The 'poor Parson', as the resident rector of his parish, is also an estate ideal, a cleric who prefers the service of God and his parishioners to the pursuit of individual profit. He has not, unlike the secular clergy denounced by Gower for their love of luxury and their pursuit of promotion, been an absentee who neglected to care for his flock or been over-zealous in excommunicating those who did not pay their tithes: 'He was a shepherde and noght a mercenarie'. Instead, he goes out of his way to visit his far-flung parishioners, instructing his flock by his example rather than just his words: he teaches the law of Christ and his apostles twelve 'but first he folwed it hymselve' (*CT*, I: 477-528; *VC*, 3: 16-20). His brother, the Plough-man, is also an exemplary figure. Unlike the lazy, seditious grasping peasants and labourers whom Gower depicted as irrational beasts, Chaucer's Plough-man is 'a trewe swynkere' who lived 'in pees and parfite charitee', loving his neighbour and God, working for others poorer than himself without payment, and never failing to pay his tithes. Far from being realistic por-traits of actual individuals, these characters are estate ideals who are almost too good to be true (*VC*, V: 9-10; *CT*, I: 529-41).[28] Other pilgrims, such as the Clerk and the Knight's Yeoman, may perhaps also be counted amongst the estate ideals. The Clerk, who devotes his life to study, preferring books to ecclesiastical promotion, is certainly not one of those clerks condemned by Gower for falling into 'gret debat' rather than attending to the 'comun profit'. Instead, his learning has taught him how to speak with restraint, his speech being used to express 'moral vertu'. Like the Parson, he communi-cates wisdom and Christ's Law to others, as in his tale with its message that 'every wight, in his degree, / Sholde be constant in adversitee' (*VC*, Pro-logue: 372-7; *CT*, I: 285-308; IV: 1145-61).[29]

In contrast with such exemplary figures, Olson sees many of the pilgrims as perversions of their estate ideals who prefer to submit to their lower natures and seek their own pleasure rather than contributing to the common good. The Squire, for instance, is the obverse of his father, the Knight. He is 'a lovyere and a lusty bacheler' in his fashionable short gown with its long, wide sleeves. Well able to dance but, like the classic courtly lover, as unable to sleep at night as the nightingale, he represents the voluptuous, romantic love depicted in the Temple of Venus in *The Parlia-ment of Fowls* and the 'Knight's Tale' (*PF*: 211-94; *CT*, I: 1918-66). He would certainly not have met with the approval of Gower, who attacked those knights who fell captive to love's uncertainty and who were thereby deprived of their honour and reason by an affliction more deadly than a physical wound (*CT*, I: 80-100, *VC*, V: 1-4).[30] For Olson, other pilgrims represent the effects of pride, luxury and avarice amongst the first and third estates. The Monk, for instance, shows the corruption of the ideals of the regular clergy. Ignoring the rule of St Benedict, which sought to prevent the monks wandering outside their monastery as 'by no means expedient for their souls', he is an 'outridere' who prefers hunting to studying or manual work. He lives more like a 'lord ful fat and in good poynt' than a monk committed to the ascent of Benedict's ladder of humility. Gower, never willing to pass up the chance of repeating a commonplace, compares the monk out of his cloister to the fish out of water but this opinion Chaucer's Monk 'heeld he nat worth an oystre' (*CT*, I: 165-207; *VC*, IV: 5).[31] Amongst the estate of those who work, the Miller and the Reeve present a marked contrast with the patience and charity of the Ploughman. Robin the Miller is violent in his deeds and vulgar in his speech, he steals corn and charges his customers excessively, cheating them with his 'thombe of golde'. His very physiognomy points to his corrupt inner nature, his broad shoulders and wide nostrils being interpreted at the time as a sign that a man was bold and easy to anger, his short arms indicating that he is evil, foolish and a lover of discord, his fleshy face and the mole on his nose symbolising his lustful, venereal nature, and his red beard signifying that he is as treacherous as a fox. The Miller is thus a far less pleasant character than he might at first seem to be to the modern reader (*CT*, I: 545-66).[32] Oswald the Reeve is similarly loveless, even diabolical in his associations. Bromyard denounced the wicked reeves who bullied those beneath them whilst not hesitating to deceive their own masters. It thus comes as no shock when Chaucer tells us that his Reeve makes the bailiffs, herdsmen and servants below him 'adrad of hym as of the deeth' whilst at the same time winning his lord's favour and reward by 'lending' the lord's own goods to him. Even the fact that the Reeve is from Norfolk is significant, since Norfolk men had a reputation for cunning and avarice in the fourteenth century. Indeed, the early fourteenth-century *Fasciculus Morum* includes an exemplum about a tyrannical reeve from the diocese of Norwich who 'habitually tormented the poor and simple' (*CT*, I: 587-622).[33]

However, for Olson, the pilgrims are not merely an array of stock literary-characters or timeless sermon stereotypes whom Chaucer used to praise virtue and to denounce vice; they also have a more immediate and specific contemporary relevance. He argues that the three fields of the Knight's martial activities represent three particular policy options open at the time. Firstly, there was the policy of fighting against Islam in Spain, a course in which John of Gaunt may have had an interest arising from his claim to the throne of Castile.[34] Secondly, there was 'the way of Jerusalem', crusading in the eastern Mediterranean in the footsteps of King Peter of Cyprus. Thirdly, there was the 'way of Prussia', battling alongside the Teutonic knights against the pagan Lithuanians. For Olson, support for the way of Jerusalem was an alternative to the way of Prussia which was associated with Richard II's opponents such as Gloucester. In fact, as is shown by the writings of Philippe de Mézières, ex-chancellor of Peter of Cyprus and the tireless promoter of a new crusading 'Order of the Passion', and by the activities of Chaucer's crusading contemporaries (not to say Chaucer's Knight himself), support for any particular field of crusading did not necessarily preclude support for holy war elsewhere.[35] Jones has attempted to refute the view of the Knight as an estate ideal and argued that, far from being a paragon of Christian chivalry, Chaucer gives us the information which reveals the Knight to be a mercenary of the type with whom Chaucer would have been familiar from his encounter with Sir John Hawkwood in Italy in 1378. The Knight, he claims, has been involved in campaigns which were 'often appalling massacres, scenes of sadism and pillage' and one of which, the siege of Alexandria, was notorious for the disgrace which the English knights brought upon themselves. Jones's argument has, however, found little support from other critics. Modern writers may prefer those who fight for 'king and country' to those who kill the infidel in the name of 'a religion of Love and Peace' but late fourteenth-century moralists did not necessarily share this opinion. Certainly, for Chaucer's contemporary Philippe de Mézières, Peter of Cyprus's crusading battles at Alexandria, Satalye and Lyeys were not (respectively) an 'appalling massacre', a bloody outrage' and 'a worthless fiasco' but models of what could be achieved if the kings of France and England united to 'turn their weapons against the enemies of the Faith'. The Knight's involvement in them need not necessarily make us doubt his worth, at least when judged by contemporary standards.[36]

If the Knight is accepted as an estate ideal, it would seem that Chaucer, like Gower, preferred the crusade as an alternative to the continued mutual slaughter of Christians in the Hundred Years War between France and England. Whilst Chaucer's contemporaries, including the members of the Scrope family whom, in 1386, Chaucer supported in their armorial dispute with the Grosvenors, managed to combine crusading with involvement in the Hundred Years War, combat against his fellow Christians is conspicuous by its absence in the Knight's long list of battle honours. Certainly, Philippe de Mézières won support in England from Chaucer's patron, Gaunt, and from the poet's friends such as Sir Lewis Clifford and Sir John Clanvowe, when he argued that the kings of France and England should arrive at a peace in order to end 'the shedding of the blood of their Christian brothers and kin' and to permit the diversion of the martial energies of the West towards the recovery of the Holy Land.[37] It is the Squire, the Knight's son, the perversion of the ideal of the *bellatores*, who has been on *chevauchées* to Flanders, Artois and Picardy in the Hundred Years War.

This service overseas almost certainly refers to the expedition led by Henry Despenser, Bishop of Norwich, in 1383. Technically a 'crusade' in favour of the Roman pope Urban VI against the French supporters of Clement VII of Avignon, the expedition was a military disaster. Its failure and the 'exploits of an army of marauders masquerading as soldiers of the Cross' only served to bring further discredit on the Church. Like the knights attacked in Gower's *Vox Clamantis*, the Squire fights not for the good of the community but 'In hope to stonden in his lady grace'. The Squire's involvement in an expedition representing the debasement of the crusading ideal provides a marked contrast with his father's lifetime's service 'in his lordes werre' (*CT*, I: 47, 85-8).[38]

For Olson, the tales told by the Knight, Miller and Reeve, with which the *Canterbury Tales* begin, all address, albeit in Chaucer's typically indirect manner, the issues raised by these figures in the 'General Prologue': crusading, the war with France and social unrest at home. The tales begin with an *exemplum* of secular political virtue in the tale told by the worthy Knight about Theseus, the ideal ruler and great conqueror who, unlike Creon the tyrant whom he defeats, is portrayed as wise and chivalrous. He feels pity for the plight of the widows of Thebes, whom Creon refuses to allow to bury their fallen husbands, and secures justice for them. His firm rule maintains justice and order within his lands but he can also be merciful, as when Palamon and Arcite admit their fault to him. Then, unlike a wrathful tyrant, his 'resoun' quickly overcomes his 'ire': 'Fy / Upon a lord that wol have no mercy / But been a leon, both in worde and dede, / To hem that been in repentaunce and drede, / As wel to a proud despitous man'. However, even though Theseus has divine providence on his side (as when he is led to discover Palamon and Arcite while he is out hunting), he is not above the law himself, he is not a tyrant ruling according to his own whim or merely for his own profit. He reigns for the common good, is himself bound by natural law and determines policy with the advice of his counsellors and magnates. He wins military victory but then, as Aristotle advises Alexander in the handbook for princes included in Gower's *Confessio Amantis*, secures the loyalty of his subjects and cements the peace between Thebes and Athens by the marriage of Palamon and Emily. In this perspective, Theseus is an ideal medieval ruler, the mighty conqueror who is also the bringer of peace. From Augustine to Gower, medieval writers were agreed that whilst it is good to eschew war, 'A kyng may make werre uppon his right, / For of bataille the final ende is pees'. As Honoré Bonet put it, 'the aim of war is to wrest peace, tranquillity and reasonableness from him who refuses to acknowledge his wrongdoing'.[39]

Thus, Theseus's subjects praise him for arranging the tournament between Palamon and Arcite so that no blood will be shed, a contrast with the description of the tournament in Boccaccio's *Teseida*, one of the main sources for the 'Knight's Tale', where a great many knights are killed (*CT*, I: 2537-64). Whilst Theseus is firm, making commands to Palamon and Arcite which brook no 'repplicacioun', he also rules with the advice of his parliament since, as Gower put it, 'About a king good counseil is to preise / Above all things most vailable' (*CT*, I: 1846, 2970, 3076; *IPP*: 141-2). Chaucer thus adopts the depiction of Theseus found in Boccaccio's *Teseida*, where he represents the subordination of passion to reason and of reason to divine providence, and in contemporary chronicles, where Theseus is portrayed as the founder of knighthood and parliaments, the first philosopher-king, the ruler of Athens, the city of Minerva, and the conqueror of Thebes, which, for Chaucer, represented fratricide and illicit sexuality. In this perspective, Theseus becomes 'the closest Chaucer ever got to portraying a hero'. He is an ideal chivalric warrior and ruler, just, magnanimous, gentle, benign and brave, who overcomes evil and chaos, restores order and harmony, and who, as in the classic monologic text, functions as the mouthpiece for the views of the author (*PF*: 379-81; *CT*, I: 865, 944-550, 1663-72, 1716, 1773-7, 1813-16, 2537-64, 2970, 2987-3074, 3076, 3096; *CA*, VII: 3103-24).[40]

Whilst the 'Knight's Tale' is set in ancient Athens, it is presented by Chaucer as having lessons for the society of his own day. Above all, the moral relevance of the tale can be seen in its inclusion of passages from Boethius's *Consolation of Philosophy*, the Latin text of which Chaucer himself had translated into Middle English. It is Boethius's theodicy, the justification of the ways of God to man, which eventually constitutes the explicit moral of the 'Knight's Tale' in which the theme of love is set in the broader perspective of 'the providential purpose behind the order of nature'.[41] In the *Consolation*, the unjustly imprisoned Boethius (*c*. 480-524) begins by bemoaning his unhappy fate and the way in which unfaithful, deceitful Fortune has turned against him. Lady Philosophy appears to him in his cell and explains to him the futility of submitting himself to the rule of Fortune whose wheel raises men on high only, in turn, to cast them down. In fact, 'contrarious fortune' is really more profitable to man than 'Fortune debonayre' since the latter enslaves us with 'the beaute of false goodes' whereas ill-fortune can reveal the truth to us, teaching us, for instance, who is our true friend. All men seek happiness but true happiness is not to be found in earthyly wealth, power or fame or in bodily pleasures. True happiness is to share in the perfect goodness of God, the self-sufficient regulator of the universe. Although it may seem that the wicked flourish while the innocent suffer, in fact, 'good folk ben alwey strong and myghti, and the schrewes ben feble and desert and naked of alle strengthes', a view which Lady Philosophy justifies with the argument that, since evil is actually nothing, so the power to do evil is really the power to do nothing. In reality, the good are always rewarded and the bad are always punished. Indeed, goodness is its own reward whilst wickedness, by removing man from a share of true happiness, is its own punishment. It follows, paradoxically, that 'the doere of wrong is more wrecche than he that hath suffride wrong'. Lady Philosophy argues that the world seems confused only to those who do not understand its underlying principle of love and order, a principle in accordance with the goodness of God himself who ensures that all things happen aright. Since God, the maker of all things, ordains all things to the good, it follows that, from the viewpoint of divine Providence, there is no evil anywhere in the world. All that happens to us is good fortune since it either rewards us or corrects us. Fortune does not rule us, we have our destiny in our own hands and can overcome adversity. True freedom is when we contemplate the divine thought: human souls are less free when they are bound down by the body but most enslaved of all when they give way to vice and lose all reason. Thus, despite all of the apparent suffering and injustice in the world, Boethius's Lady Philosophy defends the view that the world is controlled by a beneficent divinity (*Bo*: 397-8, 409, 415, 416, 420, 422, 432, 437-8, 440-4, 447-52, 454-6, 458).

In a monologic perspective, the 'Knight's Tale' constitutes a Boethian lesson about the suffering of those who trust in earthly fortune and who submit to enslavement by their lower natures rather than obeying the dictates of wisdom, reason and morality. The first reference to Boethius's work in the tale comes when Arcite refuses to accept that Palamon has a prior claim to Emily simply because he saw her first: 'Wostow nat wel the olde clerkes sawe, / That "who shal yeve a lovere any lawe?"'. This saying, whose source is given as a marginal gloss in many manuscripts,[42] alludes to Boethius's account of the story of Orpheus, who loses Eurydice by disobeying the god of the underworld's command not to look back at her, a story which Chaucer tells us is an allegory of those who set their thoughts on earthly things and so lose 'al that evere he hath drawen of the noble good celestial' (*CT*, I: 1163-4; *Bo*: 440). Arcite is similarly ethically confused when he laments his release from prison on the grounds that his exile from Athens means that he will no longer have sight of Emily. Since he has been granted his wish to be freed from prison but only then realises its consequences, Arcite compares humanity, which seeks after happiness but which often goes the wrong way after it, to a drunken man who knows that he has a house but does not know the right way home. In fact, in Boethian terms, it is Arcite himself who is the drunkard who has been led astray and forgotten the true good, the desire for which has been implanted in him by nature (*CT*, I: 1251-74; *Bo*: 422). Likewise, when Palamon laments being left behind in prison, he repeats the complaint of Boethius at the start of the *Consolation* that the innocent are punished whilst the evil are free to do their mischief, i.e., his state of mind is that of Boethius *before* he has been fully enlightened by Lady Philosophy (*CT*, I: 1303-33; *Bo*: 404-5).

It is Theseus, the instrument of 'destinee, ministre general, / That executeth in the world over al / The purveiance that God hath seyn biforn' (*CT*, I: 1663-5; *Bo*: 451-2), whom Chaucer makes into the mouthpiece for Lady Philosophy's defence of the ways of God to man when, at the end of the tale, he addresses his parliament and attempts to console Palamon and Emily for the loss of Arcite (*CT*, I: 2970, 2980). Theseus expounds the Boethian teaching that the 'Firste Moevere' of all things has bound the four elements, earth, air, fire and water, by 'the faire cheyne of love' and ordained a certain duration for all earthly things. This First Mover is eternal and unchanging, it is the whole from which all of nature is derived. It is the First Mover's wise purveyance and ordinance that no earthly thing should last for ever. Even the oak which 'hath so long a life' is eventually 'wasted', the 'harde stoon' under our feet is worn away, the broad river dries up and great tounes 'wane and wende', so 'al this thyng hath ende'. So all men and women must also die, either in youth or in old age, the king as much as the page. It is 'Juppiter, the kyng', the 'prince and cause of alle thyng', who makes all living things die and thus return to the original source from which they were derived. Therefore, it is wise 'to maken vertu of necessitee' and folly to complain against fate and to rebel against he who governs everything. In order to make a virtue of necessity, Theseus adds to the traditional *solacia* for the death of Arcite already provided by his father Egeus (*CT*, I: 2843-9), a variety of forms of rhetorical *consolatio mortis*, including the arguments that death is the end of our earthly troubles, that death is the common lot of all men, and that we cannot strive against the will of God. In particular, Theseus develops the *solacium* of the *opportunitas mortis* which demonstrates that death occurred at the best time for the deceased or was even a positive advantage to him, when he argues that it is better, like Arcite, to die in the flower of one's youth, when one is sure of one's good name and can die with honour, than to die in old age when all his 'vassellage' is forgotten. To question this would be wilful-ness so we should not complain that Arcite has departed from the 'foule prison of this lyf'. To do so would be to offend Arcite's spirit without making ourselves any happier. After woe, we should be merry, thanking Jupiter for all his grace, and thus, to make one joy from two sorrows, Emily and Palamon should be united in matrimony (*CT*, I: 2987-3081; *Bo*: 420, 431, 451-2, 455). As in *The Parliament of Fowls*, where Nature, the vicar of God, has bound 'hot, cold, hevy, lyght, moyst and dreye' by 'evene nombres of acord', Theseus's final speech asserts that there is a divinely established order in the universe, an order 'to which men must submit and which turns all things to good'. If death is an inevitable part of the natural cycle of life, so is birth and renewal, represented by the marriage of Palamon and Emily. *Natura*, representing moderation, cyclical order and the renewal of life is victorious over capricious *Fortuna*, representing death and the extremes of adversity and prosperity (*PF*: 380-1).[43]

Like the narrator of the 'Knight's Tale', Theseus has 'wisdom, true nobility, chivalry, pity, "gentilesse", truth, worthiness and might'. As a ruler, he is not simply strong and wise, as in Statius's work which was the source for Boccaccio's *Teseida*, he is a philosopher-king who approaches the highest secular ideal of medieval society. In his monotheistic final speech, he seems even to anticipate a Christian wisdom in his recognition of the transitory nature of human life and the vanity of human wishes. In rejecting the fatalism which Chaucer normally attributes to his pagan characters and in his recognition of the possibility of human free will, Theseus shows himself to be the wisest of pagans, even if, as Minnis argues, his moral vision focuses excessively on human fame and honour and stops short of the notion of a loving god who actively intervenes in human affairs.[44]

As Knapp argues, the Knight's character whose voice comes loaded with prior 'external' authority, in this case that of the Boethian belief in a providential order at work in the universe which makes good result even from apparent tragedy. The Knigh's ideals are those of hierarchy and obe-dience as interpreted in terms of the chivalric ideology of the late medieval aristocracy. Rebellion, represented by Palamon and Arcite, is contained and the rule of the wise Duke Theseus, who exemplifies the life style of the nobility as ruler, warrior, patron of the arts and the bestower of women in marriage, is idealised. In this outlook, experience is controlled and ritual-ised, as when Theseus ends the mortal combat of Palamon and Arcite and replaces it with the tournament; sex and labour are excluded; marriage is about cementing political alliances; women are prizes to be allotted. Since the tale deals with the realm of eternal truths it does not matter that the murals in Theseus's temple of Mars anachronistically portray the deaths of Caesar and Nero which had not then taken place (*CT*, I: 2031-2): what is important is the timeless moral message which is expressed by these events.[45]

However, the reproduction by the 'Knight's Tale' of the official ideology of the age is the function not just of the ideas which it propounds explicitly but also of its adoption of a specific literary form and generic conventions which together convey a particular view of the natural and social order. In particular, the tale's social meaning is linked to the stately pace of its narrative, which has to cover the events of a number of years, and its emphasis on symmetry and balance, such as that between the imagery and symbolism used for Arcite (Mars, red, blood, fire, strength) and that used for Palamon (Venus, white, milk, water, gentleness). Above all, this balance is personified by the character of Theseus, who combines the firmness of Mars with the affection of Venus, a synthesis symbolised by his banner of red and white which signifies that he is a figure of harmonious unity, moderation and reconciliation.[46] In shifting the emphasis of the tale away from Arcite, the focus of Boccaccio's version of the story, and emphasising both cousins equally, Chaucer tends, if anything, to enhance the balance and symmetry of his characters and narrative. The form of the Knight's speech also expresses his balanced, ordered view of life. It has the *proprietas* commended by medieval literary theory, with a style and subject matter appropriate to its speaker and subject matter: 'the wordes moote be cosyn to the dede'. There is the stylistic elaboration, eloquence and figurative language suitable for the 'curteis' or 'faire' speech of someone of the Knight's social station, rather than the 'rude' and 'large' speech of the Knight's social inferiors for which Chaucer has to apologise to his readers (*CT*, I: 725-46, 3170-86). The Knight thus makes frequent use of rhetorical devices such as *occupatio*, i.e., saying something while apparently refusing to say it, as when he recounts how Theseus conquered the Amazons and married Hippolyta while explicitly telling us that 'al that thyng I moot as now forbere' (*CT*, I: 885, see also *CT*, I: 994-1000, 1187, 2206, 2963). He also employs epic similes such as his comparison of the confrontation of Palamon and Arcite to that of a hunter with a lion or a bear (*CT*, I: 1638-48, see also 2626-36).[47]

The world-view of the Knight also requires an appropriate literary genre for its expression. Indeed, Chaucer's notion of literary *proprietas* seems more concerned with generically appropriate style than with the distinctions between the 'high', 'middle' and 'low' styles traditionally expounded by rhetorical handbooks.[48] The 'Knight's Tale', although incorporating elements of works of philosophy and the chronicle, is essentially a romance narrative but – crucially – one which has been grafted on to an epic. Unlike the traditional romance, where the key issue is whether or not the lover will win his lady, the epic is concerned with broader social issues. Thus, in the epic perspective of the 'Knight's Tale', Emily's desires for chastity count for nothing. Marriage is seen in social and political, not individual, terms; individual desire is not to be admired but here leads to chaos and disaster. The 'Knight's Tale' thus presents us with a wise father-figure who overcomes the threat of disorder represented by Palamon and Arcite, the young lovers who, in their pursuit of Emily, abandon their reason and mutual friendship, submit to their own lower natures and indulge in the follies depicted in the Temple of Venus built by Theseus. Its relevance to the Knight's son, the Squire, a fashionable and accomplished courtier who, like Arcite, cannot sleep because of love, is obvious (*CT*, I: 97-8, 1361).[49]

In its celebration of hierarchy and order at the personal, social and cosmic levels, the 'Knight's Tale' is, in Bakhtinian terms, a monologic 'epic' rather than a dialogic 'novel'. Yet, at the end of the tale, when the pilgrims, and particularly the 'gentils', have praised its nobility, Robin the drunken Miller ignores the Host's invitation to the Monk to tell the next tale and insists on telling his 'cherles tale' with which he will 'quite' (i.e., pay back) the Knight (*CT*, I: 3109-43). In turn, the Reeve, angered by tale told by the Miller at the expense of a carpenter (the craft in which the Reeve was originally trained), takes his revenge in narrative form by recounting the tale of a miller who attempts to trick two clerks but is bettered by them (*CT* I: 614, 3144-9, 3860-2, 3913-20, 4324). For Olson, the tales told by the Miller and the Reeve are exactly what we should expect from characters who represent the perversion of their estate ideals. They are demonstrations of the workings of the sins of pride, avarice and luxury which are the root of social decay and disorder. Modern readers might be inclined to admire the Miller's literary Peasants' Revolt in which the bawdy world-view of the *fabliau* is pitted against the high seriousness of the epic. In fact, the Miller's refusal to know his place in the social hierarchy simply prepares the ground for his quarrel with the Reeve, a quarrel which represents the disorder into which society would fall without the firm rule of the first estate extolled in the 'Knight's Tale'. The Miller and the Reeve are thus followers of Venus and of Mars. With, at the very most, only a retributive justice at work (and in the Miller's Tale hardly even that), their tales can provide only a negative parody of the

'Knight's Tale' (for further discussion of these tales, see below, pp. 47-
9).[50] Here, as in Bakhtin's account of Tolstoy's work, Chaucer's stylistic
variety within the *Canterbury Tales* seems to be perfectly compatible
with the existence of a hierarchy of discourses, one of which is privileged
as truth.

Finally, those who see the *Canterbury Tales* as the expression of a consistent, conservative world-view would argue that if the tales begin with
the chivalric, secular wisdom of the Knight, they culminate in the peniten-
tial, spiritual wisdom of the Parson.[51] Both the beginning and end of the
Canterbury Tales provide us with privileged standpoints from which to
judge the values, attitudes and outlook of the other pilgrims and their tales.
Certainly, the comprehensive and authoritative spiritual system set out in
the 'Parson's Tale' would seem to be an obstacle for those who wish to
present the *Canterbury Tales* as a dialogic text in which no pilgrim has the
final word. After the Manciple has told his tale, the Host announces that all
the pilgrims but one have spoken and invites the Parson to tell his tale (*CT*,
X: 1-29). In response, with Libra in the ascendant (*CT*, X: 11), perhaps as a
reminder to the pilgrims of the scales of God's final judgement, the Parson
offers what is often referred to as a sermon but is in fact a treatise on penitence based on a thirteenth-century work by Raymund of Pennaforte, two
abbreviated versions of William of Peraldus's encyclopedia of sin, and the
Summa Virtutum de Remediis Anime.[52] The Host had earlier referred to
the Parson as a 'Loller' (i.e., a Lollard) (*CT*, II: 1173, 1177) but, in practice,
his 'tale' seems totally orthodox in its belief in the pains of Purgatory, its
emphasis on the obligation of the individual to submit to the Church's
authority, injunctions and sacraments and, in particular, its stress on the
need for oral confession (*CT*, X: 315-20, 808). The confusion, multiplicity
of voices and emphasis on worldly occupation, experience and outer
appearances characteristic of the 'General Prologue' thus give way at the
end of the tales to order, univocal truth, accepted authority and inner spiritual reality. The 'game' of artistic play gives way to the 'earnest' of the
vision of the Jerusalem Celestial.[53]

The Parson locates his moral and social teaching within a broader
vision of rightful hierarchy at all levels of existence. 'God hath creat all
thynges in right ordre, and no thyng withouten ordre, but all thynges been
ordeyned and nombred.' Those that are damned 'been nothyng in ordre,
ne holden noon ordre'. Sin is then presented as a rebellion against this
divine order. Rightfully, 'God sholde have lordshipe over resoun, and
resoun over sensualitee, and sensualitee over the body of man. / But soothly,
whan man synneth al this ordre or ordinaunce is turned up-so-doun'.

Human reason should be subject and obedient to God 'that is his lord by right'; in rejecting this rightful hierarchy, humanity loses its own lordship over sensuality and the body (*CT*, X: 218, 260-70).[54] Similarly, true order demands hierarchy and inequality within society as a whole and 'reason' requires that there should be 'degree above degree'. It is God who has 'ordeyned that som folk sholde be moore heigh in estatt and in degree, and some folk moore lough'. True humility requires us to receive gladly the decisions of our rulers 'or of hyem that is in hyer degre', servants should not 'seyn harm and grucche, and murmure prively' when given lawful commands by their masters, nor should anyone envy the prosperity of others. Nevertheless, even though 'thraldom' is the consequence of human sin and of our fallen condition, those in authority should not be like wolves and extort or devour unmercifully the possessions of the poor folk in their authority: even the lower should 'be served in his estaat and in his degree'. All of the estates should work for the good of the others and the common profit of all: the knights, for instance, should defend the Holy Church, not despoil it. But where those in authority do not practise the charity expected of them, the Parson offers to their subjects only the spiritual benefits of 'suffrynge paciently wronges that been done to thee' and the promise that 'hunger and thurst' in this life will bring the reward of 'plentee of joye' in heaven: the punishment of the extortionate rich, like the reward of the patient poor, will come only in the next life (*CT*, X: 314, 482, 490, 499, 505-7, 763-75, 1055, 1080).

For many critics, the Parson's outlook possesses a monologic authority, either as the expression of a morality which implicitly or explicitly underpins all of the *Canterbury Tales* or as a new and higher moral perspective which forces us to revise our previous opinions of the other pilgrims and their tales. For both Cooper and Patterson, the tale told by the Parson transcends the rest of the *Canterbury Tales*, showing up the moral imperfections of the earlier tales 'as strikingly as the goodness of his life shows up the imperfection of most of the other pilgrims'. Here the 'dramatic' fit of tale with its teller does *not* relativise the speech of the Parson so that he becomes just another character on the road to Canterbury. Rather, the correlation between his words and his ideal deeds monologically privileges his message. 'For all the relativism of which Chaucer was so conscious, for all the different readings of the world embodied in the various tales and all his other works, he never lost sight of the Boethian belief that God's vision was single.'[55]

(iii) The *Canterbury Tales* as dialogic text

If many critics present the *Canterbury Tales* as a work which is monologic in form and 'conservative' in its social outlook (whether they regard this outlook as characteristic of 'medieval man' in general or as an ideology propagated by particular social groups), others adopt the second of our main approaches and see Chaucer's works as disruptive of the claims of the dominant social ideologies of their day. Indeed, this view of Chaucer as radically unorthodox, at least in the realm of religion, can be traced back to the sixteenth century when Chaucer, to whose Ploughman was attached an early fifteenth-century Lollard tract on the wealth and corruption of the Church, was seen as an early Protestant and a follower of Wyclif, a view which was to last until at least the nineteenth century. In particular, those critics who see Chaucer as offering a challenge to the official world-view of his age tend to present the *Canterbury Tales* as a dialogic text which, in its insistence on the clash of different world-views embodied in the pilgrims' tales, undermines the claims to authority of any single dominant discourse. David Aers, for instance, presents Chaucer's work as a comprehensive challenge to the claims of the medieval ideology of the three estates. For Aers, 'Chaucer's work represents society as a composite of *inevitably* competing groups motivated by individualist forms of material self-interest ... In this vision all claims to be pursuing an allegedly *common profit* are exposed to a sceptical examination which subverts the very notion of a unified society and a harmonious common profit. With this goes a critical reflexivity which desublimates all attempts to erect ideologically secure, impersonally authoritative discourses. His texts continually return such discourses to the social processes within which they are generated and to which they contribute. Contrary to the dominant ideology of late medieval England, his work represents long-term *antagonism* between social groups as an altogether predictable, even inevitable, state of affairs, while the literary modes he constructs subvert attempts to impose traditional social ideology and moralisations on what is exhibited as intractable material'.[56]

As we have seen, those critics who see Chaucer in monologic terms assume firstly that the 'General Prologue' supplies us with the information about the pilgrims which allows us to accept or reject their world-view by depicting them as ideal or perverted embodiments of their estate and, secondly, that the voice of certain characters (such as the Knight and the Parson) can be equated with the views of Chaucer himself. Both of these assumptions have necessarily to be criticised by those who see the

Canterbury Tales as a dialogic text which relativises and personalises the discourses of its characters and privileges none as the 'final word'.

Firstly, if the 'General Prologue' simply provided us with stock-judgements with which to judge the pilgrims, it would be little different from traditional estates satires, such as those of Gower, which urge the reader to repent his own sins by offering clear denunciations of the vices typical of each estate of society. Yet this is not the experience of most modern readers when they read Chaucer's 'General Prologue'. Far from reproducing the didacticism of the traditional estates satire, Chaucer seems to transform and undermine the conventions of the genre by replacing heated invective and moral denunciation with ambiguity, irony and detachment. The customary monologic discourse of the genre is replaced by a multiplicity of voices, none of which can easily be equated with Truth. Certainly, when we look at the descriptions of the pilgrims set out in the 'General Prologue', we have at least four different perspectives. Firstly, there is the viewpoint of Chaucer the protagonist, i.e., Chaucer the pilgrim, who is himself one of the characters on the road to Canterbury. This Chaucer should not be confused with Chaucer the poet. Instead, like Dante in *The Divine Comedy* or Gower in the *Confessio Amantis*, Chaucer the pilgrim is presented as naive and fallible. Thus the courtly Prioress, whom Gower would have denounced as a follower of Venus and of the laws of the flesh (*VC*, IV: 13-15), is portrayed by Chaucer the pilgrim with 'a wide-eyed wonder at the glamour of the great world. It is just what one might expect of a bourgeois exposed to the splendours of high society'.[57] Medieval literary theory was well acquainted with the distinction between the poet who wrote a text and the poet who appears as a character within his own text where he speaks '*in persona aliorum*' rather than '*in propria persona*', as in the *Consolation of Philosophy* where Boethius the fictional character has to be enlightened by the words of Lady Philosophy, words which, of course, have actually been written by Boethius the author.[58] Secondly, in addition to the voice of Chaucer the pilgrim, there is the voice of Chaucer the poet which reveals to us aspects of the characters which Chaucer the pilgrim at the Tabard could not know. For instance, we are told of the Sergeant of Law that 'Nowher so bisy a man as he ther was. / And yet he seemed bisier than he was' (*CT*, I: 321-2). Thirdly, within the 'General Prologue', there is the voice of the conventional estates satirist, of the stock moral judgement of the age. This judgement can either be explicit, as when we are reminded of the saying that a monk outside the cloister is like a fish out of water (*CT*, I: 180-1), or left implicit, as when we are told that since gold is a medicine for the heart, the Doctor of Physic 'lovede gold in special' (*CT*, I: 443-4). Finally, and unusually for an estates satire where characters tend to be judged from the outside, there are the voices of the pilgrims themselves, as when the Friar tells us that 'it is nat honest' for such a worthy man as himself to mix with lepers and beggars (*CT*, I: 240-8), voices which we also hear between the tales, as in the Wife of Bath's lengthy, self-justificatory 'Prologue'. In particular, the characters anticipate or respond to external evaluations of them, a classic characteristic of Bakhtin's dialogic text, as when the Monk rejects criticism of his lifestyle as being 'nat worth an oystre' (*CT*, I: 182).[59]

For Donaldson and for Mann, this multiplicity of voices creates an ambiguity of response which means that it is not always possible to determine 'which of them has the last word'.[60] We have seen how much the portraits of the pilgrims in the 'General Prologue' owe to the stock literary and scientific conventions of the day (Chapter 1). Yet, if this is the case, why do modern readers so often respond to the pilgrims in terms of their 'realism' rather as a collection of stereotypes? Mann's answer is that this impression of realism is not derived from a correspondence to external reality but is rather an effect produced by specific literary techniques and devices.[61] In particular, it is evoked by the complexity of our responses to the multiplicity of voices heard in the 'General Prologue'. Firstly, the portraits of the pilgrims mix moral responses with emotional and personal ones. The Friar and the Summoner may both be corrupt when judged by traditional moral standards, the Friar preferring the company of innkeepers and barmaids to lepers or beggar women, the Summoner being willing to overlook people's crimes for 'a quart of wyn'. Yet, Mann argues, we judge the easy going Friar, with his twinkling eyes and his singing and harping less harshly than the Summoner, with his leprous complexion which terrifies children (*CT*, I: 240-2, 266-7, 625-8, 649-50).[62] Secondly, there is the accumulation of apparently unmotivated detail, as when we are told that the Wife of Bath is somewhat deaf or that the Squire 'carf biforn his fader at the table' (*CT*, I: 100, 446), a technique which also creates an impression of realism: we seem to be presented with individual characters with a life of their own not just with stock types who exist to be condemned by us.[63] Finally, in the case of the corrupt characters, there is the omission of the victim, which again inhibits any easy denunciation of them as stock depictions of vice. Gower and Langland might explicitly mention the corruption of sergeants of law, Chaucer simply tells us that his Sergeant excels in his profession. The emphasis is on the pilgrims' professional skill, such as the Wife surpassing the cloth-makers of Ypres and Ghent or the Shipman who has the best knowledge of sea and tides of any 'from Hulle to

Cartage' (*CT*, I: 448, 401-4), rather than on the effects of the pilgrims' actions on others which would allow us to arrive at some stock moral judgement. We should not, therefore, judge the pilgrims on the basis of standards laid down outside the *Canterbury Tales*. A Gower or a Langland might have judged the pilgrims by such criteria but Chaucer nowhere tells us that we should do so or provides the context to permit such judgements. Although, in terms of medieval literary theory, the *Canterbury Tales* is a 'mixed' text which incorporates speech by the author in his own person *and* that of the characters he has created (as opposed to an exegematic one, i.e., where the author simply speaks in his own voice, or a 'dramatic' one, in which only the fictional characters speak), the balance is overwhelmingly in favour of the voices of the characters with relatively little overt authorial comment.[64]

If the first assumption of those who see Chaucer as a monologic, conservative writer is that the 'General Prologue' provides us with the information with which to judge individual pilgrims and their tales, the second is that the voice of Chaucer the author can be equated with that of the particular characters within his text. In fact, most of the debates about the meaning of the *Canterbury Tales* come down to this issue of whether or not we can identify the voice of Chaucer the author with the voices of particular pilgrims and, if so, which ones. Those for whom the *Canterbury Tales* are a dialogic text necessarily reject the view that Chaucer's voice can be easily equated with that of the Knight or of any of the other pilgrims. Instead, critics such as Rogers, Cooper and Sklute present the *Canterbury Tales* as a collection of particular world-views, each of which reveals a dissatisfaction with the preceding tales but none of which is presented as a definitive or final answer. The structure of the work as a whole is, therefore, the 'movement of the mind as it proceeds, restless and dissatisfied, from one of its worlds to another'. It thus forms a dialectical whole whose meaning is greater than the message of any one of its parts. The world-view of the Knight or of the Parson is not to be taken as valid above all others; each simply provides us with one of a number of possible, provisional world-views produced by particular individuals with their own partial viewpoints, none of which is authoritative and each of which the reader has to judge for himself or herself. Similarly, for Strohm, much of the attraction of Chaucer's works lies in their 'provisional and unfinished qualities, their willingness to entertain alternatives without pressing for premature resolution'. Chaucer's texts are not simply the expression of some hegemonic ideology but are rather the sites of 'unresolved contention, of a struggle between hegemony and counter-hegemony', as places 'crowded with many voices representing many centres of social authority'. Explicitly invoking the work of Bakhtin, Strohm argues that Chaucer rejected a 'single, univalent "truth"' in favour of a multiplicity of voices, each with its own partial truth. No voice goes unchallenged but no voice is totally devoid of all truth.

There is no equivalent in the *Canterbury Tales* of the figure of Genius, who leads Amans to an understanding of the meaning of love in Gower's didactic *Confessio Amantis*. Instead the pilgrims are ruled over by Harry Bailly, landlord of a tavern, leaving the message of Chaucer's work as ambiguous, ironic and elusive. Such critics offer us a dialogic, open-ended inconclusive Chaucer, one who moves away from closure and containment towards a multiplicity of perspectives, each of which is conscious of and responsive to the others and which together constitute an interpretive free-for-all in which there is no final word. This is a pluralist Chaucer who deals in disorder and disruption, who questions the ability of language in general or of any particular genre or discourse to represent reality, who recognises that divided loyalties of the age make impossible any claim to absolute certainties, and who sets out thesis and antithesis without ever providing us with a synthesis. As Fyler puts it, Chaucer shows how elaborate intellectual systems collapse as soon as they are built, how the claims of authority conflict with those of experience and how one authority contradicts another leaving us simply with a bewildering variety of perspectives rather than any final truth or definitive meaning. Chaucer thus combines an existentialist recognition of 'relativity, uncertainty and absurdity' of the human situation with a postmodern 'awareness of the contingent and arbitrary nature of language'.[65] As Arnulf of Orléans said in his twelfth-century commentary on Lucan's *Bellum civile*, 'in the manner of the philosopher he [Lucan] puts forward three opinions, but in the manner of the poet he neither resolves nor affirms any of them'.[66]

This view of Chaucer's work as dialogic challenge to the monologic discourses of his age, is set out with particular clarity in Knapp's *Chaucer and the Social Contest*. For Knapp, the pilgrims' story-telling contest is a microcosm of the broader social contests of late fourteenth-century England. Story-telling is a way of ordering the world, a way of making sense of reality through historically specific discursive codes. Such codes do not just reflect some pre-existing world: language orders and constructs specific interpretations of reality for us. A discourse is a way of thinking and speaking, one expressed not just in a set of explicit religious, political and philosophical claims but also by what it takes for granted and presents as 'natural'. Discourses are about power, about repression and the maintenance of order or ways of resisting such order. Taken individually, Chaucer's tales do often have a dominant, hegemonic voice, as in the Knight's rehearsal of the dominant social and philosophical theories of the day. Yet, for Knapp, these discourses are contested by other voices, voices which do not, as Olson claims, simply end up by confirming the truth of the dominant ideology of the day but instead offer a genuine challenge to it. The monologic discourses of particular tales are relativised when placed within the dialogic framework of the tales as a whole.[67]

In particular, Knapp, like many critics, sees the 'Miller's Tale' as burlesquing and ridiculing the hierarchical world-view set out in the 'Knight's Tale'. In both tales, two young lovers compete for the love of one woman, but whereas in the Knight's hands this material becomes the occasion for a moral epic, in the Miller's hands it provides the raw material for a bawdy *fabliau*: the contest of world-views is expressed as a contest of genres, each with its own chronotope. Whereas the 'Knight's Tale' is concerned with the stately passage of years in the history of ancient Greece, the humour of the Miller's tale depends upon split-second timing of a farce set in modern Oxford. The 'Miller's Tale' mocks both the solemnity of the sober moral formulations of the Knight and the 'high' literary form in which they are expressed; it is both a counter-vision and a counter-art to the 'Knight's Tale'. Whereas the 'Knight's Tale' is concerned with eternal truths and exemplary morals, the 'Miller's Tale' is local, immediate and particular; it is, as Strohm calls it, an 'unfettered attack on all forms of transcendence'. When the Knight attempts in his tale to reproduce the official ideology of medieval society, he can do so only by a systematic exclusion or repression of the worlds of labour and of sex. It is precisely these aspects of human existence which are foregrounded in the 'Miller's Tale', which thereby exposes the structuring absences of the Knight's discourse, i.e., those things which his ideology does not, will not and cannot say if it is to present itself as coherent.[68] In the 'Knight's Tale', the desires of Arcite and Palamon are a force for disorder which result in the death of the former and have to be tamed by marriage in the case of the latter; in the amoral 'Miller's Tale', there is no suggestion that Nicholas has been improved by his experiences. The tale offers no guarantee of order, justice or moral retribution as is shown when the adulterous Alison escapes scot-free. The main butt of the tale is John, the gullible carpenter who takes the place in the Miller's narrative of Theseus the wise father-figure. The Knight's hierarchical emphasis and transcendent philosophy in which earthly events are linked to a divine providence are replaced by the Miller's egalitarian insistence on sex and excretion, the material bodily functions which we all have in common, and his dismissal of John the carpenter's belief in divine intervention in human affairs as 'fantasie' and 'vanytee' (*CT*, I: 3835). Whereas the 'Knight's Tale' shows courtly love to be tragic, the 'Miller's Tale' burlesques its ritualised codes through the figure of Absolon. For the Miller, what is real is the body and bodily desire. Whereas Emily is not even aware of Palamon and Arcite's existence, Nicholas, on encountering Alison alone, takes 'hire by the queynte' and holds 'hire harde by the haunchebones'. Whereas the world of the Knight's Tale is the realm of abstraction and ideals, the *fabliau*-world of the Miller is natural, material and tangible: Emily is compared to a goddess or a heavenly angel; Alison, amongst other things, to a weasel, a kid, a calf and a colt. The 'Miller's Tale' is, therefore, the literary and philosophical anti-type of the tale which precedes it (*CT*, I: 3276-9, 1101, 1055, 3233-70).[69]

In Bakhtinian terms, the 'Miller's Tale' is an example of a 'double-voiced' form of speech, that of the 'hidden polemic' in which statements do not simply describe some object (in this case, the travails of married life in fourteenth-century Oxford) but are so constructed that they strike a blow at another person's language and statements about the same topic. In the case of the 'Miller's Tale', it is the language and social claims made in the 'Knight's Tale' which, though left implicit, structure everything the Miller says. Indeed, at one point, hidden polemic passes into a more blatant form of double-voiced speech, that of open parody, when the Miller adopts the Knight's description of Arcite lying in his cold grave 'Allone, withouten any compaignye', but applies it to Nicholas who lives in his elegantly adorned chamber, 'Allone, withouten any compaignye' (*CT*, I: 2779; 3204).[70] Naturally, if we assume the standpoint of the Knight, the Miller and his view of human experience will appear as the embodiment of the 'discord nourished on gluttony, vainglory and avarice' and the 'threatening forces of chaos' which the Knight's own hierarchical world-view is meant to contain.[71] On the other hand, if we stand on the ground of the Miller, the Knight's outlook will seem humourless and pretentious. By putting these world-views into the mouths of particular characters, Chaucer relativises them, personalising them and depriving them of any ultimate authority. In its parodic conversion of the events of the Knight's philosophical epic of chivalry into the form of a *fabliau*, the 'Miller's Tale' would seem to be a classic instance of the 'novelistic' force which lays bare the limits and the artificial constraints of a particular literary system. In its focus on the concrete, on sex and the body instead of the Knight's emphasis on the transcendent, the abstract and the supramundane, in dealing with the present rather than the mythic past, the 'Miller's Tale' represents a carnivalesque exposé of the official culture of the Middle Ages.[72] If the Knight's discourse comes buttressed by ready-made external authority, the 'Miller's Tale' constructs its own *internal* authority, above all, by its use of humour, ridiculing the dominant world-view of medieval society under cover of the 'legitimised freedom' of jointly shared laughter. In literal terms, the 'Miller's Tale' is scandalous, as Chaucer himself warns us, but, through its humour, it wins the laughter of all the pilgrims – with the exception only of the Reeve (*CT*, I: 3860). As Knapp puts it, to laugh with someone else, to accept their joke, is also to accept, at least temporarily, their premises and to put oneself on their ground: 'By his wit, the Miller wrests an improbable victory from the forces of hegemony'.[73]

Once we break with any simple identification of the views of Chaucer the author with those expressed by the Knight, it then becomes possible not just to pit the standpoint of the Miller in opposition to that of the Knight but also to argue that the logic of the 'Knight's Tale' is in opposition to itself. A gap then emerges between what the Knight as narrator is explicitly *telling* us and what Chaucer the poet is implicitly *showing* us, the latter supplementing and even contradicting the former. In other words, the voice of the Knight cannot simply be equated with that of Chaucer the poet who, in fact, exposes, rather than merely reproducing, the problematic and ideological nature of the Knight's discourse. Thus, whilst Theseus is undoubtedly the hero of the Knight as narrator of his tale, a number of critics have argued that Chaucer also supplies the reader with the information to arrive at an alternative assessment of the supposedly noble duke. For instance, Knapp claims that Theseus can be seen as the wise guardian of Emily, deciding her future for her good and that of society *or* she can be seen as his prisoner of war, the booty of his defeat of the Amazons who exists to be disposed of to Theseus's own political advantage: 'the text offers *both* alternatives'. Similarly, Theseus wages war on Creon when the latter refuses to allow the burial or the cremation of the bodies of his defeated enemies, leaving them to be eaten by dogs, yet, having defeated Creon, Theseus himself then allows the bodies of his enemies to be ransacked and stripped of their armour and clothing (*CT*, I: 944-7, 1005-7). Finally, on returning to Athens, Theseus is honoured with the laurel crown of the conqueror yet in the Temple of Mars the figure of 'Conquest' is portrayed in another light, sitting in great honour but 'With the sharpe swerd over his heed / Hangynge by a soutil twynes threed' (*CT*, I: 1027, 2028-30). Whereas the narrator of the 'Knight's Tale' explicitly shares the self-conception of Theseus the conqueror, the Temple of Mars shows us the reality of war from the viewpoint of the vanquished. As Aers put it, the tale exposes the self-interested motives underlying the rhetoric of chivalry and the continuities between state violence and other forms of murderous aggression: 'St Augustine himself likened the order of king-doms to that of robber bands, asserting that the only difference between them is the impunity of the offical rulers'. Despite its attempt to depict the world from a particular perspective, Aers, Knapp and the other critics who read Chaucer's work in dialogic terms see the 'Knight's Tale' as containing latent contradictions and inconsistencies which, though repressed, con-stantly threaten to return to disturb the orderly surface of the tale. It is these inconsistencies which suggest to us that, far from being the ideal philosopher-king, Theseus is a tyrant whose philosophical discourse is actually self-interested propaganda. He offers only a garbled perversion of Boethius's philosophy, one which should be distinguished from the views of Chaucer himself, and his is only one voice in the on going dialogue and debate of world-views of the tales as a whole. Those who see Chaucer's Theseus as a heroic figure argue that Chaucer *omits* those elements from his sources which might cast doubt on Theseus's virtue, such as his destruc-tion and punishment of Thebes. By contrast, those who see Theseus in a more negative light maintain that Chaucer *adds* elements which emphasise Theseus's cruelty, replacing Boccaccio's depiction of Teseo giving medi-cal help to the wounded Thebans and burying their dead with a new passage in which his men pillage the dead Thebans for their harness.[74]

A third approach to the 'Knight's Tale' would argue that the tale assumes neither a monologic unanimity of opinion between the voices of Chaucer the poet, the Knight-narrator and Theseus, nor a gap between poet and narrator with Chaucer satirising the Knight's view of Theseus. In this third approach, the Knight himself, as narrator, is aligned with Chaucer in his satire of Theseus's attempts to make sense of the world. As we shall see, exactly the same three positions have been adopted in regard to the voices of Chaucer and the narrator of the 'Nun's Priest's Tale' (below, pp. 93, 105-6). In this third perspective, the 'Knight's Tale' is seen as built around the stock characters of the Menippean dialogue: the 'know-it-all', representing authority and philosophical abstraction (Theseus), and the human struggler, representing experience and suffering (Palamon and Arcite). In the Menippean satire, neither of these protagonists has the final say for both are subject to comic and ironic attack. Thus, far from Theseus's 'final mover' speech representing the ultimate truth of the 'Knight's Tale', it is, in its mismatch between the claims it makes and the events we as readers have actually witnessed, simply another of humanity's philosophically insufficient attempts to impose order on the world on the

basis of a few selected facts. It is 'an eclectic selection of random philosophical thoughts', the inadequacies of which are 'evident at every turn',
one which reinforce the Knight's portrayal of Theseus 'as incapable of
comprehending the levels of complexity in the universe which intrude
upon the life surrounding him'. Faced with the bleak truth about the
world, a truth which the suffering portrayed in the 'Knight's Tale' reveals
to us, all we can do is seek consolation in 'beautiful half-truths which make
life a little more bearable'. Far from showing Theseus to be the embodiment of Boethian wisdom and an agent of Boethian destiny, the 'Knight's
Tale' undermines the idea of a benevolent destiny and parodies Boethius's
theories. The Knight exposes such theories as 'words which override actual experience'.[75]

Finally, if neither the 'General Prologue' nor the 'Knight's Tale' provides the reader with reliable grounds for judging the pilgrims and their
tales, what of the encyclopedic moral scheme offered in the 'Parson's
Tale'? For many readers, the Parson's monologic seriousness provides a
'drab conclusion' to the *Canterbury Tales*, and constitutes a 'betrayal of all
that is most Chaucerian'. As a result, one past response to the 'Parson's
Tale' was to deny that it was actually Chaucer's work and to ascribe it instead to 'a bungler of the lowest order'. In fact, there now seems no reason
to doubt that the 'Parson's Tale' *was* the work of Chaucer.[76] But in that
case how does it relate to the rest of the tales? For some critics, far from the
'Parson's Tale' being an explicit statement of Chaucer's own morality, it
lacks any definitive authority; it is either a pious gesture, foreign to the rest
of the *Canterbury Tales* in its style and concerns, or it is simply another
tale, one with an appropriate subject matter and which is told in an appropriate manner for its particular speaker. In this perspective, the 'Parson's
Tale' is 'no more valid than any other' and, like all the other tales, only
further reveals Chaucer's 'multidimensional ambiguity'. It 'has truth in it.
But this is not the whole truth of the *Canterbury Tales*', which are seen as
resisting closure to the very end, so denying to any one pilgrim the finality
of utterance to which the Parson himself aspires. Rather than reading all
the other tales in the light of the morality of the 'Parson's Tale', we should
read the 'Parson's Tale' in the light of the satiric tone and multiplicity of
perspectives of the tales which have preceded it.[77]

Such critics therefore refuse to accept that the 'Parson's Tale' is
intended as a monologic conclusion to the pilgrims' contest of world-
views or to equate the voice of the Parson with that of Chaucer the poet. In
this perspective, the Parson's didactic literalism and his conflation of
fiction with falsehood do not constitute the culmination of the *Canterbury*

Tales so much as their complete negation. After all, when asked for a 'fable' by the Host, the Parson, like other fourteenth-century preachers, replies by rejecting 'fables and swich wrecchednesse' in favour of 'Moralitee and vertuous mateere' (*CT*, X: 30-41; 1 Timothy 1: 4; 2 Timothy 4: 4). Indeed, his tale lacks even the narrative *exempla* commonly used in such works to make the relentless didacticism of the genre more palatable to its audience.[78] As Whittock puts it, moral didacticism may suffice for the Parson but it can hardly do so for the poet. There is, therefore, a problem in identifying precisely who is speaking when the 'Parson's Tale' induces Chaucer, in his 'Retraction', to renounce his 'translacions and enditynges of wordly vanitees' including those of the *Canterbury Tales* 'that sownen into synne' and excepting only his translation of Boethius and 'othere bookes of legendes of seintes and omelies, and moralitee and devocioun' (*CT*, X: 1084-7). It may be artistically appropriate for Chaucer the pilgrim on the road to Canterbury to make such a renunciation but it is hardly sufficient for Chaucer the poet who is writing the text, otherwise 'the *Canterbury Tales* could never have been written in the first place'. Chaucer's retractions are thus part of the artistic strategy of the works in which they appear, 'not failed attempts to suppress them'.[79] After all, Chaucer the poet could have had the Parson tell his tale much earlier, before his readers have worked their way through all those tales which 'sownen into synne'. Indeed, the Host first invites the Parson to tell a tale once the Man of Law has told his (*CT*, II: 1166-7, 1178-80), but it is essential, if the rest of the tales are to go ahead without being damned, for Chaucer to postpone the Parson's rejection of fables, in this case by having the Shipman insist on telling a tale. Again, a gap appears between the voice of Chaucer's fictional characters and that of Chaucer the author and, unlike the monologic text, there can be no easy equation of one with the other, even in the case of the morally upright Parson with his doctrines backed by the authority of the Church.

For those who see Chaucer in monologic terms and who equate his voice with that of the Parson, Chaucer the poet adopts what Kolakowski calls the standpoint of the 'Priest', a standpoint which perpetuates the absolute: 'the priest is the guardian of the absolute; he sustains the cult of the final and the obvious as acknowledged by and contained in tradition'. For those who interpret the *Canterbury Tales* as a dialogic work, Chaucer becomes the 'Jester', a character whose task is to challenge and question traditional absolutes: 'the jester is he who moves in good society without belonging to it, and treats it with impertinence; he who doubts all that appears self-evident'. He thus seeks to 'unveil the non-obvious behind the obvious, the non-final behind the final; yet he must frequent society so as to know what it holds sacred and to have the opportunity to address it impertinently'.[80]

(iv) Conclusion

It is hard to imagine a more polarised set of readings than those currently on offer about the meaning of Chaucer's *Canterbury Tales*. On the one hand, the tales are presented as a monologic reassertion of the orthodox ideology of social hierarchy and order familiar from the traditional teachings of the medieval Church. On the other, they are seen as a carnivalesque disruption of hierarchy and order which dialogically subjectivises and relativises all social norms and values and so renders Chaucer's text rather unsuitable as a vehicle for the reproduction of any established ideology. Such critical disagreements seem to provide us with a classic instance of the incommensurable paradigms of interpretation which so frequently characterise literary criticism. How can we decide between these wildly divergent views of Chaucer's work? Is a monologic or a dialogic reading of Chaucer the more plausible? This conclusion attempts to answer these questions by addressing three main issues. Firstly, it argues that the absence of explicit moral judgements of the pilgrims in the 'General Prologue' does not mean that the text lacks a set of coherent underlying moral assumptions and that such seemingly 'open' texts could have very different meanings in the Middle Ages from the ones which we would tend to ascribe to them today. Secondly, it asks whether any of the competing voices of the pilgrims on the road to Canterbury can be equated with that of Chaucer the poet. For instance, is the discourse of the Knight undermined and relativised by that of the Miller? Is the Knight's discourse shown by Chaucer to be internally contradictory? Its answer is that the apparent inconsistencies and contradictions of the 'Knight's Tale', which make Theseus seem a tyrant to many modern critics, would not have been so evident when seen in the context of late medieval ethics, philosophy and political thought and that the tale is intended as the statement of a serious secular morality. Thirdly, it examines the 'Parson's Tale' in terms of the literary theory of the medieval period and argues that such theory would have granted an authoritative standing and privileged status to the Parson's voice as the ending of the *Canterbury Tales*.

Firstly, what of the view that the multiplicity of voices at work in the *Canterbury Tales*, above all in the 'General Prologue', creates an open-endedness and ambiguity of response which means that it is not possible to determine which of the pilgrims' voices has the last word? Interestingly, medieval literary theorists themselves commented on the use of such open-ended literary formulations. For instance, in his rhetorical hand-book, the *Poetria Nova*, Geoffrey of Vinsauf gives, as an example of understatement, a straightforward description of a woman who 'went wandering about with hair adorned' but then concludes that 'this manner of speech indicates that she was wanton'. Such description, indirectly showing the nature of a character rather than directly telling it to us, 'can enclose the whole strength of a discourse in half a statement' since it addresses part of the discourse to our ear and reserves part for the intelli-gence. Similarly, Geoffrey claims, the statement 'he is an extraordinary man' implies that he is a very good man, 'but the hint that he is a very bad man indirectly peers out at us, for this also is implied'. Thus, as Geoffrey says earlier, 'the discretion of the wise man observes what is said through what is left unsaid'.[81] Grammatical and rhetorical handbooks thus listed a variety of tropes and figures related to '*allegoria*' (apparently saying one thing while actually meaning another) and '*significatio*' (leaving more to be suspected by the reader than is explicitly asserted). Medieval writers such as Langland and the Gawain-poet commonly used such ironic tech-niques, allowing the gap between the ideal and the actual to speak for itself rather than moralising explicitly. It was this assumption that inspired the countless medieval defences of the description of immoral acts in the works of Ovid and other pagan poets on the grounds that 'ill-done things are written in books so that one can flee them and avoid them'.[82]

It was for this reason that Chaucer the poet did not need to offer an explicit moral judgement of the behaviour of the Monk who prefers to go out hunting to observing the rules of his order. Chaucer's failure to specify the response expected from his readers was *not* intended to allow his read-ers to make up their own minds about the Monk, rather it assumed that readers already knew what opinion they were supposed to have: the text could be left open precisely because the reader's response was presumed to be closed. The indirect techniques which make the character portraits of the 'General Prologue' so ambiguous to us could thus have a rather different significance in the medieval period itself. Indeed, much of the humour in the pilgrims' portraits arises from the contrast between what the pilgrims are are expected to be according to their estate ideal and what they are actually like. It is a commonplace of aesthetics that works of art do not simply consist of a prior content or paraphraseable argument which is then given a specific artistic form. Rather, as we saw in the contrasting literary form of the tales told by the Knight and by the Miller, form and content constitute a unity in conveying ideological meaning. However, whilst accepting this view, we also need to emphasise that the meanings ascribed to particular literary devices and forms are themselves historically specific.[83] Thus, even if we accept that the *Canterbury Tales* is an 'open' text which lacks any direct authorial comment and leaves the response to the reader, the implications of such a literary form could be far more monologic in medieval literary culture than tends to be assumed by modern audiences. If Chaucer's work escapes the shackles of overt didacticism and adopts instead a literary form in which moral judgements become more subtle and elusive, this does not mean that Chaucer 'refuses to evaluate or to judge' his characters.[85] As Manly long ago said, Chaucer did not indict and sermonise to the extent that other late medieval poets did. Nevertheless, he still manages to shows us folly and vice in such a way that even though we *seem* to arrive at our own opinion, we 'necessarily think of them as he would have us think'. After all, we would have to be as naive and credulous as Chaucer the pilgrim himself (see p. 43) to miss the irony in the portraits of the Monk and the Friar. Indeed, in the case of the Friar, Chaucer's description seems to pass from a stance of cynically detached amusement to one of outright sarcasm (see above, p. 13-14). In such cases, Chaucer's comedy does not seek to overturn a social norm or invite us to sympathise with its transgression but rather reminds us of the norm's existence through his characters' blatant disregard of it. If the gap between ideal and reality arises from observed detail rather than explicit authorial comment, the ideal itself is still evident. As Geoffrey of Vinsauf said, 'if you wish to inveigh fully against foolish people, attack in this way: praise, but facetiously; accuse but bear yourself good humouredly and in all ways becomingly'.[85]

The second issue which has to be addressed in any assessment of monologic versus dialgoic readings of Chaucer is whether the voices of any of the pilgrims in the *Canterbury Tales* should be equated with that of Chaucer the author. In particular, does the 'Knight's Tale' provide the beginning of the story-telling contest with an ideal of social order against which the world-views of the other pilgrims, such as the Miller, should be judged? Is it possible to decide between the views of those critics who see Theseus as the ideal philosopher-ruler and those who see him as a self-interested tyrant? Here I argue that the 'Knight's Tale' does indeed open the *Canterbury Tales* with a vision of justice in this world, the virtue which, according to medieval texts such as the twelfth-century *Moralium Dogma Philosophorum*, preserves 'human society and the life of the community'. It is this vision which prepares the way for the account offered in the 'Parson's Tale' of the spiritual justice involved in the penance for sin which readies us for the next life.[86]

Is the explicit description of Theseus in the 'Knight's Tale' as an ideal ruler who is 'wise', 'chivalrous', 'pitiful' and 'gentle' (CT, I: 865, 1761) undermined by the tyranny implicit in his actual deeds? One solution to this problem is to look at the conventions of medieval literature and to adopt Blake's argument that medieval narratives were was not based on consistent characters in the way which modern readers expect but instead were constructed around 'themes', traditional literary set-pieces which could be added together in new patterns. As in Jordan's characterisation of Gothic art in terms of a multiple, rather than an organic, unity, medieval literature is constructed as an additive totality made up of distinct or even of incongruent and detachable parts. As a result, characters are not the driving force of the narrative, as they are in much modern literature, but are secondary to the story. The result is often startling *voltes faces*, as in the case of Athelston, the noble hero of a late fourteenth-century romance, who, on learning of his wife's supposed treachery, kicks her in the stomach so that their child is still-born. Yet, once convinced of her innocence, he reverts to the role of noble ruler, unwilling to break his oath or to act unjustly: 'The portrayal of the king in one theme is quite contrary to that in another, for such themes were designed to promote the narrative and not for the internal cohesion of the characters'.[87] Perhaps, as in Lydgate's *Siege of Thebes*, which describes Theseus pulling Thebes to the ground, 'the howsys brente, the puple slough for al her crying loude' and the city turned to a wilderness, yet continues to regard him as a 'worthy duk', we simply have to accept the heroic status of Theseus as the explicit premise of Chaucer's 'Knight's Tale' (*ST*: 4501-99, 4639)?

But perhaps a more convincing resolution of the apparent contradiction between what the Knight explicitly says about Theseus and what his tale implicitly seems to show to the modern reader would be to ask whether, in a fourteenth-century perspective, such inconsistencies would have been apparent in the first place. For instance, the pillaging of the bodies of Theseus's enemies has been seen as undermining Theseus's moral justification for waging war on Thebes; in fact, the laws of medieval warfare *did* explicitly allow the pillage of a defeated enemy.[88] Even Theseus's refusal to ransom Palamon and Arcite (*CT*, I: 1024) may not have been the unchivalrous act that it at first appears to be since although a chivalric writer such as Honoré Bonet condemned as tyrants those who demanded an excessive ransom, he also emphasised that the right to reasonable ransom applied *only* to wars between Christians and that in ancient civil law a prisoner could be enslaved or even killed by his captor.[89] More generally, unlike modern glorifiers of mighty conquerors, medieval authors, as we have already seen in the case of Lydgate, seem to have been perfectly capable of graphically depicting the horrors of war and praising the virtues of peace while simultaneously glorifying their warrior heroes as 'worthy conquerors'. For example, the main purpose of the *Gesta Henrici Quinti* (1416-17) was to present Henry V as a devoutly Christian prince, one who was 'honourable, considerate and humble' in diplomacy and in war and who secured his victories with the help of God and his saints. Nevertheless, its author did not hesitate to describe Henry's soldiers as 'butchering' their French enemies, pillaging the dead and searching through piles of bodies for those who were still alive who could be taken as prisoners. Nor did this chronicler shrink from portraying the king himself burning down villages which refused to pay him a 'ransom'.[90] As Augustine said, in defending the notion of the just war, 'it is the injustice of the opposing side that lays on the wise man the duty of waging wars' but this did not mean that we should overlook the slaughter and miseries involved in even the most just of wars.[91]

Similarly, the apparent inconsistency between the depiction of the perilously enthroned Conquest in the Temple of Mars and the description of Theseus himself being honoured as a conqueror and as later 'Arrayed right as he were a god in trone' may not constitute the critique of the duke which it first seems (*CT*, I: 1027, 2028-30, 2529).[92] It was, after all, Theseus who commissioned the image of Conquest in the first place. In this perspective, the temple of Mars (like that of Venus or of Diana) does not provide a critique of Theseus's actions but is actually an expression of his own moral vision. Theseus here seems to be displaying the self-awareness and sense of perspective extolled in the *Confessio Amantis* where Gower describes the jester who rode alongside the Roman emperors at their 'triumphs' with the task of reminding them that, though they were now victorious, the Wheel of Fortune might one day turn against them since all things last but a little time (*CA*, VII: 2381-411). In like vein, in his *In Praise of Peace*, Gower applauds King Solomon, who asked God for wisdom, in preference to Alexander, who asked to conquer the world (*IPP*: 31, 38). Far from constituting an implicit critique of Theseus, the depiction of Conquest in the Temple of Mars which he commissions emphasises – at least from a fourteenth-century perspective – his wisdom and his awareness of the transience of earthly power and glory.[93]

Much of the debate about the meaning of the 'Knight's Tale' revolves around Theseus's concluding speech which extols the wisdom of the

'First Mover'. For many critics, Theseus's speech is an ideological instrument of political control, an expression of political opportunism by which he ensures his own personal and political power, secures the marriage of Emily and Palamon against Emily's wishes and thereby furthers his own imperial ambitions and the subordination of Thebes.[94] This would certainly be a valid reading if we assumed that Chaucer possessed a rather Machiavellian outlook in which the state and political power are seen simply as an 'instrument of domination by certain groups over other groups, utilised by the former to their own advantage and to the disadvantage of the latter'. But, in fact, the dominant view in the Middle Ages was exactly the opposite of this since it saw the rightful business of politics as the 'attempt to establish order and justice' for the common good. As we saw in the case of Gower, 'mirrors for princes' offering guidance in kingship presented politics as the extension of ethics into the public realm and as essentially concerned with the production of justice, order and virtue in the body politic. Politics is a form of morality, and morality is a form of politics, since it involves the rule of the lower human faculties by the higher. The state is, as Giles of Rome argued, politically useful and morally right; it is a perfect community which subsumes other human institutions, such as marriage which is itself a microcosm of the body politic.[95] Of course, modern readers are (quite rightly) likely to be suspicious of the specific content which was, in practice, given by medieval writers to such worthy abstractions as 'order', 'justice', 'love', 'reason' and 'common profit', as when Philippe de Mézières saw Richard II's 'love of God and, hence, of his neighbour' as being demonstrated by Richard's subjugation, without bloodshed, of 'a race of people as savage and uncivilised as the Irish'.[96] However, we should not assume that medieval readers necessarily shared our suspicions.

Thus, if we judge Theseus by the political standards of our own day, his requirement that Emily should comply with his 'will' and acquiesce to a marriage which runs counter to her own personal wishes is likely to seem rather 'coercive', making Theseus himself into a tyrant, albeit one who 'consults his parliament'.[97] Yet, Theseus's actions would have seemed less reprehensible when seen in the context of medieval views of the political functions of marriage. For instance, Philippe de Mézières urged the twenty-eight-year-old Richard II to marry Isabella, the seven- or eight-year-old princess of France, so that through their alliance 'all unease will be banished from both countries' and 'the two kingdoms will become as one'. Philippe did not stop to consider Isabella's wishes in the matter. Instead, he compared the princess to a horse, elephant or camel, all of which are best trained when young and impressionable. Through such an education, the king would obtain a wife with the 'marvellous patience' of Griselda, one instructed according to the will of her 'lord and husband'. In this perspective, the marriage of Emily and Palamon which cements the union of Athens and Thebes is, far from being the expression of Theseus's opportunistic 'will to power'. Instead it becomes an example of the bringing together of nations by treaty and by chaste married love which Boethius saw as instances of the working of the chain of Love which binds the entire universe in harmony.[98]

With their ethical view of what kingship *should* be, medieval political theorists certainly did not think that political power was good *per se*. On the contrary, they criticised those 'tyrants' who would not be governed by their own laws and ruled for their own personal benefit without the advice of wise counsel, exactly the charges made to justify the deposition of Richard II in 1399.[99] As the 'Manciple's Tale' says – echoing St Augustine – the only difference between a tyrant and a bandit is that a tyrant has a great army and does more damage than an outlaw's band (*CT*, IX: 223-34). However, Augustine did *not* equate kingdoms *per se* with tyranny or with robber bands. What he said was that kingdoms became 'gangs of criminals on a large scale' *once* justice was removed from them. Even a kingdom's just wars should not be the occasion for rejoicing because they are the result of the wickedness of others. At best, the just war is a 'stern necessity' although 'since it would be worse that the unjust should lord it over the just, this stern necessity may be called good fortune without impropriety': 'it is beneficial that the good should extend their dominion far and wide and that their reign should endure'.[100] In this context, it becomes difficult to see why Theseus's arranging of the marriage of Palamon and Emily with the aid of 'al the conseil and the baronage' of his land falls into the category of tyrannical acts as defined in medieval terms, particularly when we are told that, after their marriage, the couple lived happily ever after with never a cross word between them (*CT*, I: 3094-108). It has been argued that 'this utopian claim is not easy to judge', as if Palamon and Emily were actual people whose real lives could be judged against the Knight's claim. But, of course, Palamon and Emily exist only within their tale, their living happily ever after is no more or no less real than Palamon and Arcite's imprisonment. Nor can the plausibility of their happiness be judged against the depressing images of love in the Temple of Venus since for medieval writers there was a crucial difference between the chaste love of husband and wife ordained by natural law, where each loves the other 'with all their heart', and the irrationality of the 'wild and wanton' servants of Venus who had yet to acquire the 'sadness and wisdom' of maturity (*CT*, I: 3094, X: 915, 920, 936-7; *Bo*: 420; *TC*, V: 1824-48). In this perspective, the depictions of love in the Temple of Venus do not cast doubt on the happiness of Palamon and Emily. Rather, their happiness within marriage is based on the renunciation of the kind of love depicted therein, a love based on the victory of the body and the flesh over reason and self-control.[101]

Many critics argue that even if the First Mover speech was not intended by Chaucer to demonstrate Theseus's *political* opportunism, it is, despite all the duke's supposed wisdom, evidence of his *philosophical* deficiencies. Again a gap is opened up between the voice of Theseus (and the Knight) and that of Chaucer the poet, thereby undermining the monologic certainty of Theseus's discourse. Thus, Theseus has been seen as at fault in his 'First Mover' speech in lacking any reflexivity about his own discourse, he fails 'to qualify his statements' or to recognise 'the provisional nature of his picture of the world'. It is certainly true that Theseus claims to know what the First Mover's 'entente' was when he created the 'faire cheyne of love' which binds the universe. But this claim to know the 'devyne thought' comes straight from Boethius, a text translated into English by Chaucer himself. Twentieth-century critics understandably find certainty in such matters astonishing, but fourteenth-century readers may have had less difficulty with the notion that God had bound the universe with a fair chain of love, whether this claim was put into the mouth of Lady Philosophy by Boethius or into the mouth of Duke Theseus by Chaucer (*CT*, I: 2987-91; *Bo*: 451).[102]

Perhaps the most powerful point in favour of those who see a gap between Theseus's world-view and that of Chaucer is the argument that, far from offering a satisfactory conclusion to the tale, Theseus's claims for the beneficent omnipotence of the First Mover seem to be refuted by the very events of the tale itself. After all, whilst Theseus's speech emphasises the omnipotence of Jupiter, it is actually the malign and capricious Saturn, a figure added to the story by Chaucer himself, who intervenes to resolve the dispute of Mars and Venus over the prayers of Arcite and Palamon when Jupiter himself could scarce 'stente' the conflict (*CT*, I: 2438-78, 3035-6). Saturn's speech, in which he claims 'moore power than woot any man' makes clear his malign influence when he says that to him belong drowning, imprisonment, strangling and hanging by the throat, 'murmure and the cherles rebellyng', secret poisoning, vengeance and correction, the destruction of cities, 'maladyes colde', dark treasons, plots and pestilence (*CT*, I: 2453-70). As Brown and Butcher have shown, Saturn's astrological influence can be found even in minor details of the tale, such as Arcite's careful handling of money as squire to Theseus or the specific tasks he performs as servant to Emily. For many critics, it would seem that, in introducing an emphasis on Saturn not found in any of his sources, Chaucer 'takes care that his audience understands Theseus to be mistaken', depicting a world in which, despite Theseus's optimisic claims, 'disharmony, evil and suffering' are the dominant force rather than justice or love. The emotions evoked in the reader by the horror of Arcite's death and the effect on us of the depiction of the world as a prison-house ruled over by the malign Saturn thus far outweigh the abstract, philosophical consolation offered by Theseus at the end of the tale.[103]

However, we should not necessarily assume that the metaphysical inconsistencies which modern readers are likely to identify in the Knight's outlook were equally apparent to a medieval audience. For instance, Aers finds it ridiculous that Theseus can cite the fact that all things in this 'wrecched world' must one day die as an 'experiential proof of a stable and eternal first mover who binds all in a chain of love' (CT, I: 2994-3004, 3011-15).[104] It is certainly possible that Chaucer accepted the view that this world was 'wrecched' and this life to be a 'foule prisoun' (CT, I: 2995, 3061; Fo: 1). He had, after all, translated into English Innocent III's De Miseria Humane Conditionis (LGW, 'G': 414-15), a work which argues that man is conceived in sin, born to pain, lives a life of unlawful, shameful, indecent and unprofitable deeds before dying and becoming fuel for the fire and food for worms. This does not mean that either Innocent III or Chaucer believed that this world was *simply* a foul prison. Innocent had, after all, intended to write a sequel to De Miseria extolling 'the dignity of human nature'. As so often in medieval thought, the moral critic is not pretending to offer a simple, empirical description of the world. Rather, he is recommending a particular outlook or attitude for specific purposes: in Innocent III's case in De Miseria, that of *contemptus mundi* with which to humble the mighty; in Theseus's case, that of a *consolatio* for the death of Arcite.[105]

Medieval thinkers certainly found an awareness of the miseries of this world perfectly compatible with a belief in an omniscient, omnipotent, loving God. After all, Christianity had long been committed both to a belief in a benevolent God and to a view of world history as a series of evils, troubles and disasters: war, disease, famines and earthquakes. Indeed, medieval Christians, such as the author of *The Goodman of Paris* (c. 1395), believed that it was their loving God who was directly responsible for sending them tribulations such as 'the death of friends, the loss of goods and children and lineage, discomfiture by enemies, captures, slayings, losses, fire, tempest, storms of weather, [and] floods of water'. In return, said the Goodman, our response to such miseries should be (like that of Griselda in the 'Clerk's Tale') to 'suffer patiently' and to seek to be reunited with our tormentor.[106] The modern attitude (thankfully) tends to be that suffering is wrong *per se* and consequently looks for ways to remove suffering and injustice. Medieval moralists, by contrast, were more interested in humanity's *reactions* to suffering. As Augustine put it, 'when the good and the wicked suffer alike, the identity of their sufferings does not mean that there is no difference between them. Though the sufferings are the same, the sufferers remain different ... The violence which assails good men to test them, to cleanse and purify them, effects in the wicked their condemnation, ruin and annihilation. Thus the wicked, under pressure of affliction, execrate God and blaspheme; the good, in the same affliction, offer up prayers and praises. This shows that what matters is the nature of the sufferer, not the nature of the sufferings.'[107]

The *Consolation of Philosophy* addresses the problem of suffering directly: if God knows all things and can only will good things, then how is it that evil not only goes unpunished but actually seems to flourish whilst virtue 'is cast undir and fortroden undir the feet of felenous folk' (*Bo*: 440)? Upon reading Philosophy's sophistic answers (i.e., that since evil is nothing, the wicked can in fact do nothing; that goodness is always rewarded and wickedness punished; that God's love rules the universe; and that, despite all appearances to the contrary, all fortune is good fortune (*Bo*: 443, 444, 455)), students have sometimes wondered whether Boethius was being serious. Yet, as far as we know, the *Consolation* was not intended to be read ironically, tempting though it is to do so.[108] Significantly, as evidence for the divinely inspired 'accordaunce' which rules the universe and overcomes all 'discordable bataile', Boethius explicitly cites the fact that Love, which brings forth all living things, also seizes, hides and takes away all things, engulfing them in the final death: 'ravysschynge, hideth and bynymeth, and drencheth undir the laste deth, alle thinges iborn' (*Bo*: 454-5). As in Theseus's 'First Mover' speech, death is explicitly cited by Boethius as part of the divine plan.[109] It is for this reason, in *Troilus and Criseyde*, when 'by Goddes wille' Troilus has died at the hands of Achilles, Troilus's soul then rises to the eighth celestial sphere from where he sees 'this wrecched world' in its true perspective and realises that we 'sholden al oure herte on heven caste' (*TC*, V: 1805-25). Similarly, Gower was able to combine a conviction that God rules all things with the belief that 'all things change and die' and that, as the world sinks into moral decay, it is the good who die whilst bad men endure and live again (*VC*, II: 7; VI: 19-21). This was an idea which went back to Augustine who argued that we, as mortal creatures, share in the alternation and succession of the passage of nature and thus often find it hard to appreciate the ordered beauty of God's creation: 'Hence the right course for us, when faced with things in which we are ill-equipped to contemplate God's providential design, is to obey the command to believe in the Creator's providence. We must not, in the rashness of human folly, allow ourselves to find fault, in any particular, with the work of that great Artificer who created all things'.[110]

The apparent discrepancy between the beneficient role which Theseus claims for the First Mover in his final speech and the capricious actions of the gods which we have witnessed in the tale itself may be further reduced when we recall that, in a Boethian perspective, Saturn and the other pagan deities are far from being merely malevolent individuals who act according to whim so that human affairs become matters of chance. For Boethius, as later for Dante (*DC*, VII: 61-96), 'chance' is a matter of our perspective since, in reality, Fortune is subject to a higher power so that it becomes an instrument of destiny. Fortune is simply a name for providence misunderstood since, in reality, what seems to be cruel and capricious is actually part of a beneficial providential order. Since God rules Fortune, she ultimately works for good; the real mischief in human affairs lies in our response to her rather than in her deeds *per se*. Similarly, human free will is not the opposite of destiny but an integral part of it. In this sense, the deities are not simply external agents but are personifications of Palamon, Arcite and Emily and their own inner qualities. In particular, the power of Saturn does not simply represent some irresistible external force or capricious fate since, in Boethian terms, it is those who abandon their reason and allow themselves to be ruled by their passions and lower natures, such as Palamon's Venusian concupiscence and Arcite's Martian wrath, who are most subject to external necessity. Palamon and Arcite are not ruled by some irresistible fate, rather they have willingly fallen in its trap through their own folly and submission to their lower appetites.[111]

Nevertheless, the pagan gods can also be seen as personifications of the astrological influence of the planets, as Palamon, Arcite and Emily recognise when they time their prayers to Venus, Mars and Diana (the latter's planet being the Moon) to coincide with each planet's maximum power. But, once more, in a Boethian perspective, the influence of these planets works not according to some capricious whim but is rather as a result of their inner nature, a nature which, in turn, is determined by the First Mover. Far from the workings of the planets providing a refutation of

Theseus's view of the universe, the astrological deities function here as an allegorical way of referring to the workings of Providence: they are instruments or aspects of the First Mover not an alternative to it. As the *Boece* makes clear, Divine Providence ('purveaunce') controls the motion of all things through Fate ('destyne'), whether it works through nature, individuals, the 'celestial moevynges of the sterres' or even the 'divers subtilte of develis', which is how medieval writers often portrayed the deities of antiquity. As the devil in the 'Friar's Tale' says of his work: 'somtyme we been Goddes instrumentz / And meenes to doon his comandementz, / Whan that hyn list, upon his creatures, / In divers art and in diverse figures. / Withouten hym we have no myght, certayn, / If that hym list so stonden theragayn' (*CT*, III: 1482-7). Boethius thus presents as a unity forces which we are more likely to see as opposites (*Bo*: 451). As a result, the events of the 'Knight's Tale', in which Saturn, the cause of disorder, becomes, as the agent of Jupiter, the efficient cause of restored order, are perfectly compatible with the medieval view, as expressed by Bartholomaeus Anglicus, that the beneficent influence of Jupiter tempers that of all the other planets that come within its range, its goodness abating even the malice of Saturn, which itself then becomes a force for order. It is, therefore, to Jupiter that the dying Arcite, who has come to see the consequences of his devotion to Mars, commends his soul (*CT*, I: 2792). If the gods (in astrological form) can be cruel and contrary, then they can also, on occasion, come into a peaceful and beneficient conjunction. Even Augustine, who attacked the pagan gods as 'wicked demons' and specifically denied the powers claimed by the Romans for Jupiter, was prepared to praise the ancient philosophers who 'refer to destiny under the name of Jupiter, whom they suppose to be the supreme god' since they anticipated the Christian sense of destiny to mean a chain of causes dependent upon the will and power of the supreme God.[112]

Furthermore, if Theseus's speech seems, at least to the modern reader, 'to transcend difficulties, rather than to analyse and solve them', this seems to imply that there *is* some adequate solution to the problem of suffering and death at which Theseus should have arrived.[113] But what is this solution? It is true that Theseus fails to consider one possible option, i.e., that an argument from design, when applied to the events of the 'Knight's Tale', might lead the reader not to a belief in a loving, omnipotent first mover but to the conclusion that the world has been made either 'by a crippled or apprentice deity' or, as in 'some manichean or gnostic traditions', by some fallen and evil principle, or by a deity who, if not malevolent, is quite unconcerned with the world he had created.[114] But is Theseus's failure to arrive at this conclusion really to be read as implying that his speech is unconvincing and inadequate when judged by the standards of the late fourteenth century? We may see Theseus's use of death as an example of the workings of a loving First Mover as a proof that his examination of such matters lacks 'scrupulousness', but Boethius – and perhaps his English translator – was rather more impressed with the wisdom of this line of argument. It would seem then that wisdom itself is a historically specific concept: the profundities of one age become the 'commonplaces' or even the absurdities of another.[115]

None the less, Theseus's First Mover speech can be seen as being signalled by Chaucer as containing a number of philosophical inadequacies. However, such inadequacies are the result not of the speech's (inevitable) implausibility when assessed by modern standards but rather, as Minnis has argued, of its deficiencies when judged from the standpoint of medieval Christianity. It has often argued been that the Middle Ages lacked a sense of anachronism, i.e., of the difference of the people of the past from those of the society of their own day. The past lost its distance, reinterpreted through *exempla*, became 'a part of present moral experience'.[116] By contrast, Minnis, like C. D. Benson, argues that Chaucer was acutely aware of the essential differences between the pagan past and the Christian present and did his best, given the sources available to him, to represent classical antiquity in historically authentic terms. Hence the fatalism of Emily, who, as late medieval writers would have expected of a pagan, passively accepts her destiny. Even Theseus, who does possess a belief in the freedom of the will and an understanding of the importance of human action, is of limited wisdom when judged by the standards of Christian theology. For instance, in order to make a virtue of the necessity (a phrase which Chaucer takes from his source, Boccaccio's *Teseida*) of Arcite's death, Theseus argues that it is better for a man 'to dyen in his excellence and flour', when he is sure of his good name and honour, than in old age, when his name is faded and his prowess forgotten. Here Theseus seemt to be guilty of the excessive concern with one's earthly good name for which Christian writers, including Boethius, had long criticised the pagans (although Boethius did still value the 'honourable renoun of this world' brought by a glorious death). Certainly, theologians from the time of Augustine onwards had, following classical writers such as Sallust and Cicero, depicted the ancients as motivated primarily by a a desire for earthly fame, glory and renown. This motive was, of course, inferior to the true virtue of the Christian, whose glory lay in God and his own conscience, but at least had the beneficial effect of making men 'less depraved' than they would otherwise have been. As the fourteenth-century allegorist Pierre Bersuire put it, 'the ancients performed all their lofty deeds for the sake of acquiring fame, and they longed for glory and fame as the final reward of their deeds; and this they did because they were ignorant of the true glory of heaven and the true, everlasting reward' (*CT*, I: 3041-66; *Bo*: 418-20, 426-7, 453).[117]

The 'Knight's Tale' can therefore be seen as an attempt by Chaucer to depict ancient Greece in authentically historical terms. In this perspective, Chaucer's Duke Theseus is not merely the embodiment of some vague princely virtue. Rather, his portrait is based upon a particular classical ethic, that contained in the works of the Stoic philosophers, including Seneca's *De Clementia* and Cicero's *De Officiis*, as these works were interpreted by medieval writers such as Abelard, Alanus de Insulis, Jean de Meun, William of Peraldus and Petrarch. For the Stoics, this world is a realm of chaos, disorder, passion, destruction, death and the turns of Fortune. Indeed, Nature in general was seen as an endless cyclical process of death–birth–death, a view of the world which was perfectly compatible with Christian orthodoxy 'as long as there is no suggestion either that this activity was without beginning' and as long as it does not lapse into pantheism. However, for both pagan and Christian Stoics, humanity could still achieve at least some temporary victory over the Saturnine forces of chaos and disorder since, even if it lacks control of events in the external world, it can control its inner self by exercising its reason and virtue and by cultivating the virtues of moderation, self-restraint, humility, patience and sobriety, In Augustine's words, 'The good man, though a slave, is free; the wicked, though he reigns, is a slave, and not the slave of a single man but – what is far worse – the slave of as many masters as he has vices' (see 2 Peter 2: 19). As Seneca put it, 'the most degraded slavery is that which is self-imposed'. In this outlook, even prosperity is to be feared, since it breeds excessive pride, let alone the inevitable down-turn of the wheel of Fortune which inevitably occurs in the affairs of this world. Petrarch thus argued that one should neither boast of one's good fortune nor bewail one's bad fortune: if you are born of a good family, think that both you and the poor husbandman will soon both be the food for worms; if you are blind, count your blessings that you can no longer have to see spectacles of foul wantonness.[118]

Chaucer himself was described by the French poet Eustache Deschamps as a Seneca in his morality, and Seneca's advice against excessive mourning, even for the death of one's own child or friend, is cited with approval in the 'Tale of Melibee' told by Chaucer the pilgrim (*CT*, VII: 984, 991-2).[119] But it is in the 'Knight's Tale' that the Stoic outlook is most fully developed. Reason and harmony, personified by Theseus, who represents the peak of pagan wisdom, his father Egeus and the chastened Palamon, can prevail against the ever-threatening forces of disorder: fortitude can overcome adversity, temperance conquer desire and, as in the 'Tale of Melibee', those who govern themselves with wisdom and moderation can 'put awey sorwe' (*CT*, VII: 990-3). Evil, represented by the tyrannical Creon, is not always victorious, suffering can be ameliorated, and justice, the key social virtue, can prevail. Pagans and Christians are not simply opposites even though pagan philosophy *is* inferior to Christian wisdom. If pagans cannot attain the theological virtues of Faith, Hope and Charity, they can exercise the four cardinal virtues of Prudence, Justice, Fortitude and Temperance. Theseus's First Mover speech may lack a specifically Christian revelation or a knowledge of the immortality of the soul and, instead of Boethius's theological consolation for earthly suffering, can offer only the earthly consolations of honour and legitimate marriage. Nevertheless, the 'Knight's Tale' still manages to combine reasons for optimism alongside its awareness of human suffering and, in its portrayal of the virtue achievable even by pagans, provides a viable moral example to the Christians of Chaucer's day. As the preachers' commonplace had it, if pagans could achieve such virtue then how much more should Christians be able to achieve?[120]

It would seem then that many of the apparent contradictions which modern critics have identified in Chaucer's presentation of Theseus disappear if we see the 'Knight's Tale' in its historical context and interpret it in terms of fourteenth-century understandings of antiquity and, in particular, of late medieval conceptions of 'political power' and 'love', rather than loading such abstractions with their modern connotations. Once we adopt this approach, there is no need to resolve the apparent discrepancy between the Knight's description of Theseus as an ideal ruler and the seemingly tyrannical nature of Theseus's actual actions by reading his praise of Theseus as ironic.[121] In fact, it may well be that, by late medieval standards, there was no discrepancy to resolve in the first place. The 'Knight's Tale' may then be seen as rather more internally consistent – or monologic – than many recent critics have allowed.

In comparison with the authority of the Knight, the ideal representative of the second estate, the voice of Robin the Miller has little authority. As we have seen, the Miller is described in the 'General Prologue' as thieving, boorish and deceitful. His animosity to the Knight comes not from just a lower-class hostility to the pretensions of the gentle but reflects a more general lack of charity and love of discord. As in many other medieval depictions of millers, the golden-thumbed Robin is just as willing to steal from his neighbours as he is from anyone else (*CT*, I: 562-3).[122] In comparison with the combination of Stoic morality and Boethian philosophy contained in the 'Knight's Tale', the tale told by the Miller offers, in medieval terms, only a negative vision of society in which people are reduced to their lowest natures, however attractive its egalitarian hedonism may be to modern audiences. In the world which it portrays, the likelihood of morality and the possibility of justice are absent and there is no means of bringing humanity into harmony with the divine or natural orders; even the perfunctory moral usually tagged on to the end of a *fabliau* is missing. In the context of the Knight's vision of social order, this tale confirms, rather than refutes, the vision of social hierarchy as 'natural, inevitable and required'. The Miller's nihilism, however entertaining in its own terms, is not particularly effective as a refutation of the Knight's idealism but works only in terms of the 'myopic circumscription' characteristic of the *fabliau*. Its humour, rather than unmasking the Knight's chivalric ideology, works, like that of many *fabliaux*, at the expense of the pretensions of the lower orders of society, the 'bumbling peasants and small-town manipulators who amuse the more sophisticated audience with their simple wit'. Thus, whilst the love of the two Theban knights for Emily is represented as an irrational force in the 'Knight's Tale', it is still in some sense understandable and tragic. In the 'Miller's Tale', the imitation of courtly love by Absolon the parish clerk is seen as an absurd comic pretension. Similarly, the portrait of John the carpenter, the ignorant and credulous cuckold who would be lord of the world (*CT*, I: 3581-2) but who ends up being humiliated in front of his neighbours, is typical of the lack of personal or communal solidarity which the tale takes for granted as the human condition. It is not difficult, therefore, to see why the 'Miller's Tale' provokes a reply from Oswald the carpenter-reeve (*CT*, I: 3859-60) rather than from the Knight himself. For all its humour, the tale told by the drunken Miller presents lower-class revolt as itself laughable and impotent, as 'based on the systematic destruction of the decorum of established rule in life *and* art'. It 'would have been a good deal more congenial to the tastes of Chaucer's predominantly gentle audience' than the Miller's aggressive tone and social hostility might initially seem to imply.[123]

What of the status of the Parson's discourse about sin and penitence at the end of the *Canterbury Tales*? Is the Parson's voice simply one amongst many or does an ideal cleric enjoy a more authoritative status than that of a drunken miller? There is no doubt that the literary theory of the medieval period itself tended to privilege the message offered at the end of a text. For instance, in his highly popular commentary on the book of Ecclesiastes, St Bonaventure considered the argument that since this book includes the teachings of a foolish and carnal man which could lead readers astray, it should be removed from the canon of the Bible. St Bonaventure replied by arguing that 'to say something in the character of a foolish or carnal person' *can* lead people into error but that this is *not* the case with Ecclesiastes since the author of this book explicitly gives his own opinion at the end of the text. It is this unambiguous ending which allows us retrospectively to assess which opinions he agrees with and those which he disagrees with as foolish and vain: the 'book cannot be understood unless attention is paid to its totality'.[124] Similarly, in her attack on Jean de Meun's *Roman de la Rose*, Christine de Pizan argued that 'a work stands or falls by its conclusion', just as in council, 'whatever may have been previously said, people rely on the closing argument'. Thus it may be permissible to have literary characters speak sinfully provided that the writer concludes 'in favour of the moral way of life' (*QR*: 132). As Dante put it, 'what a speaker is most intent upon conveying must always be reserved for the end, for what is said last makes the most enduring impression on the mind of the listener'.[125] Pandarus repeats this idea in Chaucer's *Troilus and Criseyde* when he says that although men delight to tell tales with subtle art, still they write toward 'som conclusioun': 'th'end is every tales strengthe' (*TC*, II: 256-60). When applied to the *Canterbury Tales*, this privileging of the conclusion of a work of literature by medieval literary theory would seem to render Chaucer's text rather more monologic than many modern readers would care to admit. As Cooper argues, when the Parson begins his tale his words *are* merely the 'dramatic voice of one character, not Chaucer's own', he is simply 'one pilgrim among many, telling a tale that is rhetorically and dramatically appropriate for him; one voice to set besides all the others'. But by the end of the tale, and in Chaucer's 'Retractions' which form the conclusion to the *Canterbury Tales*, 'Chaucer and the Parson are speaking with a single voice'. Chaucer's moral Parson is thus not just another voice amongst the pilgrims, his is 'an exceptional, authoritative voice' whose privileged status is signalled by his personal virtue and by its position as the culmination of the pilgrimage to Canterbury?[126]

Finally, if the *Canterbury Tales* does invest certain voices with a monologic authority, why have so many critics been able to read Chaucer's text as a dialogic work which undermines and relativises established authority? Here it would seem that the literary form of the tales posed problems for the transmission of the dominant ideology of Chaucer's day to those readers who were not already convinced of the virtues of that ideology, a category which (hopefully) is likely to include most of the text's modern audience. In particular, the fact that the *Canterbury Tales* lacks any consistent authoritative voice, whether of an external narrator or of a protagonist within the diegesis of the pilgrimage, means that readers will tend to judge the pilgrims and their tales according to their own particular values. As a result, Chaucer's pilgrims, with their first-person mono- logues, tend to produce sympathy and identification on the part of the modern reader. Geoffrey of Vinsauf was able to assume that his readers would realise that a woman who went out with her hair adorned was sup- posed to be a 'wanton' (above, p. 000) but such a response can no longer be relied upon from a modern audience: the disparity between the ideal expected and the reality actually observed no longer 'speaks for itself'.

Thus, in the absence of any consistent authorial or narratorial com- mentary, the 'Truth' revealed at the end of the *Canterbury Tales* does not, unlike that of Dante's *Divine Comedy*, appear as the logical culmination or fulfilment of a gradual progression towards knowledge on the part of its protagonist (in this case, Chaucer the pilgrim). Despite the interplay of the pilgrims on the road to Canterbury, the frame of the tales does not take the form of a journey towards understanding and the allegorical potential of the pilgrimage is invoked only twice. Firstly, it appears at the start of the journey, in the 'Knight's Tale', when Egeus describes this world as a thor- oughfare full of woe in which we are 'pilgrymes, passynge to and fro' (*CT*, I: 2847-8), and secondly at the very end of the tales when the Parson offers to show his companions 'the wey, in this viage, / Of thilke parfit glorious pilgrymage that highte Jerusalem celestial' (*CT*, X: 49-51). Yet even the Parson, despite beginning his tale by referring to the 'righte wey of Jerusa- lem celestial', makes little of the possibilities of the metaphor of the 'weyes espirituels that leden folk to oure Lord Jhesu Crist' (*CT*, X: 75-80). If the *Tales* begin with the secular virtue of the Knight and end in the religious virtue of the Parson, it is nevertheless rather difficult to identify any arc of spiritual development running between them. Unlike the allegorical journey to the New Jerusalem described in Guillaume de Deguileville's *Le Pèlerinage de Vie Humaine*, where the pilgrim is aided by the armour of virtue and the staff of hope etc. etc., the structure of the *Canterbury Tales* resembles, as Howard has argued, the labyrinths depicted in medieval cathedrals which have Jerusalem at the centre but which are reached by a meandering path, one which symbolises the confusion and puzzlement of the world. Given the absence of any growing spiritual knowledge or self- awareness on the part of the pilgrims, we are unprepared for the shift of tone represented by the 'Parson's Tale', which comes as an abrupt resolution and external imposition of seriousness on the story-telling contest. The totality of the interaction of the pilgrims thus tends to overwhelm the didacticism of any individual narrator. As a resault, the 'game' of the motif of the story-telling on the road to Canterbury, a self-contained arena in which 'the valuations of virtue and vice do not apply', comes to supplant the 'ernest' of the metaphor of life as a pilgrimage and the creative vision of art takes priority over any specific moral vision or ethical system.[127]

This difficulty in understanding the meanings and morals left implicit in their works by medieval authors is not simply a problem which confronts modern audiences. On the contrary, in their debate with the Col brothers and Jean de Montreuil on the *Roman de la Rose* in 1401-3, Jean Gerson and Christine de Pizan argued that a lack of explicit authorial commentary in work of literature such as the *Rose* created problems even for the transmission of authorial intentions to a contemporary audiences. They attacked Jean de Meun's continuation of the *Rose* as an 'exhortation to vice' and, against those who defended the moral intentions underlying Jean de Meun's depiction of vice, argued that it was insufficient for an author simply to *portray* folly or sin in the hope that readers would therefore eschew such sin themselves. Even *if* Jean de Meun's intentions were moral (which Gerson and Christine thought was in itself unlikely), the literary techniques he had adopted were ill-suited to such purposes and would lead readers astray, seducing them into the very vices which his defenders claimed he had set out to attack. It is not enough, claimed Gerson and Christine, simply to describe foolish and sinful deeds. Instead, the author himself has the responsibility of explicitly *condemning* such folly since 'mankind is naturally inclined to evil' and cannot be trusted to recognise such folly for itself.[128] One wonders, if they had been confronted with Chaucer's text, whether Gerson and Christine would have made similar criticisms of the *Canterbury Tales*. If allowing contemporary readers to draw their own conclusions was a rhetorical strategy fraught with potential dangers, such risks were inevitably exacerbated once Chaucer's works came to be read by audiences unfamiliar with the literary conventions and the socially dominant values of Chaucer's own day and when the apparent openness of his text allowed readers to interpret the text in ways which were anachronistic by the standards of the fourteenth century. Benson argues that in the varied world-views of the *Canterbury Tales*, Chaucer can 'wander far afield because he always knows where home is', but an audience which lacks a fourteenth-century world-view is more likely to remember the wandering along the way than to share its conception of what constitutes our true home.[129]

It would seem, therefore, that it *is* possible to reconcile the apparently contradictory 'monologic' and 'dialogic' interpretations of the *Canterbury Tales*. Even if we accept that Chaucer himself intended his work to buttress the hierarchial, official world-view of his day, such intentions could come into conflict with the dialogic potential inherent in his story-telling contest and with his adoption of a literary form which, with its lack of any consistent, authoritative voice, was ill-equipped to constrain later interpretations or to prevent diametrically opposed readings of his text. However, if the *Canterbury Tales* left itself open to being read as a dialogic work by modern critics, it could be argued that, given medieval notions of the purposes of literature, such a reading was far removed from that of Chaucer himself and hardly available to readers in Chaucer's own day. It is, therefore, to the literary theory of the medieval period itself that we now turn our attention.

Notes

1 Althusser, 1971: 203-5.
2 Emerson, 1986: 23-4; Volosinov, 1986: 58-61, 67-8; Bakhtin and Medvedev, 1985: 159; Bakhtin, 1992: 259, 333; Morson, 1986b: vii; Lodge, 1990: 1-8; Bennett, 1981: 71-2, 77; Holquist, 1990: 109-15; Bakhtin, 1986: xiv, xvi, 10-19.
3 Lodge, 1990: 21, 90; Morson, 1986c: 83-4; Bakhtin, 1973: 64-7.
4 Bakhtin, 1992: xxxi, 6; Ganim, 1990: 19-20; Bakhtin, 1973: 153-65; Lodge, 1990: 59-60; Kristeva, 1969: 43-4; Lawton, 1985: 3-5.
5 Holquist, 1990: 69; Forgacs, 1986: 195; Lodge, 1990: 61; Hirschkop, 1989: 12; Todorov, 1984: 63-4; Bakhtin, 1992: 283, 349; Bakhtin, 1973: 56-60, 64, 71, 80, 150-1.
6 Bakhtin, 1992: 17-18; Barron, 1990: 132.
7 Duby, 1980; Owst, 1966: chapter 9; Fletcher, 1991; Rigby, 1995: chapter 9.
8 Coffman, 1965; Bennett, 1966: 61; Minnis, 1980: 172-6; Peck, 1978; Strohm, 1979; Minnis, 1983b; Wickert, 1981; Coleman, 1981: 126-56; Olsson, 1982: 195-6; Porter, 1983a; Yeager, 1990: 265-79. Wetherbee sees Gower's conclusions in the *Confessio Amantis* as less certain and more tentative than many earlier critics have suggested (Wetherbee, 1991: 31) whilst Olsson argues that Gower's shifts of meaning in this work 'have the effect of weaning readers away from the false security of a single-valenced argument, or from a facile morality and illusory wisdom'. Nevertheless, even if Gower does not allow us to settle 'prematurely' into 'superficially "correct" judgement', it does seem possible to defend a view of the diverse elements of the *Confessio* as 'wholly congruous' with each other (Olsson, 1992: 12-15, 247-8; Minnis, 1991b: 54-5).
9 Bakhtin, 1984: 5, 9-20, 49, 81, 83, 87, 89, 97; Bakhtin, 1973: 100-13; Mackenzie, 1987; Clopper, 1990; Dinn, 1990, I: 232-4; Rimbault, 1875; Andreas, 1990; Howard, 1987: 421-6; Pearsall, 1987: 38-9; Gash, 1986.

10   Cook, 1986: 177-8; Bakhtin, 1973: 106-7; Bakhtin, 1984: 4-5, 9, 72-82, 88, 90, 92, 94-6; Rimbault, 1875: xviii, xxv; Ganim, 1990: 11.

11   Eco, 1984: 60; Barber, 1959: 6, 36-49, 213-14; Ladurie, 1980; Hilton, 1992: 125-6; Kendrick, 1988: 127, 156; Mâle, 1972: 60-1; Strohm, 1992: 45-6.

12   Bakhtin, 1973, 87-99, 110; Payne, 1981, 4-14, 21, 27-31; Kristeva, 1969: 52-5.

13   Lodge, 1990: 96.

14   Knight, 1986: 92; Bishop, 1988: 25; Brown and Butcher, 1991: 69-70, 76; Patterson, 1991: 27-8.

15   Cooper, 1989: 301.

16   Wood, 1991: 77; Huppé, 1967; Olson, 1986; Delany, 1990: 143. On Olson, see below, pp. 29-33, 39-40.

17   Crone, 1989: chapter 6; Fourquin, 1978, 37-8; Blum, 1978: 3-6; Mousnier, 1973: 10-11, 20; Keen, 1990: 3-5; Robertson, 1968: 4-5; Britton, 1977: 167-71; Rigby, 1995: chapters 3, 5.

18   Robertson, 1980: 270, 293-4, 301; Robertson, 1969: 51, 74-5, 260, 265; Clogan, 1992: 138, 149.

19   See above, pp. 1-2 and also Hilton, 1977; Hilton, 1985: chapter 9; Dyer, 1981; Dyer, 1984; Razi, 1979: 152-7; Razi, 1983; Rigby, 1995, chapter 3.

20   For references to Marx and Engels on ideology, see Rigby, 1987: chapter 12; Rigby, 1992: 77-81, 166-7.

21   Robey, 1986: 78-9; Patterson, 1991: 165; Graff, 1989: 169; Bennett, 1981: 19.

22   Greenblatt, 1992: 12, 18, 75-6; Lapsley and Westlake, 1988: 19-20; Sarup, 1988: 80-8; Montrose, 1989: 15, 17, 20; Dollimore, 1985: 4, 10; Newton, 1989: 152-3; Bennett, 1990: 19, 21, 52-3, 69, 72-5, 108, 141. For cultural materialism, see Barrell, 1988: vii–viii, 12, 36.

23   Lentricchia, 1989: 234; Greenblatt, 1992: 3.

24   Burrow, 1992: 129; Olson, 1986: 4, 30-1, 298.

25   Huppé, 1967; 56; Delany, 1990, 111, 143; Olson, 1986: 28-33, 44.

26   Olson, 1986: 22, 27-8, 30-1, 44.

27   Bowden, 1954: 46-50; Mehl, 1986: 133-4; Owst, 1966: 332-3; Donaldson, 1977: 8, 60; Manly, 1907: 49-59; Hatton, 1968.

28   Horrell, 1939; Benson, 1986: 7.

29   Olson, 1986: 28-37, 99, 257-62; Owen, 1977: 45-6, 73; Howard, 1987: 410.

30   Olson, 1986, 29-30, 33-4, 40; Fleming, 1985: 162.

31   Olson, 1986, 39-40; Bowden, 1954: 108-9.

32   Curry, 1960: 79-90; Jones, 1955: 4-5; Steele, 1898: 114, 229.

33   Olson, 1986: 38-9; Ellis, 1992; Owst, 1966: 324-5; Fletcher, 1983; Mann, 1973: 166, 284; Wenzel, 1989: 339.

34   Goodman, 1992: 136.

35   Olson, 1986: 10-11, 19-20, 50-1; Manly, 1907: 57-9.

36   Jones, 1980: 2, 35, 42-9, 69-70, 94-100; Coopland, 1975: 14-15; Minnis, 1982: 176; Keen, 1983; Porter, 1983b; Pearsall, 1985: 116; Pearsall, 1986: 140; Pearsall, 1992: 44-5, 200; Pratt, 1987; Tyerman, 1988: 259-62.

37   Manly, 1907: 56-8; *IPP*: 250-1; Loomis, 1940: 298-9; Hatton, 1968; Olson, 1986: 31-2; Coopland, 1975: 14-16, 30-3, 44, 63-72.

38 McKisack, 1971: 145-6, 429-33; Bowden, 1954: 83-4; Olson, 1986: 33-4.

39 Knowles, 1972: 861-2; Keen, 1965: 8, 66; *IPP*: 64-7; Coopland, 1949: 81, 125.

40 Olson, 1986: 49-50, 101, 129; 62-3; Bishop, 1988: 41, 47-8; Boitani, 1977: 143-6; Boitani, 1985a: 195; Burnley, 1979: 25-30, 44, 79, 116, 127, 127; Clogan, 1992; Cooper, 1983: 104; Finlayson, 1992: 131-2, 143; Frost, 1949: 122, 130-1; Kean, 1972, II: 19; Kolve, 1984: 101, 129; McCall, 1979: 66-7; McCoy, 1974: 1; Minnis, 1982: 109, 120-31, 141-3; Muscatine, 1957: 183; Nicholson, 1988: 194-99; Patterson, 1991: 75-6, 198, 200; Pearsall, 1985: 135; Ruggiers, 1967: 161-2; Bakhtin, 1973: 64.

41 Gleason, 1987; Minnis, 1987b; Wetherbee, 1991: 8.

42 Manly and Rickert, 1940, III: 484.

43 Jefferson, 1917: 131; Bartholomew, 1966: 10-17, 76-7, 88, 98, 101-5; Kean, 1972: 5, 28-9, 41-51; Muscatine, 1972: 126; Bishop, 1968: 15-23; Bishop, 1983: 43-44; Bishop, 1988: 45, 47; Olson, 1986: 66-8; Huppé, 1967: 54-7, 73-4.

44 Knapp, 1990: 27; Minnis, 1982: 121, 127-31, 142-3; Clogan, 1992: 138.

45 Jordan, 1967: 152-3, 157, 184; Knapp, 1990: chapter 2; Patterson, 1991: 168-74, 178, 198, 200-1.

46 Mâle, 1972: 9; Boitani, 1977: 127, 134; Knapp, 1990: 19; Muscatine, 1957: 178-81; Jordan, 1967: 155, 161, 175; Blake, 1973: 4-5; Patterson, 1991: 207; Howard, 1976: 234; McCall, 1979: 66, 83-4; Cooper, 1983: 94; Benson, 1986: chapter 4; Blanch and Wasserman, 1986.

47 Minnis, 1982: 28; Burnley, 1983: 167, 185-200; Knight, 1973: 240; Kendrick, 1988: 101; Knapp, 1990: 18-23.

48 Aers, 1991; Bennett, 78-9, 106; Burnley, 1983: 184-5, 200; Miller, 1977: 71; Fisher, 1973.

49 Muscatine, 1957: 185; Muscatine, 1972: 125; Knapp, 1990: 28-31; Leicester, 1990: 226; Neuse, 1962: 259; Huppé, 1967: 54.

50 Olson, 1986: chapter 2; Miller, 1970, 159-60; Patterson, 1991: 40, 245.

51 Lawler, 1980: 161, 167-9; Huppé, 1967: 58.

52 Wood, 1970: 275-97; Cooper, 1989: 400-1. Wood emphasises that the scales of Libra were associated not just with the idea of divine judgement but also with crucifixion and pennance. Peck argues that the number symbolism of the 'Parson's Prologue' also emphasises pennance (Peck, 1967).

53 Strohm, 1989: 177; Joseph, 1970: 95.

54 Owst, 1966: 551.

55 Huppé, 1967: 239-40; Jordan, 1967: 239-40; Howard, 1976: 380; Howard, 1987: 425-6, 495-6; Baldwin, 1955: 39-45; Wood, 1991: 79; Kendrick, 1988: 129; Cooper, 1989: 397, 403-404, 412; Patterson, 1978: 379-80.

56 Cooper, 1989: 417-18; Georgianna, 1990: 55-8; Heffernan, 1990: 160-1; Pratt, n.d., II: 357-63; IV: 248-50; Aers, 1986a: 24, original emphases.

57 Donaldson, 1977, 4, 9-10; Kendrick, 1988: 142.

58 *CA*, I: 60; Minnis, 1991a: 16-17; Minnis, 1991b: 52-3; Nolan, 1986: 157.

59 Bakhtin, 1973: 58.

60 Donaldson, 1977: 10; Mann, 1973: 189-90, 193, 197-202.

61 Lumiansky, 1980: 12; Barthes, 1968: 88.

62 Mann, 1973: 192; Patterson, 1991: 27; Nolan, 1986: 161.

63 Mann, 1973: 180, 183-4.

64 Mann, 1973: chapters 4, 9; Kendrick, 1988: 97; Minnis, 1991a: 15; Andrew, 1989.

65 Rogers, 1986: 24-7, 65; Strohm, 1979; Strohm, 1989: xii-xiii, 171-2; Benson, 1986:
    22, 25, 36, 64, 85, 87; Børch, 1982; Cook, 1986: 190; Cooper, 1983: 49, 53, 55, 85,
    202, 208, 221, 240-4; Fyler, 1979: 20-2, 148-9, 161-3; Ganim, 1990: 65-6, 68, 107,
    129, 134-5; Jordan, 1987: 1-10, 169-72; Josipovici, 1979: 52-4, 56, 73, 80, 97;
    Justman, 1976; Kiser, 1991: 1-9; Koff, 1988: 10, 102-3, 108; Kolve, 1974: 317-18;
    Kolve, 1984: 82, 217-19; Mann, 1973: 189-90, 197-202; Minnis, 1991b: 51, 65;
    Neuse, 1991: 7, 36, 52, 85, 87; Patterson, 1991: 168; Riddy, 1993: 104; Root, 1994:
    253; Sklute, 1984: 4-5, 10, 21, 95-9, 115, 130, 134-8; Wetherbee, 1991: 8-9.

66 Minnis, 1991b: 55; Minnis, Scott and Wallace, 1988: 115.

67 Knapp, 1990: chapter 1; Kendrick, 1988: 99, 116-26; Patterson, 1991: 168.

68 Knapp, 1990: 36-41; Macherey, 1978: 52, 64-8, 133, 154; Eagleton, 1976: 89;
    Strohm, 1989: 133. On the competing conceptions of space in the tales of the
    Knight and the Miller, see Joseph, 1970: 84-9.

69 Knapp, 1990: 36-41; Jordan, 1967: 187; Dane, 1980: 215, 223; Shoaf, 1983: 168-9;
    Kolve, 1984: 118, 172-3, 185, 215, 252; Benson, 1986: chapter 4; Bishop, 1988: 59,
    61; Kendrick, 1988: 19; Strohm, 1989: 133; Muscatine, 1986: 59-61, 73-84, 92-103,
    154; Andreas, 1990: 140; Cooper, 1983: 110-14.

70 Bakhtin, 1973: 161-2; Kristeva, 1969: 44.

71 Robertson, 1969: 243; Muscatine, 1957: 189-90.

72 Bakhtin, 1992: xxxi, 6; Bakhtin, 1973: 88-9, 101; Benson, 1986: chapter 4; Cook,
    1986: 181-2; Knapp, 1990: 37-42; Pearsall, 1992: 156.

73 Muscatine, 1986: 159; Bakhtin, 1973: 104; Knapp, 1990: 33, 42-4; Patterson, 1991:
    245.

74 Underwood, 1959: 466; Rogers, 1986: 26-7; Patterson, 1991: 168-9, 202, 230;
    Knapp, 1990: 22-3; Reiss, 1980: 396; Ferster, 1985; 34, 40; Aers, 1980: 176, 189-91;
    Aers, 1986a: 25-6; Clogan, 1992: 146, 149. For Blake (1973), Theseus is well
    intentioned in his world-view but still misguided in his faith in the benevolence of
    Jupiter and his ignorance of the malign influence of Saturn on human affairs.

75 Payne, 1981: 12, 34, 208, 219-20, 229-33, 236-9, 253-5, 257.

76 Eilers, 1884: 609; Patterson, 1978: 331.

77 Finlayson, 1971; Mann, 1973: 190; Donaldson, 1977: 172-3; Cooper, 1983: 54, 199-
    201, 243-4; Rogers, 1986: 25, 121; Whittock, 1968: 293-6; Burrow, 1992: 128;
    Strohm, 1989: 180.

78 Smalley, 1960: 43, 299; Cooper, 1983: 200-1.

79 Josipovici, 1979: 80, 90-1, 97; Kolve, 1984: 370; Whittock, 1968: 295.

80 Kolakowski, 1971: 55-6; Aers, 1979: 196-7.

81 Gallo, 1971: 51, 97-9.

82 Haidu, 1968: 14-23; Howard, 1966: 282, 286; Allen, 1982: 6-11, 18, 217, 288, 293;
    Minnis, 199b: 39, 55-6.

83 Børch, 1982: ii; Pearsall, 1992: 122-3; Prince, 1991: 157-8.

84 Eco, 1992a: 23-4; Jordan, 1987: 125-6; Sklute, 1984: 96.

85 Manly, 1926b: 294-5; Owen, 1977: 5-6, 56-7, 65-6; Reiss, 1979: 81; Benson, 1986:

27; Havely, 1985: 250; Eco, 1984: 6; Gallo, 1971: 37 (translation of Vinsauf from Rowland, 1985: xviii).

86 Nolan, 1992: 263, 356; Wenzel, 1989: 497-507.

87 Blake, 1979: 128-30; Jordan, 1967: ix, 130-1, 238-9.

88 Knapp, 1990: 22; Keen, 1965: 70, 137, 140; Leicester, 1990: 229; Coopland, 1949: 152-4.

89 Aers: 1980: 176-7; Coopland, 1949: 134, 151-4.

90 Taylor and Roskell, 1975: xxiii, 71, 79, 91, 99, 125.

91 Knowles, 1972: 6, 12, 861-2.

92 Knapp, 1990: 22; Aers, 1980, 178; Pearsall, 1985: 116-17.

93 Gaylord, 1974: 175; Patterson, 1991: 198; Nolan, 1992: 275.

94 Neuse, 1962: 250-2; Jones, 1980: 202-16; Aers, 1980: 188-95; Payne, 1981: 219, 254; Ferster, 1985: 34-5; Aers, 1986: 29-30; Knapp, 1990: 27-8; Brown and Butcher, 1991: 233.

95 Duverger, 1972: 18-19; Porter, 1983a: 135-9; Minnis, 1983b: 71.

96 Coopland, 1975: 65, 139; McKisack, 1971: 470-3.

97 Ferster, 1985: 33, 35, 42, 44.

98 Coopland, 1975: xx, xxxii, 42, 68, 69; Neuse, 1962: 252; *Bo*: 420; Leicester, 1990: 350.

99 Coopland, 1949: 115-16, 209-13; Barron, 1968.

100 Knowles, 1972: 138-9, 154, 214.

101 Ferster, 1985: 40-2; Hanawalt, 1993, 6, 199-202; Moffat, 1908: 49; Robertson, 1969: 370-5.

102 Ferster, 1985: 40, 42, 44; Aers, 1980: 191.

103 Underwood, 1959: 462-3; Spearing, 1966: 75-9; Fifield, 1968: 95; Blake, 1973: 12, 16-19; Salter, 1983: 168; Aers, 1980, 179-80, 189-90; Payne, 1981: 256; Cooper, 1983: 103-5, 213-14; Ferster, 1985: 34; Knight, 1986: 87-8; McAlindon, 1986: 54-5 (for McAlindon, both pity, kindness, reason and ceremonious order *and* cruelty, fury, blind will and anarchy are inevitable parts of the cosmic order and of human affairs); Mehl, 1986: 162; Luxton, 1987: 96-102 (but see also pp. 105-9); Bishop, 1988: 47; Strohm, 1989: 133; Brown and Butcher, 1991: 212-29; Patterson, 1991: 203, 213; Finlayson, 1992: 141-2, 146.

104 Aers, 1980: 189.

105 Lewis, 1978: 92, 94.

106 Coopland, 1949: 42-3, 64, 118-19; Power, 1928: 137; McNamara, 1973.

107 Knowles, 1972: 14, 39-40, 139.

108 Payne, 1981: 59-62, 73-5, 78, 81 accepts this temptation.

109 Jefferson, 1917: 118.

110 Knowles, 1972: 475.

111 Jefferson, 1917: 50, 59, 64, 68; Bartholomew, 1966: 16-19; Kean, 1972: 27-51; Gaylord, 1974: 177-82; Elbow, 1975: 45; Kolve, 1984: 332; Leicester, 1990: 303, 313-14; McCall, 1979: 75; Finlayson, 1992: 138.

112 Lowes, 1934: 10-13; Kean, 1972: 28-51; Gaylord, 1974: 182-3; Minnis, 1982: 33-6; Mann, 1986: 79-80, 87-90; McAlindon, 1986: 41, 52-3; Ruggiers, 1967: 156-7; Kolve, 1984: 123-6; Pearsall, 1985: 126; North, 1988: 402, 420-1; Pearsall, 1992: 155, 157;

Knowles, 1972: 44, 155-6, 188-9 ('Augustine thus denied any sense of destiny as an inevitable sequence of events, independent of the will of God or man', *ibid.*, 179).

113 Salter, 1983: 168-81; Benson, 1986: 86-7.

114 Aers, 1980: 190; Haldane, 1968: 43-5.

115 Aers, 1980: 189-90; McCall, 1979: 80-3; Nolan, 1992: 60-8. Luxton argues that for medieval writers, proverbial commonplaces were likely to satisfy only if they were, like those of Theseus in his First Mover speech, the result of a lengthy period of reflection rather than a stock response which closed down thought. See Luxton, 1987: 105-9.

116 Burke, 1969: 1-6; Smalley, 1960: 10; Payne, 1973: 81.

117 McCoy, 1974: 315; Jefferson, 1917: 87-8; Knowles, 1972: 197-213; Benson, 1968; Minnis, 1982: 21-2, 29-30, 63-4, 127-35; Bishop, 1988: 45; Pearsall, 1992: 158. Fourteenth-century preachers were not necessarily opposed to the pursuit of a good name *per se*. Robert Holcot, for instance, argued that although virtuous men should not be excessively concerned with their earthly reputation, a desire for good fame could be a useful stimulus to goodness, even though one which was inferior to the promise of eternal glory (Smalley, 1960: 184).

118 Norton-Smith, 1974: 143-4, 229-54; Knowles, 1972: 139, 177; Myles, 1994: 56-7; Rawski, 1991, I: xxiii–xxiv, 1-7, III: 57, 96, 298; Scattergood, 1991.

119 Brewer, 1978: 41.

120 Bishop, 1968: 16-23; Benson, 1968: 123; McCall, 1979: 84, 111, 156; Cooper, 1983: 100; Kolve, 1984: 86, 142, 149-52; Nolan, 1992: 248-52, 260-8, 278-81; Neuse, 1991: 123; Finlayson, 1992: 144-7.

121 Webb, 1947: 289, 296; Jones, 1980: 195; Leicester, 1990: 361.

122 Jones, 1955.

123 Muscatine, 1957: 66; Nykrog, 1957: 95, 104; Kolve, 1984: 252; Pearsall, 1987: 41-2; Crane, 1992: 217; Cooper, 1983: 115-16; Olson, 1986: chapter 2; Kendrick, 1988: 60-1; Strohm, 1989: 139, 153-4, 168, 174; Pearsall, 1992: 237.

124 Minnis, Scott and Wallace, 1988: 231-2; Minnis, 1991a: 16.

125 Ryan, C., 1989: 58 (II, viii, 2-3).

126 Cooper, 1989: 397, 404; Pearsall, 1992: 269; Dean, 1989: 72-4; Wood, 1991: 76.

127 Cooper, 1983: 54-5, 73; Henry, 1985; Finlayson, 1971: 103-4; Robertson, 1969: 373; Norton-Smith, 1974: 155-7; Howard, 1976: 67-73, 326-32, 385-6; Howard, 1987: 441-2; Kolve, 1984: 156; Kirkpatrick, 1985: 205; Benson, 1986: 64, 85; Kendrick, 1988: 161; Neuse, 1991: 32, 85; Owen, 1977: 3-8; Manning, 1979; Huizinga, 1970: 25. On the notion of 'game' in the *Canterbury Tales*, see also Lanham, 1967. For the Pilgrimage of Life genre, see Wenzel (1973).

128 Minnis, 1991a: 17, 25, 27; *QR*: 55, 63, 74, 80-2, 130-7, 149.

129 Benson, 1986: 149.

3

Allegorical versus humanist
Chaucer

> For seint Paul seith that al that writen is,
> To oure doctrine it is ywrite, ywis;
> Taketh the fruyt, and lat the chaf be stille. (*CT*, VII: 3441-3)

DESPITE the multiplicity of new approaches to Chaucer's work, such as
the Bakhtinian and the New Historicist, which have been popular in
recent years, it is still true to say that many of the present generation of
Chaucer critics have been trained either as 'Robertsonians' or as
'Donaldsonians'. These great scholars, D. W. Robertson and E. Talbot
Donaldson, personify the two major schools of Chaucer interpretation
considered in this chapter: the 'allegorical' and the 'humanist'.[1] The contradictory assumptions underlying these two approaches provide, if it
were still needed, further evidence for the seeming incommensurability of
critical paradigms which characterises Chaucer studies. For Robertson,
the founder of 'patristic criticism' (or, as he preferred to call it, 'historical
criticism'), Chaucer is a poet of profound Christian faith; for Donaldson,
Chaucer takes our sinfulness for granted and is more interested in 'the
marvellous variety of life in a world which, however sinful, is the only
world we've got'. For Robertson, even those medieval poems which do
not explicitly address religious issues were frequently intended to promote the Augustinian doctrine of charity beneath a pleasing surface; for
Donaldson, there are 'no such poems in Middle English'. For Robertson,
the theological doctrines which underlie the *Canterbury Tales* in their
entirety are explicitly set out in the 'Parson's Tale'; for Donaldson, the
'Parson's Tale' is alien, in its morbid negativity, to the healthy
affirmativeness of many of the other tales. For Robertson, the mentality
underlying medieval poems such as the 'Nun's Priest's Tale' was profoundly different from that of the modern world and can thus be grasped
only by an effort of the intellect on our part; for Donaldson, the 'Nun's

Priest's Tale' is more immediately accessible, it is about more timeless concerns, about how the men of western civilisation 'have always behaved'.[2]

Debates about the validity of the patristic approach have raged ever since Robertson's earliest statements of his method yet, over forty years on, they seem no nearer to a resolution. On the one hand, those who reject patristic criticism argue that it is 'ahistorical' and 'reductive' and that Robertson himself eventually realised its shortcomings. On the other hand, patristic readings of Chaucer's poetry continue to be offered, even by those who disagree with particular aspects of Robertson's work, whilst, more generally, the admirers of patristic criticism claim that it has continued to gather support since it 'has proved so fruitful' for Chaucer studies.[3] Certainly, although patristic criticism has been around for a long time, it is perfectly capable of being updated to address more recent theoretical concerns. Indeed, it would be perfectly possible to see the patristic approach as an early instance of the now-fashionable emphases on the need to understand works of medieval literature in terms of their 'intertextuality' by which they are 'more often in dialogue with other works of literature than with any secure extra-textual concept of life'.[4] Similarly, the Donaldsonian humanist approach continues to be of enduring vitality since, as we shall see, it too can be recast into new vocabularies, such as the Marxist or the feminist. This chapter sets out the basics of the Augustinian doctrine of charity and of medieval allegorical theory and examines 'patristic' interpretations of Chaucer's work, particularly of the 'Nun's Priest Tale' (section i). It then goes on to look at the humanist alternative to the patristic method (section ii) and then concludes with an assessment of the strengths and weaknesses of the patristic approach (section iii).

(i) Patristic (or 'historical') criticism

Although 'historical criticism' has been seen as 'badly misnamed' by those who reject it,[5] Robertson's fundamental point *was* thoroughly historical, i.e., that the very notion of literature itself, its nature, purpose and reception, is historically specific, differing according to time and place. If this is the case, then to understand medieval poetry we need first to understand the literary theory of the medieval period itself. For the patristic critics, such theory saw poetry, or at least serious poetry, as primarily moral in its purposes. Literature pertains to ethics, '*ethice subponitur*' or, in St Paul's words, cited at the end of the 'Nun's Priest's Tale', 'Al that writen is, / To our doctrine it is ywrite' (Romans 15: 4; *CT*, VII: 3441-2).[6] Of course, medieval writers believed that poetry should amuse and entertain us but it should do so as the means to a higher end, rather than as an end in itself. As Richard de Bury said in his *Philobiblion* (1345), just as children have to be given rewards so as to persuade them to learn what they would otherwise be unwilling to study, so, 'since our fallen nature does not tend to virtue with the same enthusiasm with which it rushes to vice', poets provide us with 'delight' in order to lead us on to 'profit'. Nevertheless, such delight is merely the 'shell' of the nut whereas the profitable message is its nourishing 'kernel'.[7] Alternatively, literary form could be referred to as the dispensable 'chaff' of a text whilst its 'sentence' or moral message was its 'fruit, as when the Nun's Priest asks us to 'Taketh the fruyt' of his animal-fable 'and lat the chaf be stille' (*CT*, VII: 3443). But however it was expressed, it was a medieval commonplace that, as Boccaccio put it, 'fiction is a form of discourse, which, under the guise of invention, illustrates or proves an idea'. It is for this reason that, at the start of the tales, the Host offers the prize of a supper to the pilgrim who tells the tale providing not only the 'moost solaas' but also that of the 'best sentence' (*CT*, I: 798). It would seem then that, as Allen has argued, medieval thinkers lacked the notion of an autonomous category of 'literature'. Rather, as medieval commentators on Ovid's works never tired of saying, Ovid's intention was 'to delight as much as possible, and by delighting to instruct in behaviour, because virtually all authors have to do with ethics' (see, however, below p. 109).[8]

More specifically, the moral sentence underlying medieval poetry was, according to the patristic critics, formulated in accordance with St Augustine's doctrine of charity. Augustine's teaching was set out in his *On Christian Doctrine* (A.D. 427), the work which remained the standard introduction to the study of scripture throughout the medieval period: 'Chaucer views his pilgrims with the same attitude as St Augustine viewed his world'. According to St Augustine, 'Scripture teaches nothing but charity, nor condemns anything except cupidity', charity being defined as 'the motion of the soul toward the enjoyment of God for His own sake, and the enjoyment of one's self and of one's neighbour for the sake of God'. Cupidity, by contrast, is 'a motion of the soul toward the enjoyment of one's self, one's neighbour, or any corporeal thing for the sake of something other than God'. As Thomas Bradwardine, archbishop of Canterbury (d. 1349) explained: 'God must be loved in respect of himself and everything else must be loved in respect of God'. Charity is the source of all virtue and requires the exercise of our higher faculties, of our reason, the possession of which distinguishes us from the beasts. It represents the New Law brought by Christ to allow the salvation of mankind and which replaced the Old Law under which salvation was not possible. Cupidity, by contrast, is the source of all vice and represents the victory of our lower natures, of the flesh which should be subordinated to our reason. Man is a creature who is divided: he shares reason and spirituality with the angels, yet is also a material creature with fleshly, animal desires. The human condition is thus one of continuous tension between charity and cupidity. Man must choose between his two natures, between his higher nature, which includes his reason, virtue, spirit, and his lower nature, which includes his lust, sin and flesh, these two realms often being metaphorically equated by theologians with the masculine and the feminine respectively (see below, pp. 122-3). More generally, for a man to love any worldly thing before God, even his own wife and child, is an act of cupidity which, as the Parson says in his tale, makes that thing into his 'mawmet' (idol) and himself into an 'ydolastre' (idolater) (*CT*, X: 859).[9]

For the patristic critics, the aim of serious medieval poetry (like that of the scriptures) was that of leading its readers towards Truth but the methods it employed to do so were indirect, being figurative and allegorical rather than literal. As St Augustine explained, figurative language, in which a thing is used as a sign of some other meaning, was particularly well suited as a means of guiding us to Truth since it provides the pleasures of solving the difficulties and puzzles contained within a text: 'What is attended with greater difficulty in the seeking gives greater pleasure in the finding'. Such pleasures were not, however, intended as ends in themselves but were simply the means of leading us on from the 'letter' of the text to its higher spiritual meaning. To take figurative expressions as though they were literal is to be like a beast. One should not mistake signs for things but, using one's reason and intellect, 'raise the eye of the mind above things that are corporeal and created, to drink in eternal light'. As St Paul put it, 'The letter killeth, but the spirit quickeneth' (2 Corinthians 3: 6).[10] Medieval theorists, such as Hugh of St Victor (d. 1141), thus distinguished between the 'letter' of a text (i.e., its grammatical construction), its literal 'sense' or meaning, and its deeper significance or 'sentence', the first two merely constituting the 'husk' of the text, the latter providing its valuable 'kernel'. For Alanus de Insulis (1128-*c.* 1203), those who ignored the higher, spiritual truth of a text and remained at the literal level were 'puerile' readers: 'Do not read my poem if you seek only sensual pleasure'.[11]

Such allegorical modes of interpretation were modelled on the methods commonly used to explicate scriptural meaning. The types of significance to be found within a scriptural text could be classified in a variety of ways, but a common one, from the time of Origen and Clement of Alexandria

onwards, was a fourfold division into its 'literal', 'allegorical', 'tropological' and 'anagogical' meanings. The literal meaning included the supposed historical reality of Biblical events and requires little elaboration
here. An 'allegorical' meaning in the context of this fourfold division is one
which refers to what we should believe, including meanings to do with the
Church and Old Testament prefigurations of the events of the New Testament. The 'tropological' meaning is that concerned with morality and
what we should do. The 'anagogical' meaning is that concerned with the
after life, towards which our actions in this world are leading us.[12] Thus, to
take a stock medieval *distinctio* which illustrates these four modes of reading, the word 'Jerusalem' has a literal or historical sense: it is a real place
which the Wife of Bath has thrice visited on her wanderings by the way
(*CT*, I: 463). But, it can also be read allegorically, as the Church Militant
(Revelation 21: 2), tropologically, as the faithful soul (Isaiah 52: 2), and
anagogically as the 'Jerusalem celestial' to which the scriptures and the
Parson's teachings will lead us (*CT*, X: 51; Galatians 4: 26).[13] Any one text
is thus polysemous, i.e., capable of being read in a variety of different ways.
However, provided such readings promote the reign of charity, they are all
valid.[14] In practice, Biblical images, though not fixed in their meaning, as
when the scriptures use the lion *in bono* as a symbol of Christ but also *in
malo* to represent the Devil (Revelation 5: 5; 1 Peter 5: 8), did tend to
acquire standard interpretations through their explication by the Church
Fathers and by later Biblical commentaries, above all by the *Glossa
Ordinaria* of Anselm of Laon (d. 1117) and his associates, which ousted its
rivals and established itself as the standard Biblical gloss.[15] Chaucer himself was certainly aware of Biblical commentaries such as the *Glossa
Ordinaria*, as is shown by the 'Merchant's Tale' where Prosperyna uses it
to expound the meaning of Ecclesiastes 7: 28 (*CT*, IV: 2247-8, 2287-90;
PL, 113: 1124, see below, p. 156). Indeed, he could hardly have failed to
have been aware of such commentaries, given their centrality to medieval
learning and culture.[16]

It is true that from the twelfth century onwards there was a renewal of
interest in the literal sense of the Biblical text and an awareness of the need
for a mastery of Greek and Hebrew in order to comprehend this literal
meaning fully. Yet, even those who emphasised the need for us to comprehend the literal sense so as to avoid imposing a fanciful spiritual interpretation on a text still accepted that a full understanding of the literal
sense was a means to the end of grasping a text's higher spiritual meaning.
As Hugh of St Victor said, we should not 'strive superstitiously to find a
mystical sense and a deep allegory where none is' but neither should we

deny the spiritual sense when it is there. It is an understanding of this spiritual level which allows us to resolve the apparent inconsistencies and contradictions of the scriptures when read literally.[17] By the fourteenth century, the excesses of 'glossing' were acquiring a bad name, as when Chaucer's Squire and Parson contrast glossing with speaking the plain truth (CT, V: 166; X: 45). Writers such as Wyclif and Langland criticised sophistic and negligent glossing which perverted the authorial intention behind the Biblical text, ignored the literal and historical sense of the original and imposed an alien meaning on to the scriptures by quoting out of context. Nevertheless, just as Langland continued to offer his own allegorical meanings, so Wyclif continued to expound the meaning of the scriptures in terms of the traditional fourfold modes of reading: the literal or historical, i.e., that which has been done; the allegorical, which teaches what we ought to believe; the tropological, which teaches what we ought to do to avoid vice and embrace virtue; and the anagogical, which teaches what we ought to hope for in heaven. He did not reject spiritual readings *per se* but only those that were not 'groundid opynly in the text of hooly writ'. Despite the growing interest in the literal meaning of the scriptures represented by fourteenth-century commentators such as Nicholas of Lyre (although the 'literal' sense of the scriptures did also come to include a number of figurative meanings), Biblical exegesis remained 'largely Augustinian' in character in its basic distinction between the literal and the spiritual sense of the text. Allegorical interpretations remained particularly popular in sermons, whilst the fourteenth century even saw a renewal of interest in the moral and allegorical, rather than literal, meanings of the scriptures in the works of the English 'classicising friars' such as Robert Holcot. Even William of Auvergne, who argued that it would be wrong to see the adultery of David with Bathsheba as actually *signifying* Christ's union with the Church (its standard allegorical interpretation), was nevertheless prepared to accept the comparison of the two for the purposes of analogy.[18]

However, it was not only the scriptures which could be interpreted in terms of their concealed meaning, since almost anything was open to allegorical reading, from natural objects to the works of pagan poets such as Ovid. Nature was, after all, the Book of Creation written by God in which 'the invisible things of him ... are clearly seen, being understood by the things that are made' (Romans 1: 20). This semiological view of the universe can be seen in the works of Hugh of St Victor, who claimed that 'in the divine utterance not only words but even things have a meaning'. Indeed 'the significance of things is far more excellent than that of words' since the latter are a perishable human creation. The meaning of particular words is conventional and arbitrary whereas the meaning of things is necessary and natural. Creation is thus 'the voice of God speaking to men': 'all nature speaks of God, all nature teaches man'.[19] For instance, medieval depictions of the crucifixion frequently include a pelican nesting on the top of the cross. This is not because the gospels refer to the presence of such a bird at the time of Christ's death but because, as a fourteenth-century English Franciscan tells us, the pelican symbolises Christ's sacrifice: the pelican kills its own offspring through anger but then, moved by compassion, brings them back to life by piercing its own body to the heart with its beak and sprinkling them with its blood. Similarly, Christ, through shedding his blood on the cross, 'has brought sinners back to the life of grace after they had spiritually died by offending God'. As the *Bestiary* put it, 'the birds are there to teach man, not man to teach the birds': 'divine providence would not have revealed the natural qualities of birds so clearly if we had not been required to gain some advantage from it'.[20] As in Biblical exegesis, natural symbols were also polysemous but, in practice, they too acquired stock meanings, meanings which were set out in symbolic dictionaries such as Bartholomaeus Anglicus's *On the Properties of Things* (*c.* 1250).[21]

Furthermore, whilst the late medieval period did see an undoubted shift of attention towards the literal sense of the scriptures, this shift was also accompanied by a rise of interest in the allegorical and even spiritual meaning of non-scriptural works, although fictional works had been read in the same way as Biblical texts and in order to find the same meanings since at least the time of Fulgentius (fl. 468-533).[22] Such readings of secular works of fiction for their spiritual sense were denounced by John of Salisbury in the twelfth century but, despite continued opposition from certain theologians, were a commonplace by the fourteenth century when even pagan poets such as Virgil could be read allegorically and tropologically, if not anagogically.[23] Thus the French Benedictine, Pierre Bersuire (d. 1362), whose descriptions of the pagan deities may have been used by Chaucer in the 'Knight's Tale', was able to offer a moralised version of Ovid's *Metamorphoses* on the grounds that both the scriptures and the poets habitually used fables and inventions 'so that from them some truth may be extracted or deducted'. Even the mysteries of faith can be confirmed 'by using the very fictions of men'. For instance, the goddess Diana, depicted holding a bow and arrow, chasing horned stags and surrounded by the nymphs of the woods, hills, springs and seas and by horned satyrs, can be read *in bono* as a symbol of the Virgin Mary who 'is armed with the bow of pliant mercy and the arrow of prayer' with which she overcomes the horned stag of the Devil. The four types of nymphs who cluster around her represent 'souls who dwell in the rivers of the Scriptures', whilst the horned satyrs, the gods of the fields, symbolise the sinful mighty men who are thought of as gods in this world and 'dance hither and thither round her, begging pardon and mercy from her'. Read *in malo*, by contrast, Diana 'represents the evil woman' who wounds foolish men with the arrows of temptation and lust, her nymphs then become the 'young women who are deceived by her example' whilst the horned satyrs are the 'wanton men who are puffed up with the horns of high office'. Even the immoralities of the pagan gods could be interpreted *in bono* by those intent on finding an allegorical meaning.[24] Thirteenth-century mendicants, such as Aquinas, had argued that the scriptures were unique in having a higher spiritual sense but, by the following century, learned friars were offering moral and even spiritual readings of secular works of fiction and expressed a growing interest in pagan authors, deities and heroes as sources for their sermon *exempla*. Thus, fourteenth-century biblical commentators such as John Lathbury and Robert Holcot equated Christ and Hercules whilst a commentator on Virgil's *Eclogues* was even able to find references to Christ, St Paul and St Augustine in Virgil's text. Even Wyclif accepted that pagan poets such as Homer and Virgil could reveal '*multe veritates scripture sacre*', even though, naturally, their works lacked the absolute and ultimate authority which lay behind the scriptures. Virtually anything, therefore, whether in sacred or secular history, in nature or in fiction, could be used to provide a moral or a spiritual meaning. It was this 'analogical sensibility', rather than any strict application of the fourfold levels of allegorical meaning, which was the dominant medieval 'mental procedure for dealing with interior and exterior reality' and which remained very much at the heart of the culture of the later Middle Ages despite a growing number of challenges to it.[25]

Finally, it was not only ancient poets such as Ovid and Virgil who could be read allegorically by medieval commentators. If allegorical exegesis was primarily a mode of reading rather than writing, some medieval poets do also seem to have seen themselves as writing in an allegorical fashion for their own readers. For instance, in his 'Letter to Can Grande', Dante says of *The Divine Comedy* that 'there is not just a single sense in this work', rather there are several meanings, not just the literal or historical but also the 'mystical senses' derived from them: the anagogical, the moral (i.e., tropological) and the allegorical.[26] Similarly, at the end of his translation of Boccaccio's story of Griselda into Latin, Petrarch explains that the story of how Griselda patiently endures the 'unjust' and bitter sufferings heaped on her by husband Walter should *not* be seen literally as an inducement for women of his own day 'to imitate the patience of this wife' but was rather intended to lead his readers 'to emulate the example of feminine constancy and to submit themselves to God with the same courage as did this woman to her husband'. We should 'suffer without a murmur for God, what this poor peasant woman bore for her mortal husband'.[27] For Boccaccio himself it was such deeper levels of meaning which provided the justification of poetry since, as Quintilian said, 'the real power of eloquence is inconsistent with falsehood'. For Boccaccio, poets such as Virgil, Petrarch and Dante did not merely write to demonstrate their eloquence or their dexterity in composing metrical narrative: Virgil was a philosopher of deep learning, Dante a great theologian, Petrarch a moral philosopher. Boccaccio even implied that his own eclogues were possessed of a deeper meaning of this sort.[28]

Chaucer himself was well aware of such allegorical techniques of reading and writing. For instance, in the 'Tale of Melibee' the rich and mighty Melibeus goes out to the fields 'for his desport', leaving his wife, Prudence, and his daughter, Sophie (i.e., wisdom), at home where they are attacked and his daughter wounded in five places by three foes who enter his house through its windows. Prudence then offers an allegorical explanation of these events to her husband: his name, 'Melibeus', means 'a man that drynketh hony' (from the Latin *mel*, i.e., honey), in this case the 'hony of sweete temporeel richesses and delices and honours of this world' which have made him forget his Creator; he has been guilty of cupidity. As Ovid said, 'Under the hony of the goodes of the body is hyd the venym that sleeth the soule'. Melibeus's three foes are also interpreted allegorically to represent the three enemies of mankind, 'that is to seyn, the flessh, the feend and the world', who have entered his heart by the 'wyndowes' of his body, i.e., his five senses (*CT*, VII: 1409-25).[29] Similarly, at the end of his translation of Petrarch's tale of Griselda, the Clerk repeats Petrarch's rejection of the literal interpretation of the story as a recommendation that wives should follow Griselda in humility and offers instead an allegorical reading of it, i.e., that 'every wight in his degree, / Should be constant in adversitee', since if a woman was so patient to a mortal man 'wel moore us oghte / Receyven al in gree that God us sent' (*CT*, IV: 1142-62). Finally, as we have seen, at the end of his tale, the Nun's Priest warns us that his animal-fable should not simply be read literally and invites us to find a deeper meaning within it (*CT*, VII: 3438-43).

However, for the patristic critics, an allegorical interpretation of the *Canterbury Tales* is not only legitimate when Chaucer himself explicitly gives or invites such readings. Rather, Chaucer's sentence is more usually concealed under a veil of fiction but is none the less signalled by the presence within the text of Biblical allusions, of which there are perhaps over thirty in the course of the 625 lines of the 'Nun's Priest's Tale' alone, and by the use of stock allegorical symbols.[30] For instance, it has been claimed that the description in the 'General Prologue' of the Prioress daintily wiping her lip so clean that not a speck of grease was seen on her cup (*CT*, I: 133-5) was intended by Chaucer as a reference to Matthew 23: 25-6 where Christ says 'Woe to you scribes and Pharisees, hypocrites; because you make clean the outside of the cup and of the dish, but within you are full of rapine and uncleanness. Thou blind Pharisee, first make clean the inside of the cup and of the dish, that the outside may become clean'. Far from Chaucer decontextualising the pilgrims so that moral judgement becomes difficult (see above, pp. 43-4), his Biblical allusion provides us here with an context which allows us to realise the Prioress's hypocrisy, provided, that is, we recognise this 'deftly interwoven' scriptural reference in the first place.[31]

However, according to the patristic critics, even a knowledge of the original Biblical passage is often insufficient for an understanding of Chaucer's text: we may also require a knowledge of the exegesis of this passage by later commentators. For instance, in the 'General Prologue', Chaucer provides us with a description of the physically repulsive and morally corrupt Summoner who, we are told, loved 'garleek, onyons and eek lekes' (*CT*, I: 634). For Kaske, this latter point is not simply some personal detail or realistic trait of the Summoner but is an allusion to Numbers 11: 5 where the Hebrews, tired of having only manna to eat, remember 'the fish that we ate in Egypt free cost: the cucumbers come into our mind, and the melons, and the leeks, and the onions, and the garlic'. For Biblical commentators from St Gregory onwards, this passage was understood allegorically: since leeks and onions make us cry they represent the delights of this world which are really full of tears. Similarly, in works such as the *Liber de Mortalitatibus*, the stink of garlic was likened to the stench of evil practices; it upsets the stomach like avarice disturbing the family; it ulcerates the body like the corrupting influence of evil; it generates leprosy (which Curry sees as the medieval physiological explanation of the Summoner's appearance), inflames the body, excites frenzy and generates red choler like the effect of the love of the world on the soul. When consumed in excess it produces weakness of vision, just as lust prevents an awareness of spiritual things. It was for this reason that, in the tenth century, Liutprand of Cremona could praise Otto I for *not* eating garlic, onions and leeks and that Chaucer's friend Gower used the text in his *Vox Clamantis* to symbolise the worldly, carnal churchman (*VC*, III, 2: 85-90). We need not see the naturalistic explanation of this line, i.e., that the Summoner loved the foods which, according to medieval medicine, worsened his condition, as being in opposition to a spiritual reading of it: both physically and spiritually the Summoner loves those things which aggravate his own discomfort. In a sense, the Summoner is a real, historical character; his office was, after all, very much specific to a particular time and place. Nevertheless, Chaucer, through his use of this Biblical quotation, also points towards the Summoner's moral significance as 'a reprobate pilgrim lusting after the fleshpots of Egypt'.[32]

Armed with this approach, patristic criticism can offer an allegorical interpretation even of those comic or immoral characters who would seem, from a Bakhtinian perspective, to represent a carnivalesque disruption of the hierarchical order and moral certainty of official medieval culture. In an allegorical perspective, such characters can be seen as examples of the 'grotesque', of a humanity which is monstrous, reduced to a bestial condition by its abandonment of reason and its embrace of vice. The depiction of the rebels of 1381 as farmyard creatures in Gower's *Vox Clamantis* is a classic example of such grotesque imagery. It is used too in the 'Nun's Priest's Tale', where Chauntecleer is at once a cock and a man, and even, Robertson argues, in the iconographic traditions which underlie the descriptions in the 'General Prologue' of characters such as the Prioress and the Monk.[33] One of the most startling examples of such grotesque imagery comes at the end of the 'Summoner's Tale'. Here, when the wrathful Friar John complains to the local lord about the fart which Thomas has donated to him to be divided between the friars of his house, Jankyn, the lord's squire, suggests how this operation might be performed: Thomas should sit at the hub of a cartwheel with twelve spokes with a friar at the end of each spoke so that 'equally the soun of it wol wende, / And eke the stynk, unto the spokes ende' (*CT*, III: 2273-4). The Summoner's ribald conclusion to his tale at first seems to be simply a crude revenge for the tale told by the Friar about a summoner carried off to hell by the Devil. Yet, in fact, Jankyn's solution to Friar John's problem owes much to Biblical, exegetical and iconographical representations of Pentecost. It is a witty, satirical reversal of the descent of the Holy Ghost when a 'mighty wind filled the whole house' (Acts 2: 2), one which bolsters the charge that the friars are hypocrites and undermines their apostolic pretensions (see above, pp. 13-14).[34]

Thus, for the patristic critics, we cannot understand Chaucer's text simply by offering a close reading of the interplay of its internal elements (unity and diversity, order and disorder, etc.) as a New Critic might do.[35] Meaning is not purely internal to the text but also has an external dimension in the work's allusions to other texts and its reliance upon shared ways of reading which, unfortunately, the modern reader can recapture only by arduous labour. In this perspective, the 'Nun's Priest's Tale' ceases to be an example of the ahistorical universality of great literature which speaks to all people in all times. Rather, it was written by and for people with a very different mentality from our own: it is the alterity of the medieval worldview, rather than its similarity to that of the modern day, which is the cornerstone of the patristic approach.[36]

Finally, Robertson presented his reading of the *Canterbury Tales* in conscious opposition to the 'dramatic' readings of Chaucer's work by those such as Kittredge and Lumiansky, an approach oten associated with 'humanist' readings of Chaucer's work (see section ii, below). For these critics, the *Canterbury Tales* is a work of 'dramatic realism' in which Chaucer, using his 'amazing understanding of human psychology', treats his pilgrims as 'a group of real pilgrims on a real pilgrimage' and presents their tales as dramatic speeches which reveal the minds and hearts of their narrators to us, even allowing us to speculate about their lives prior to the pilgrimage. Such critics place their emphasis very much on the relationship between the tale and the description of its teller given in the 'General Prologue' and also on the interactions of the pilgrims within the pilgrimage-frame of the tales: the stories exist for the sake of the pilgrims rather than vice versa. The 'Nun's Priest's Tale', for instance, contains a wide variety of digressive material (such as Chauntecleer's numerous *exempla* of prophetic dreams) but, it has been claimed, can still be seen as an 'artistic unity' when interpreted 'in the light of the Priest's personality', in particular of the resentment he feels at his subservience to the Prioress on whom he is attendant. His tale about a cock and a hen thus becomes a wish-fulfilment fantasy of the restoration of male supremacy.[37]

Despite frequent criticism, 'dramatic' readings of Chaucer's work as inhabited by 'psychologically verisimilar human beings' with an interiority analogous to our own remain extremely popular to the present day and are capable of being translated into a variety of critical vocabularies, such as the feminist or even the psychoanalytical.[38] Yet, for Robertson, Chaucer was not concerned with characters in the modern sense at all. Instead, Chaucer's descriptions of the pilgrims and of the characters within the tales are composites of revealing qualities and iconographic details which are intended as manifestations of some underlying abstraction. For instance, eating garlic, leeks and onions is not something which the Summoner does in the course of the pilgrimage. It is a typifying action, an iconographic detail, just as medieval depictions of the vices and virtues portray them by means of standard images, such as the mirror and comb used to depict Lady *Luxuria*. For the patristic critics, Chaucer's characters have much in common with such personified abstractions. Indeed, in the 'Tale of Melibee', Melibeus's wife explicitly takes her name from the cardinal virtue she personifies: the prudence which enables us to know what we should desire and what to avoid. Even when a character's moral nature is not indicated by an appropriate name, he or she can still, in practice, be little more than a personification. Thus Griselda in the 'Clerk's Tale', whose submissiveness is so unattractive to modern readers, can be seen as an instance of the virtue of Justice as defined in the medieval sense of rendering to each what is their due, including, in the case of Griselda, the obedience due to her father and her husband.[39]

In general, the patristic critics offer a particular inflection of the interpretation of the *Canterbury Tales* as a monologic text: i.e., they perceive a thematic univocity underlying the diversity of the tales, a clearly formulated vision, guaranteed by external authority, of rightful moral and social hierarchies. Patristic criticism might therefore seem to be guilty of imposing a high seriousness on to Chaucer's poetry, emphasising his piety and moral purposes and transforming the *Canterbury Tales* into a series of gloomy, Biblically based homilies whilst neglecting the comic playfulness of his work.[40] The patristic critics would reply that, in fact, much of Chaucer's humour arises from the irony at work in having his characters invoke Biblical passages and their exegetical interpretation whose message they themselves ignore or distort. An awareness of such allusions, distortions, partial quotations and misquotations should therefore add to, rather than detract from, our appreciation of the irony and satirical humour which Chaucer employed. This method reaches its peak in the 'Wife of Bath's Prologue', which constitutes a *tour de force* performance of Biblical and exegetical allusion (see below, pp. 142-9). But the method is found throughout the *Canterbury Tales*, as Chaucer's false exegetes misinterpret their sources in order to justify their own philosophy of life, as when the Man of Law distorts the meaning of a number of Biblical passages and of Innocent III's *De Miseria Condicionis Humane* in order to buttress his attack on the hateful condition of poverty.[41]

Armed with these assumptions about Chaucer's use of biblical exegesis, the patristic critics have felt able to respond positively to the Nun's Priest's invitation to find the 'moralite' of his tale. Certainly, medieval preachers did frequently use animal-fables as *exempla* to illustrate their sermons. John Bromyard even told a story very similar to that of the 'Nun's Priest's Tale', although without Chauntecleer and Pertelote's debate over dreams, as an illustration of how God can cause nefarious men to outwit themselves, whilst the author of the twelfth-century *Gallus et Vulpes* interpreted his mock-heroic tale of a cock tricked by a fox into closing its eyes as an allegory of the man of faith deceived by a heretic.[42] However, the polysemous nature of allegorical symbolism (see above, p. 82) and the fact that the Nun's Priest does not himself explain the moral sentence of his tale to us means that particular patristic critics have been able to arrive at very different readings of Chaucer's meaning. Dahlberg, for instance, sees it as particularly significant that the fox of the tale is called Russell (*CT*, VII: 3334) as this identifies him with Rousiel, the son of Reynard the fox, who is used to satirise the mendicant orders in the late thirteenth-century *Renart le Nouvel* in which he rises to become head of the Franciscans. Certainly, the treachery and deceitfulness traditionally ascribed to the fox by medieval bestiaries such as the *Physiologus*, a work cited in the 'Nun's Priest Tale' itself (*CT*, VII: 3271), were used to attack the friars by fourteenth-century writers and artists who depicted foxes as friars preaching in cowls to congregations of ducks and geese, their favourite prey. In particular, anti-mendicant writers attacked the friars for their use of flattery which is, of course, the means by which Russell deceives Chauntecleer and by which Chaucer's Friar Huberd insinuates himself into wealthy households (*CT*, I: 250; VII: 3437).[43] If the fox symbolises the friars, the cock was commonly used from the time of St Ambrose, through Hugh of St Victor, Alanus de Insulis and the writers of medieval bestiaries, to late medieval preachers such as John of Sheppey, bishop of Rochester (d. 1360), as a symbol of the priest: just as the cock should know the hours of darkness for his crowing, so the preacher should know the degrees of moral darkness.[44] For Dahlberg, the 'Nun's Priest's Tale' shows that Chauntecleer, in being 'recchelees' (*CT*, VII: 3436), is guilty of the sin of sloth in the sense that he ignores the rules which he should obey and is heedless of the warnings of danger which he receives. Chauntecleer represents the proud, slothful cleric who, closing his eyes when they should be open, falls prey to the flattery of the friars but who still has the chance to open his eyes and take control of his own destiny. Certainly, the theme of sight is stressed in the tale and it is significant that, when the five senses were represented in animal form, the cock symbolised sight, just as the boar signified hearing; the spider, touch; the monkey, taste; and the vulture, smell. As the *Ancrene Riwle* says, quoting St Gregory, 'the flatterer blinds his victim by piercing his eye with a pin'. Later critics have been willing to adopt Dahlberg's interpretation of the tale, seeing it as the 'story of a priest who falls into the clutches of a friar but escapes just in time' when he discovers the essential weaknesses of the friar's – and of his own – nature.[45]

Yet, when offering an allegorical reading of the 'Nun's Priest's Tale', we should bear in mind the words of Hugh of St Victor who, though himself a Biblical exegete, criticised what Smalley calls 'the sublime disregard' of the literal sense of the Biblical text characteristic of the Gregorian commentary tradition: 'When we read the holy books, let us rather choose from the great multitude of patristic explanations ... that which appears to have been certainly intended by the author'. We should not force 'the thought of the Scriptures to be identical with our own' but instead should wish our thought to be 'identical with that of the Scriptures'.[46] With these words in mind we might then ask why the fox of the 'Nun's Priest's Tale' should be equated with the friars and particularly with the Franciscans? After all, with his black-tipped feet, ears and tail, Russell the 'colfox' would seem a candidate for membership of the Dominican Blackfriars rather than the Franciscan Greyfriars, provided, that is, we were ever told anything about him to suggest that he was a mendicant in the first place (*CT*, VII: 3215). More generally, the fox not only could be used to symbolise the friars but was also depicted as, amongst other things, a hermit, a priestly confessor or preacher, a bishop and even the pope himself. Bromyard, for instance, used the deceitful fox to represent the hypocritical clerics who only pretend to be virtuous so as to win ecclesiastical promotion whilst Bozon equated foxes with those predatory men who seek their quarry by night.[47] Medieval allegorists would, like Dahlberg, have been perfectly capable of interpreting the 'Nun's Priest's Tale' as a warning against mendicant deceitfulness since they were prone to producing allegorical readings which seem, at least to us, to have very little to do with their controlling literary context. Nevertheless, in the absence of any explicit allegorisation of the tale by the Nun's Priest himself, it would require the provision of far more cues and markers within the text if we were to be expected to deduce this specific moral (rather than any other) from this particular narrative. In the absence of such explicit exegesis within the text itself, a convincing allegorical interpretation of the 'Nun's Priest's Tale' by the reader must arise from the narrative of the tale itself rather than being imposed on it from the outside.[48]

If this is the case, perhaps the interpretation of the 'Nun's Priest's Tale' offered by Donovan is more convincing than that attempted by Dahlberg.

Like Dahlberg, Donovan sees Chauntecleer the cock as representing a cleric, but he interprets Russell the fox in general terms as a deceiver, a heretic or the Devil, a reading which seems to fit the action of the 'Nun's Priest's Tale' rather more comfortably than the overly specific reading of Russell as a member of the mendicant orders. There is certainly no doubt that the fox *was* commonly used by medieval writers and artists as a symbol of deceit in general and of the Devil in particular. For instance, medieval bestiaries describe the fox as feigning death, so that 'when birds fly down in order to eat him up ... he springs up and catches them and eat them up', just as those who seek to partake of the flesh of the Devil, through adultery, covetousness, lust and murder, will themselves suffer the spiritual death of damnation. In this perspective, the 'Nun's Priest's Tale' becomes the tale of the man who should be alert but, blinded by the pleasures of the things of this world (represented by Chauntecleer's sensual delight in his wife Pertelote), is tempted by the flattery of the Devil and is saved only by praying to God for help (*CT*, VII: 3342-5).[49] The Nun's Priest shows that *spiritually* we have reason for optimism: though humanity has fallen, we can escape the wheel of Fortune by use of our own free will, opening our eyes so as to achieve spiritual salvation: we can be lifted up as well as cast down.

Huppé develops this approach to the tale but sees it more specifically as an allegory of disorder within marriage and even as Chaucer's own preferred solution to the 'marriage debate' which so many of the pilgrims address in their tales (see below, p. 119). It is thus the relationship between Chauntecleer and Pertelote which is at the heart of the tale, as is suggested by the title of the tale in the Ellesmere Manuscript: 'The Nonnes Preestes Tale of the Cok and the Hen'.[50] For Huppé, the tale illustrates the orthodox medieval view of marriage in which rightful order depended upon the supremacy of the husband. As the Parson says, when he equates Adam with reason and Eve with the flesh, just as it is wrong for the lower to rule the higher so it is wrong for the wife to rule the husband (*CT*, X: 330, 924-30). The 'Nun's Priest's Tale' shows the consequences of a husband putting his love for his wife before his love for God: he will fall into the snares of the Devil. It is not that woman is *either* man's ruin (*hominis confusio*, as Chauntecleer puts it) *or* 'mannes joye and al his blis' (as he mistranslates the phrase) but rather that *because* she is all his bliss, his love for her will be his ruin. Chauntecleer is like Adam in ignoring the warning of future danger with which he has been provided and in being led to his fall through his excessive uxoriousness: 'Wommenes conseils been ful often colde; / Wommannes conseil broghte us first to wo / And made Adam fro Paradys to go'. Chauntecleer is therefore punished as a servant of Venus who takes a cupidinous delight in sex 'moore for delit than world to multiplye', a delight which, as the Parson grimly reminds us in his tale, is adulterous even when it takes place between man and wife. Nevertheless, as Chauntecleer's eventual escape from the fox proves, even fallen man has reason and free will so that escape from the Devil's snares is possible (*CT*, VII: 2874-5, 3160-71; 3177, 3200, 3342-5, 3256-8; X: 904-5).[51]

Huppé thus emphasises the similarities which he sees between the story of Chauntecleer and that of the fall: like Adam, Chauntecleer falls into the clutches of the Devil through 'wommanes conseil' which, '*in principio*', was the cause of man's ruin (*CT*, VII: 3163-4, 3256-9). However, he is mainly concerned with how such parallels illustrate the relationship of man and wife between Chauntecleer and Pertelote. For Levy and Adams, by contrast, the story of the Fall and its theological significance lies at the heart of the allegorical meaning of the 'Nun's Priest's Tale'. Certainly, there are undoubted parallels between the story of the Fall and the events of the tale: Chauntecleer falls into the clutches of the Russell the fox when he ignores the warning of danger which has been given to him, just as Adam, through his pride and his lustful obedience to his wife, ignored the prohibition to eat the fruit of the Tree of Knowledge and was deceived by the Devil. For Levy and Adams, it is no accident that the tale takes place on a Friday on the third of May (*CT*, VII: 3187-9) since this is the date of the feast commemorating the 'Finding of the Cross' in Jerusalem by Helena, the mother of Constantine, in A.D. 326. In the Middle Ages, it was believed that the True Cross was made of wood from the Tree of Life of the Book of Genesis (Genesis 2: 9). The Cross was perceived as a 'cosmological tree' which stood at the centre of the Earth (Jerusalem), its branches covering the Earth and forming a ladder between heaven and Earth by which the souls of the righteous could ascend to God. Thus, Chauntecleer 'falls' when he comes 'doun fro the beem' on which he and Pertolote had been perched but is saved from the fox when he flies up into a tree (*CT*, VII: 3172, 3417) just as it was the suffering of Christ, the second Adam (Romans 5: 14), on the cross which remedied the sin of the first Adam and allowed us to be saved. This Tree of Life was often represented by a tree from which a child picks fruit, i.e., the purified soul which picks the fruit of blessedness on its ascent to heaven. In a scene reminiscent of the 'Nun's Priest's Tale', an early fourteenth-century Book of Hours depicts just such a tree in its margin complete with a woman chasing a fox which is running away with a cock in its mouth. In this perspective, the tale's warnings about flattery and even about the falsity of women are the trivial chaff of the tale, whilst its fruit is its comic recapitulation of the Fall and of our salvation. More recently, Neuse has developed this allegorical approach, presenting Chauntecleer as 'a multiple and complex *imitatio Christi*' whose encounter with the Fox is meant to evoke both the crucifixion of Christ and also the temptation in the wilderness. Thus, even if the 'Nun's Priest's Tale' is comic in tone and contains a multiplicity of morals, this does not mean that it has no serious meaning. On the contrary, its apparently banal truisms are presented elsewhere in the tales in all seriousness, as when the Parson warns us to beware of flatterers who 'been lyk to Judas that bitraysen a man to sellen hym to his enemy; that is to the devel' (*CT*, X: 611-16).[52] If, as its opponents claim, patristic criticism is now on the wane, this would seem to be more the result of a growing preference amongst literary critics for the application of modern literary theory to medieval texts rather than of any shortage within Chaucer's works of the Biblical or iconographical cues which make allegorical interpretation possible.

(ii) Humanist criticism

At the other extreme from the patristic critics are writers in the humanist tradition who reject the patristic method in general and who argue, more specifically, that the 'Nun's Priest's Tale' was not intended as the vehicle for any profound moral truth but is in fact a parody of glib moralising and even of allegorical exegesis itself. These critics emphasise the 'consistent, witty and generous humanity' of the 'Nun's Priest's Tale' and the timeless significance of its message. Far from being the expression of some historically specific morality or mode of allegorical reading, it is a poem about the 'human condition', the 'human spirit' and 'human weakness', an exposé of how the men – and roosters – of western civilisation 'have always behaved'; it is a 'living picture of a man and his wife' in which 'Chauntecleer and Pertelote become people we know, people we may become, people we may already be'.[53] For these critics, it is wrong to paraphrase the meaning of the tale into the form of a Christmas-cracker motto. Rather, the tale's literary form, its so-called 'chaff' is as central to its meaning as the supposed 'fruit' of its explicit moral sentence. How convincing are the humanist criticisms of the patristic method and how persuasive is their own alternative interpretation of the 'Nun's Priest's Tale'?

Firstly, the humanist critics, like many of the opponents of the patristic method, reject what they see as its 'reductionism', its tendency to create a 'common dead level of expectation' that all medieval literature should demonstrate the truths revealed in scriptural exegesis. To impose such readings on to every medieval text is to deny all individuality and imaginative power to its author and, more broadly, contradicts the very nature of 'imaginative writing', i.e., its ability to enhance our understanding in new and original ways rather than simply confirming received truths. 'To give a reader a flat injunction to find one predetermined specific meaning in Middle English poetry is anything but the ideal way of preparing him to understand something old and difficult and complicated; for in his eagerness to find what *must* be there he will very likely miss what *is* there.' For instance, far from the story of the fall being the centre of the 'Nun's Priest's tale', Coghill and Tolkien argued that it was only 'jestingly invoked' by means of a 'light allusion'. Whilst it is true that there was a 'large lunatic fringe of allegorists in the fourteenth century' who, since they were 'capable of anything', may well have interpreted the 'Nun's Priest's Tale' in a wild allegorical way, this approach 'tells us nothing we can credit about Chaucer's poem'.[54]

Secondly, because of their reductionism, the patristic critics are said by the humanists to twist the sense of the 'Nun's Priest's Tale' in order to make it fit the Procrustean bed of their predetermined interpretation, as when Donovan claimed that Chauntecleer is saved from the fox's clutches by opening his eyes and praying to God for help. In fact, when Chauntecleer says 'as wys God helpe me', his words are not a sign of alertness at all but are actually an oath, an instance of the taking of the Lord's name in vain which the Parson condemns in his tale (*CT*, VII: 3408; X: 587-604).[55] As a result, the allegorical interpretations of the patristic critics often seem rather arbitrary. For instance, even if Biblical exegetes could compare the Holy Church to a widow, why should the particular widow who appears in the 'Nun's Priest's Tale' be equated with the Holy Church? What does this add to our understanding of the tale given that Chauntecleer is saved not by the widow but by his own quick thinking?[56]

Thirdly, since the patristic critics are chiefly concerned with the 'fruit' of the morality of the 'Nun's Priest's Tale' they are primarily interested in its underlying moral content and its intertextual allusions rather than in the dispensable 'chaff' of its literary form. For the humanists, the patristic critics are therefore guilty of ignoring the status of the text as literature and the ways in which the tale's meaning is bound up with its literary form: they forget the *unity* of form and content. The humanist critics argue that we cannot simply paraphrase the 'Nun's Priest's Tale' so as to divorce its supposed 'chaff', its literary style, genre and form, from the 'fruit' of its underlying sentence, or moral content. Indeed, in the case of the 'Nun's

Priest's Tale', the supposed 'chaff' *is* itself the 'fruit' of the tale. The key to the literary style of the 'Nun's Priest Tale' is the way in which both Chauntecleer and the Nun's Priest speak in an ornate rhetorical manner, one which, in the context of a tale about a cock and a hen, appears inflated, self-important and pretentious. They both drop names, show off their learning and display their oratorical skills through a mass of mannered rhetoric. In particular, both Chauntecleer and the Nun's Priest follow the rules of rhetoric, composition and means of amplifying their subject matter recommended by the early thirteenth-century rhetorician Geoffrey of Vinsauf, who is explicitly named by the Nun's Priest as his master (*CT*, VII: 3347). For example, just as Geoffrey tells us that, in describing someone, a poet should start at the head and let the splendour descend to the root, letting the whole be polished to the toenail, so the Nun's Priest literally follows his advice in his description of Chauntecleer which begins with his comb and descends down to his 'nayles whitter than the lylye flour' (*CT*, VII: 2959-64).[57] The amplification of material was the key to medieval rhetorical theory and certainly the Nun's Priest makes frequent use of many of the devices listed by Vinsauf to achieve this effect.[58] For instance, he employs *circumlocutio*, as when the Nun's Priest takes a dozen lines to tells us that it is six o'clock on 3 May (CT, VII: 3187-99); *periophrasis*, where something is not named directly but revealed by its characteristics, as when Chauntecleer describes the beast 'like an hound' which he sees in his dream but which we realise is a fox (*CT*, VII: 2899-905); and *digressio*, as when the Nun's Priest gives us a learned aside on the issue of free will before concluding that he 'wil not han to do of swich mateere' in a mere tale of a cock and a hen (*CT*, VII: 3224-51).[59]

For the humanists, such excessive rhetoric is not just the outer form of the tale but the key to its inner content: the 'Nun's Priest's Tale' shows that rhetoric is used by mankind as an inadequate defence against an inscrutable reality. This is not a world of Christian certainty. On the contrary, man is lost in the world but attempts to give himself an heroic status and self-importance through his employment of rhetoric. Rhetoric orders the world, allowing us to make sense of our plight and giving ourselves the illusion that we are in control of reality. If rhetoric expresses our pompous, self-aggrandising view of our condition, it is the task of common sense to deflate this misrecognition. In this perspective, Chauntecleer is not the portrait of a sinner but the portrait of a man – or a cock – trying to impose order on the world – and failing to do so. The tale is a satire of the tendency to look everywhere for some single underlying truth and instead emphasises the multiplicity of possible perspectives, the instability of values and the bewildering array of possible morals: it is the *Canterbury Tales* in miniature. 'In brief, all the lessons drawn at the close of the story are ambiguous, and for the very good reason that the human heart is ambiguous.' This liberal humanist approach to the tale has proved extremely popular amongst modern Chaucerians and is capable of being adopted by those feminist and Marxist critics who find in the 'Nun's Priest's Tale, as in the *Canterbury Tales* in general, a dialogic subversion of accepted orthodoxies and authorities (see above, pp. 42-53, and below, pp. 117-18).[60]

If the 'Nun's Priest's Tale' is seen as dealing with 'the basic intractability of human nature and human experience and its resistance to organisation in terms of intellectual and moral analysis', this might seem to suggest, rather suspiciously, that Chaucer would have felt at home amongst modern liberal agnostics. Jill Mann, however, argues that this interpretation of the tale is not simply a projection of modern attitudes and values on to Chaucer's text. Rather, there was a genre of medieval literature in which 'serious moralising turns into a satire on the moraliser', that of the mock-heroic animal-fable. The 'Nun's Priest Tale', one of the classic works of this genre, draws our attention to another such animal-fable: the tale of 'Daun Burnel the Asse' (*CT*, VII: 3313), i.e., Nigel Longchamps's late twelfth-century *Speculum Stultorum* ('The Mirror of Fools'), which attacked the corruption of clerics and the folly of scholars in its story of an ass who goes in search of a longer tail and who, on his travels, becomes a student at the university of Paris. For Mann, both the *Speculum Stultorum* and the 'Nun's Priest's Tale' use the animal-fable to reveal the irrelevance of the moral, intellectual and aesthetic abstractions with which men organise their lives: both are comedies at the expense of those who take themselves too seriously. In Chaucer's hands, the irony and satire of the mock-heroic animal-fables such as the *Speculum* and the *Romance of Reynard* undercut the serious didacticism of the animal-*exempla* of the preachers or the allegorising of the *Physiologus*. The result is a shifting style which 'never rests long enough to serve a single view or a single doctrine' and 'celebrates the normality of differences'. In providing 'no conclusion but that sublunary values are comically unstable', the 'Nun's Priest's Tale' is the ultimate epitome of Chaucer's 'continuously human suggestion of the relativity of things'.[61]

Finally, and perhaps most crucially, the humanist critics argue that it is patristic criticism itself which is guilty of exactly the failings which Chaucer himself satirises in the 'Nun's Priest's Tale', in particular its tendency to take itself too seriously and to impose its own ready-made schematic grid upon the kaleidoscopic shape-shiftings of reality. Far from the 'Nun's Priest's Tale' being a classic instance of medieval allegorising, it is itself a satire of such allegorical techniques of interpretation. To read the 'Nun's Priest's Tale' as a serious allegory, as the patristic critics do, is to make *yourself* the butt of Chaucer's joke. The 'Nun's Priest's Tale' *is* an allegory: it is an allegory about the excesses of allegorising, a joke by the wry, satirical Chaucer at the expense of those who take allegorical meanings seriously. In its multiplicity of contradictory morals, the tale is not so much a sincere invitation to apply the methods of allegorical exegesis in order to find its moral 'fruit' but rather an ironic demonstration of the impossibility of applying such methods judiciously. Just as 'Sir Thopas' is an 'anti-romance' so the 'Nun's Priest's Tale' represents the destruction of the animal fable as a viable narrative or moral literary form. Ironically, this interpretation of the Nun's Priest's excessive rhetoric could be supported by quotation from St Augustine's *On Christian Doctrine*, the text on which the patristic critics base their allegorical readings of medieval literature, where Augustine attacks that style of speech which, though not intended to entrap listeners into falsity, nevertheless 'only aims at verbal ornamentation more than is consistent with seriousness of purpose'. Such a style, like false reasoning, deserves the title of 'sophistical', its practitioners are guilty of vanity: 'we must beware of the man who abounds in eloquent nonsense'.[62]

(iii) Conclusion

As we have seen, both the allegorical and the humanist approaches to the *Canterbury Tales* have proved extremely popular amongst literary critics. Each approach is backed up with cogent argument and each is amply supported by textual evidence – but both of them cannot be correct.[63] Is it possible to decide between these competing interpretations on any rational grounds? An initial point which needs to be stressed is that, despite the claims of the patristic critics themselves, there is no reason why allegorical interpretations of the 'Nun's Priest's Tale' should necessarily be counterposed to 'dramatic' readings of the text since, in practice, the two types of reading *can* often be combined and reconciled. We can legitimately see the 'Nun's Priest's Tale' as a 'dramatic' demonstration of its teller's character and as part of that character's interaction with the other pilgrims in the frame narrative. Indeed, since the 'General Prologue' tells us no more about 'Sir John' than the fact of his existence (*CT*, I: 164 and note, VII: 2810), we are entirely dependent upon his tale, along with its framing 'Prologue' and 'Epilogue', for our impression of him. It is particularly significant that in the 'Epilogue' to the tale, the Host compliments the Nun's Priest on his handsome masculinity – his big neck, his large chest, his bright eyes and his ruddy complexion – all of which suggest to the Host that, were the Nun's Priest a layman, he would, like Chauntecleer, be 'a trede-foul aright', needing 'more than seven tymes seventene' hens to satisfy him (*CT*, VII: 3450-60). Dramatically, one can imagine his comments as being delivered with a knowing nudge and a wink since it was a stock accusation at the time that, as Gower put it, 'the priest who visits nuns often corrupts them', even though the bride of Christ should, above all others, be chaste. Indeed, the image of the cockrel in a hen-run was a stock literary image for the man who profited sexually from his access to female recluses (*VC*, IV: 13-14).[64] The 'Nun's Priest's Tale' itself emphasises the similarities between Chauntecleer and the Nun's Priest: both speak in a highly rhetorical, rather pompous manner and both are eager to display their learning through the names of the authorities they cite (Chauntecleer's Cato, Cicero or Valerius Maximus, Macrobius, etc., the Nun's Priest's *Physiologus*, Boethius, Bradwardine, Augustine and Geoffrey of Vinsauf (*CT*, VII: 2940, 2975-6, 3123, 3271, 3241-2)); both blame women for the woes of the world (*CT*, VII: 3164, 3257); both then nervously withdraw their misogynistic comments, since, as the Nun's Priest says, perhaps with a sidelong glance at the Prioress whom he is accompanying, 'I noot to whom it myght displese' (*CT*: VII: 3166, 3260-6).[65] If the Nun's Priest's portrait of Chauntecleer is, like many of the pilgrims' tales, an inadvertent comment on his own failings, then he may have to be removed from the ranks of Chaucer's 'good priests', leaving only the Parson as the embodiment of the ideal secular cleric.[66]

Seen in the *dramatic* context of these parallels between Chauntecleer and the Nun's Priest and of the Host's suggestions that the Nun's Priest has abused his position within the nunnery for his own sexual pleasure, the *allegorical* meaning of the cock takes on a new significance. For theologians such as St Gregory and Hugh of St Victor, who used the cock to symbolise the clergyman, the latter should be like the former in the sense that just as the cock first wakes itself up by beating itself with its wings before he wakes others, so the preacher should first spiritually waken himself before he wakens others. As is said of the Parson in the 'General Prologue', the cleric should practise what he preaches: 'first he wroghte, and afterward he taughte' (*CT*, I: 497). As St Augustine warned, whatever may be the majesty of a preacher's style, 'the life of the speaker will count for more in securing the hearer's compliance' with his teaching.[67] But if this is the case, there is a dramatic irony at work in having the Nun's Priest tell a tale of a cock who defends the prophetic veracity of dreams at length but then falls into danger when, blinded by the sensual charms of his wife, he ignores his own fine words. In fact, the Nun's Priest himself, like so many of the characters in the *Canterbury Tales*, is preaching here against the very failing of which he himself is guilty. In this instance, a knowledge of the allegorical symbolism of the cock enlarges rather than undermines a 'dramatic' understanding of the tale in terms of the character of its narrator and his relationship with the other pilgrims. In other words, when the Nun's Priest tells us that 'Wommenes conseils been ful ofte colde' (*CT*, VII: 3256), we do not have to take his words literally, any more than we have to accept that Chaucer saw this life as *simply* a wretched prison (see above, p. 000). Rather, this is an attitude which he himself, as a cleric supposedly sworn to a life of celibacy, might do well to bear in mind. We do not, therefore, have to choose between either seeing Chaucer's pilgrims as personified abstractions or as full-blown, psychological portraits. Rather, there is a spectrum of possibilities between these two poles. The fact that Chaucer could portray particular characters as personified virtues and vices, particularly those *within* the pilgrims' tales, such as Prudence and patient Griselda, does not mean that he was unaware of more novelistic modes of characterisation or that dramatic readings of the tales must always be rejected. Conversely, the psychological complexity of many of his characters, particularly of the pilgrims themselves, need not rule out the possibility of their being interpreted allegorically.[68]

However, if the 'dramatic' and the 'patristic' approaches *can* be synthesised in particular instances, this does not seem to be the case with the underlying assumptions of patristic and humanist criticism.[69] Is it possible to determine whether the Robertsonian approach captures Chaucer's own meaning or simply imposes an alien sense on to Chaucer's work? One solution would be ask whether, on *a priori* grounds, it is likely that a late fourteenth-century writer such as Chaucer would have been writing Augustinian allegories. Here we have two polarised opinions: that offered by Robertson, for whom virtually all of Chaucer's work, indeed, virtually all of medieval literature, is to be read in this way, and that of Minnis for whom this type of writing 'would simply not have been a valid literary option for Chaucer'.[70] Let us consider the objections which have been raised to the patristic method in general and to allegorical interpretations of the 'Nun's Priest's Tale' in particular.

Firstly, even to those who are not devotees of the patristic approach, the *general* humanist critique of allegorical readings of Chaucer is not always entirely convincing. For instance, Donaldson attacked the patristic approach by citing Aquinas's view that whilst the Bible *could* be read in terms of its spiritual allegory, mere human productions should not be read in this way. Yet Donaldson himself admits that Aquinas may not have been typical in this respect. Certainly, there were medieval poets, such as Dante, whose works *were* sustained Christian allegories. Donaldson argues that the patristic method should not be used where Christian pre-occupations are *not* a marked feature of the work.[71] The problem is that, in general, we have no agreement as to which poems *are* Christian in their preoccupations in the first place. Besides, this objection would not seem to apply to the particular case of the 'Nun's Priest Tale', a tale told by a cleric which is offered to us as a moral *exemplum* in the guise of an animal-fable, one of the preferred popular forms adopted by medieval preachers, which ends with the words of St Paul and a blessing, and which specifically encourages us to find some underlying allegorical message within it. Donaldson argues that when writers such as Langland *are* being allegorical, they explicitly tell us so[72] just as, in Chaucer's 'Tale of Melibee', Prudence explains to us the significance of Melibeus's three foes as the flesh, the world and the Devil. But, once more, this is not an obstacle to an allegorical reading of the 'Nun's Priest's Tale' since its narrator assures us that it *does* have an allegorical meaning even though we are invited to find it for ourselves. Certainly, the 'Nun's Priest Tale' does seem to have a spiritual level of meaning which is missing in other, more straightforward versions of the fable of the cock and the fox, such as that told by Marie de France.[73]

Nor is it an indictment of the patristic critics that their allegorical readings are rather arbitrary, for instance, that they interpret the fact that Chauntecleer is a cock allegorically but not the description of him as a 'grym leoun'.[74] After all, patristic and medieval scriptural allegories tended always, by modern standards, to be extremely arbitrary, disregarding the internal consistency of the narrative they interpreted and ignoring 'all normal standards of literary decorum'. St Paul, for instance, offered an allegorical interpretation of Abraham's two sons, one by a bondwoman, one by a freewoman (Genesis 16: 15; 21: 2; 25: 2; Galatians 4: 22-4), yet neglected to tell us how Abraham's other children would affect this allegorical meaning. Such arbitrariness continued to be the case in fourteenth-century allegories which often seized upon some tenuous and, by our standards, rather arbitrary similarity or parallel in order to grind out a spiritual interpretation. Of course, there can never be a perfect correlation between literal and allegorical meaning in any figurative or metaphorical language, but such correlations tended to be particularly loose in a mode of reading which was able to interpret the golden bough of Virgil's *Aeneid* as simultaneously signifying, *in bono*, the 'virtues by which men are liberated from the hell of this life and are borne to heaven' and, *in malo*, the 'riches which cast men down to hell'.[75] The patristic approach is often objected to on the grounds that such critics cannot agree amongst themselves on the underlying allegorical meaning of the cock and the fox in the 'Nun's Priest's Tale'. Yet, since the Nun's Priest does not himself explicate his own preferred reading of his tale for us, this is not really a problem. After all, both Christian exegetes and those who allegorised classical texts emphasised the polysemous nature of allegorical symbols and were perfectly happy to accept a plurality of allegorical interpretations provided that they contributed to the reign of charity.[76] Thus many of the weaknesses and uncertainties involved in 'patristic' interpretations of the 'Nun's Priest's Tale' cannot be blamed on the patristic critics themselves but rather result from the shortcomings inherent within the allegorical procedures which the Nun's Priest invites us to apply to his tale, procedures which tended to overwhelm and, by modern standards, to distort the material to which they were applied.

Thus the frequent accusations of reductionism made against the patristic critics, their supposed imposition of a single meaning on to all medieval texts, is not really justified by the actual practice of the patristic critics themselves. In this sense, the patristic critics' insistence on the Augustinian doctrine of charity which supposedly underlies all medieval poetry is something of a red herring both for themselves and for their opponents since, in practice, the doctrine of charity cannot tell us in advance that the 'Wife of Bath's Prologue' is about the perils of ignoring the spiritual level of a text whilst the 'Summoner's Tale' is about the dangers of ignoring literal meanings. Patristic critics cannot deduce the *sentence* of these poems from medieval literary theory but, like any other critics, have to explicate them in order to establish their particular meanings.[77] Furthermore, it seems rather paradoxical that the opponents of patristic criticism should attack it *both* for offering a multiplicity of ways of reading the 'Nun's Priest's Tale' *and* for reducing all medieval literature to one predetermined meaning. Finally, it is disingenuous of the humanists to reject allegorical readings of the *Canterbury Tales* on the grounds that they are based on an *a priori* definition of literature when they base their own alternative approach on an appeal to the nature of 'imaginative writing'. Both of these schools of criticism work from an *a priori* definition of 'literature', it is simply that the patristic critics' definition is historically specific whilst that of the humanists seems to be valid for all times and places.

Where the patristic critics' opponents are often more convincing is in their questioning of the ascription of allegorical significance to *particular* images and allusions within Chaucer's work. The problem here is that, as St Augustine said, every sign is also a thing but every thing is not also a sign.[78] A classic instance is the set of bagpipes which the Miller plays as he leads the pilgrims out of London (*CT*, I: 565-6). For allegorical critics, the Miller's bagpipes should be seen as part of the iconography of the 'Old Song', the carnal life which must give way to the 'New Song' of the spiritual life. They are the 'instrument of bestial men', as Guillaume de Machaut put it, rather than the instrument of the celestial harmony which was often represented by David's harp. Yet, in fact, medieval illustrations could also depict pious clerics or even angels playing bagpipes without any carnal meaning being implied: sometimes a set of bagpipes is just a set of bagpipes. The problem of knowing when an image or allusion *is* meant allegorically is particularly problematical in Chaucer's works as here, more than anywhere else in medieval literature, there is a particular unity of the iconographic and the mimetic, of allegorical allusion and verisimilar detail.[79]

Certainly many of the Biblical parallels which the patristic critics identify within the 'Nun's Priest's Tale' do seem rather tenuous, even to a reader sympathetic to the patristic approach. This is particularly the case with those 'submerged, hypothetical' allusions and 'veiled hints' of Biblical references identified by the patristic critics but whose presence within the text Chaucer himself does not signal by means of a reference, a quotation, a misquotation or a paraphrase. For instance, there seems little reason to connect Chauntecleer's *exemplum* of the man who dies by shipwreck with Christ's walking on the water, baptismal water or the story of Noah, unless, that is, any reference to water in a medieval text can be taken in these ways (*CT*, VII: 3064-108).[80] Yet the fact that we may reject allegorical interpretations of particular elements of the 'Nun's Priest's Tale' does not mean that allegorical interpretations are invalid *per se*. On the contrary, allusions to the Bible pervade Chaucer's work: no book was more 'continually present to his imagination'.[81] Those who reject patristic criticism seem, at times, to want it *both* ways. On the one hand, the patristic critics are said to be wrong to see Russell the fox as the Devil and 'there is not the faintest suggestion' in the tale that the Nun's Priest or his audience 'had any inkling' of the allegorical overtones of his tale; on the other hand, the tale is claimed to be a parody, either by Chaucer or by the Nun's Priest, of the excesses of medieval allegorists.[82] But if the 'Nun's Priest's Tale' is a parody of allegorising then surely we would expect to find it overflowing with allegorical allusions and techniques even if they are then held up to ridicule?

Furthermore, many of the humanist attacks against the patristic critics' interpretation of the 'Nun's Priest's Tale' fail to convince. For instance, it has been claimed that the fact that Chauntecleer returns safely to his 'paradise' through the use of his own cleverness would, if read allegorically, 'make hay of Christian theology and common sense'. More generally, allegorical readings of the tale produce interpretations which are silly and blasphemous.[83] One reply to this criticism would be that since the resurrection it *has* been possible for humanity to regain paradise (or so we are told by those who claim knowledge in such matters) so that, in terms of the mysteries of Christianity, the 'Nun's Priest's Tale' is far from silly. More generally, the Church Fathers and medieval Biblical exegetes and preachers were quite capable of producing allegorical readings of the scriptures and other stories which often seem almost totally irrelevant to the particular narrative in question[84] and which, on occasion, sound shocking and even blasphemous to modern ears. This is particularly true of those cases where Old Testament passages are seen as prefigurative types of the events of the New Testament. For example, St Augustine (following Cyprian) interpreted the story of the drunken Noah who was seen naked by his sons (Genesis 9: 18-27) as actually being 'laden with prophetic meanings' concerning Christ's passion. Thus Noah's drunkenness prefigured Christ's suffering whilst his nakedness foreshadowed Christ's 'weakness' on the cross (2 Corinthians 13: 4). For Augustine, even the fact that the scripture tells us that Noah was naked in his own house 'ingeniously' indicated that Christ was to be killed by 'members of his own family, namely the Jews'. Thus whilst 'we must not suppose that all the events in the narrative are symbolical', nevertheless, 'those which have no symbolism are interwoven in the story for the sake of those which have this further significance'.[85] It would seem, that what is regarded as 'common sense' or 'blasphemous' is itself historically specific in its nature.[86]

Perhaps the strongest aspect of the humanist interpretation of the 'Nun's Priest's Tale' is its close attention to literary form and its emphasis on the inflated rhetoric which the Nun's Priest adopts to tell his tale. For Pearsall, this narratorial style is the means by which Chaucer reveals the Nun's Priest to us as 'a well-intentioned crank': his tale is a fireworks display of rhetoric but one that has 'got into the hands of a pyromaniac'. The Nun's Priest is serious about his subject matter but he is being satirised by Chaucer the poet who shows him as being overwhelmed by the complexity of his material.[87] Yet there is a strong case for arguing that it is the Nun's

Priest himself who provides the satirical voice within the tale. Certainly, there are a number of passages which suggest that the Nun's Priest is establishing an ironic distance from his material, as when he assures us that his tale is set in a time when 'Beestes and briddes koude speke and synge' and that it is as true 'As is the book of Launcelot de Lake / That wommen holde in ful greet reverence' (*CT*, VII: 2881, 3212). If this is the case then the comic effects of the mismatch between the inflated rhetorical style of the tale and its farmyard subject matter would have to be ascribed to the sophistication and irony of the Nun's Priest himself as narrator of the tale (*CT*, VII: 3348, 3355-60).[88]

Is such comedy meant to deflate the pomposity and seriousness of rhetoric or of allegorical exegesis in general? Perhaps a more likely candidate as the target of the satire of the 'Nun's Priest's Tale' is the gloominess of the 'Monk's Tale' which precedes it. The tale told by the Monk is a wearisome catalogue of rulers, ancient and modern, who, though once mighty, were eventually brought low by the Wheel of Fortune, against whose power there is 'no remedie' (*CT*, VII: 1991-7, 2811). With its one moral, one narrator, one repeated narrative, one literary form, one register and one genre, the 'Monk's Tale', as a collection of narratives, is everything that the *Canterbury Tales* is not.[89] As the pilgrims' attention wanders from the Monk's interminable and repetitive catalogue of woe, the Knight interrupts to demand an end to the Monk's tale. When the Monk declines to respond to the Host's invitation to provide an alternative tale, perhaps one to do with hunting, which would provide some 'desport' or 'game' for the other pilgrims, the Host calls upon the Nun's Priest to provide a 'thyng as may oure hertes glade' to counter the Monk's pessimism (*CT*, VII: 2767-811). In his lengthy discussion of the ability of dreams to foretell the future, the Nun's Priest takes his cue from the Monk's final tragedy, that of the rich king Croesus who dreams of his own death (*CT*, VII: 2740-60). However, the Boethian optimism of the 'Nun's Priest's Tale' offers a very different perspective on human affairs from that of the Monk. For the Nun's Priest, the Monk is correct in seeing *earthly* affairs as a realm of trouble and uncertainty, particularly for those who might seem to modern readers to be privileged and powerful. Nevertheless, humanity does still have reason for *spiritual* optimism. We do have an alternative to the ups and downs of the Wheel of Fortune, that of raising our eyes to the eternal rather than concentrating on the passing glories of this world and realising that true happiness lies in rational control of one's self rather than in earthly power and pleasure.[90]

In its comic mockery of the Monk's tragic vision of life, the 'Nun's

Priest's Tale' is reminiscent of the ending of Chaucer's *Troilus and Criseyde* where, perhaps shockingly to modern ears, Troilus, looking down at the earth after his death, laughs aloud when he sees 'the wo / Of hem that wepten for his deth so faste', realising the insignificance of human affairs when seen from a heavenly perspective (*TC*, V: 1805-25). Similarly, the implication of the 'Nun's Priest Tale' is that the sorry stories of the rulers recounted in the 'Monk's Tale' which seem so tragic and lamentable from an earthly viewpoint, become, from the perspective of the spiritual and the eternal, as trivial as the affairs of a farmyard cock, even one as 'roial as a prince is in his halle', when seen from a human perspective (*CT*, VII: 3184). The incongruity of likening Chauntecleer grubbing for corn in a farmyard to a mighty prince, having him address his wife like a lover from a courtly romance, comparing his tragedy with that of the death of King Richard and the noisy cries of Chauntecleer's wives with the lamentations of the women at the fall of Troy, all produce a mock-heroic deflation of the Monk's bewailing of the tragedies of earthly rulers (*CT*, VII: 1992, 3182-5, 3200-3, 3348). Indeed, the Nun's Priest explicitly invokes one of the tragedies told by the Monk, that of Nero who slew the Roman senators 'to heere how that men wolde wepe and crie', for one of his own mock-heroic comparisons with the lamentations of Chauntecleer's wives (*CT*, VII: 2480-1, 3369-74). In the case of the Nun's Priest at least, the identification of a spiritual message does not lead to the gloomy seriousness with which patristic criticism has so often been charged by its opponents. Rather, it is the Nun's Priest's playful allegorising which reveals the limitations of the Monk's literalism and gloomy assessment of earthly events.[91] The Nun's Priest's comically incongruous rhetoric can thus be seen as a satire of the Monk's own use of rhetoric; Manly even argued that tale told by the Monk actually employs more of the major rhetorical devices than that of the Nun's Priest. Certainly, the Nun's Priest's frequent use of apostrophe and *exclamatio* ('O destinee ... O Venus ... O Gaufred' (*CT*, VII: 3338, 3343, 3347)) echoes the rhetorical laments of the Monk's tragedies ('O Lucifer ... O noble, almyghty Sampsoun ... O noble, O worthy Petro, glorie of Spayne ... O worthy Petro, kyng of Cipre' etc. (*CT*, VII: 2004, 2052, 2375, 2391)), whilst the superlatives he uses to describe Chauntecleer have also been seen as a comic reworking of the Monk's descriptions of his heroes.[92] In short, when the Nun's Priest satirises man's use of rhetoric to give himself an heroic status and self-importance, he may have had one rather immediate exponent of rhetoric in mind rather than the use of rhetoric per se. Certainly, although Chaucer may have satirised particular devices and stylistic practices set out in rhetorical treatises such as that of Vinsauf, in general he still accepted 'their basic premises about the formal, ordered nature of art' and their 'double commitment to the moral order and to human feelings'.[93]

In other words, the Nun's Priest's rejection of the Monk's rhetorical aggrandisement of human affairs does not result from a modern scepticism about the viability of *all* over-arching intellectual schemes. Instead it is based on a theologically grounded certainty about the importance of eternal matters and the vanity of earthly concerns of which modern humanists (not to mention post-structuralists) are unlikely to approve. It is, after all, undoubtedly easier to laugh at the absurd pretensions of human affairs 'if there is something against which this comic confusion can be measured, something true, something beyond the instability, individuality, and complexity of human experience'.[94] Indeed, 'the view that man is unable to attain absolute knowledge of the truth through language or thought was one held by all medieval Christian thinkers'. Medieval writers could thus justify their critique of the inadequacies of worldly knowledge and language in terms of a claim to a higher truth, a truth which for most modern readers is likely be seen as simply one more form of worldly knowledge. Even Jordan, who insists on Chaucer's ability to anticipate postmodernist views about the 'contingent and arbitrary nature of language', recognises that Christian theology represented an absolute truth for Chaucer: if Chaucer's vision of earthly affairs was ambivalent and uncertain, his 'vision upward toward God, though not free of anxiety, expresses confidence in an absolute that endures beyond the contingencies of this world'.[95] It was on this basis that medieval writers were able to combine a scepticism about earthly affairs with a social conservatism. Modern critics are prone to finding this combination rather paradoxical and, as a result, tend only to notice Chaucer's scepticism whilst ignoring his conservatism. Unlike Chaucer, modern sceptics, in rejecting the knowability of any mind-independent reality,[96] do not have even the illusory get-out of religious faith and are left merely with the paradoxical certainty that nothing is certain, the recourse to language to tell us that linguistic meaning is always unstable and arbitrary, and the conviction, born of experience, that experience is never to be trusted. Perhaps neither the medieval nor the modern form of scepticism has much to offer us?

As a conclusion, rather than having to choose between the claim that *all* serious medieval literature was intended to be read as a spiritual allegory or that *no* Middle English poets wrote in this way, it may be useful to adopt J. B. Allen's fivefold classification of the means by which literal and

allegorical or spiritual meanings could be combined in medieval literature.[97] Firstly, there is literature which was intended to be read only on
the literal level. For instance, no one has as yet suggested that there is a
profound spiritual level to Chaucer's comic 'Tale of Sir Thopas'. Similarly, even though the description of Absolon's abundant crop of golden
hair in the 'Miller's Tale' is meant to evoke medieval depictions of
Absalom, the son of David, (CT, I: 3314-16; 2 Samuel 18: 9) and
Absolon's attempted wooing of Alisoun includes echoes of the Song of
Solomon (CT, I: 3698-9; Song of Solomon 4: 11; 4: 14), there is no contextual suggestion, in the setting of the Miller's amoral *fabliau*, that such
allusions are meant to remind us of Biblical exegesis of Absalom in terms
of the Devil, Judas or the Jews. Here Absolon's Biblical associations are
used for comic literary effect to establish his character as that of an
'effeminate small-town dandy' brought low by woman, rather than for any
serious moral point. Indeed, as Kolve argues, the insistence on the youth
of the characters of the 'Miller's Tale' and the use of animal imagery to
describe them allow their actions to be bracketed off from any external
judgement: they 'no more invite stern moral judgement than do branches
for putting forth blossom, calves and kids and colts for gambolling in
meadows ... or cats for playing with mice' – all images invoked in the
tale.[98] After all, if tales even as bawdy as that of the Miller were intended
to be read for a deeper moral or allegorical meaning it becomes rather
difficult to explain why, in his 'Retractions', Chaucer has to apologise for
those tales 'that sownen into synne' (CT, X: 1085).[99] Thus whilst there
was a pervasive or even dominant view of literature in the medieval
period as an activity justified in terms of its moral utility and its spiritual
sentence, there was also a consistent strand of thought which defended
literature in terms of promoting human health and as a form of recreation
which was justified in itself. As Aquinas put it, 'Pleasure is to the mind,
what sleep is to the body'. Works of pure amusement were regarded as
justified in their own (limited) place whilst tedious tales of pure sentence,
with 'no desport ne game', were perceived as unlikely to serve their own
improving purposes. Naturally, it was those works which combined 'best
sentence and most solass', 'lust and lore' which were seen as the finest of
all (CT, I: 798; VII: 2792; PF: 15).[100]

Secondly, in Allen's classification, there are those texts which are
straightforwardly spiritual in their meaning and explicitly divine in their
concerns. The works of fourteenth-century mystics such as Richard Rolle
or Walter Hilton are a classic instance of such texts.[101] Perhaps Chaucer's
'An ABC' in praise of the Virgin Mary or his 'Parson's Tale' could be

placed in this category. Thirdly, there are works intended as coherent allegorical fictions, whether the allegory is expounded explicitly, as in Chaucer's 'The Tale of Melibee', or left implicit, as in the 'Pardoner's Tale'.[102] Fourthly, there are those works which, though not purely or simply allegorical, *do* incorporate allegorical elements. The 'Man of Law's Tale', for instance, can be read as the true story of a real woman, Custance, daughter of the Roman emperor, who suffered for her Christian faith. Nevertheless, in its emphasis on the imagery of sea and ships, it also contains allegorical and iconographical allusions which invite interpretation tropologically (the voyage of the individual soul on the perilous Sea of the World), allegorically (the Ship of the Church journeying to the heathen) and anagogically (the journey of the soul to its final haven).[103] Finally, there are those works which use allegory and scriptural allusions for humorous, ironic or parodic purposes, including the parody of exegesis itself. Thus Robert Holcot, himself an exponent of allegorical reading, could begin his commentary on the Book of Wisdom by finding his own name within the text of the scriptures.[104] Within the *Canterbury Tales*, the tale told by Chaucer's Summoner can be seen as a satire on the excesses of illegitimate 'glosyng' of which the mendicants were often accused (*CT*, III: 1793-4). Its poetic justice of the come-uppance suffered by a friar who neglects literal meaning in favour of glossing provides a perfect riposte by the Summoner to the tale told by Friar Huberd about a summoner whose inability to see beyond the letter to the deeper meaning of the text leads to his damnation.[105]

The advantage of Allen's typology is that whilst it denies the existence of some 'univocal zeitgeist' from which the meaning of medieval works of literature can be deduced, it still permits us to use the patristic method, where it is appropriate for a particular text, 'gratefully and with profit'.[106] The problem with this typology, as with any classification which establishes the diversity of modes of medieval writing, is that its very refusal of a monolithic or reductionist approach to medieval literature makes it more, not less, difficult to determine into which category any particular work of literature falls. It remains, therefore, a matter of debate whether the 'Nun's Priest's Tale' is a secular narrative (category one), a coherent spiritual allegory (category three) as it is for the patristic critics, or whether it should be ranked amongst the satirical parodies of such allegories (category five) as Allen himself claims.[107] Here we have argued that the 'Nun's Priest's Tale' *can* be seen, as humanist critics have argued, as a satire of rhetorically inflated and over-serious accounts of the human condition but that this attack is directed against the Monk's bleak pessimism about human affairs and against the Nun's Priest's failure to follow his own good advice rather than against moralising or allegorising *per se*. It is those who, like the Monk, stick to the literal and the historical sense or who, like the Nun's Priest himself, ignore the moral and spiritual implications of their own allegorical message, whose failings are satirised in the 'Nun's Priest's Tale'.

Notes

1 The label 'humanist' is used here purely as a descriptive term rather than as the term of abuse which, somewhat bizarrely, it has now become in many critical circles.

2 Collette, 1989: 132; Robertson, 1969: 3, 6, 51, 80; Robertson, 1970: 10; Robertson, 1974; Robertson, 1984: 6; Donaldson, 1977: 134, 149, 172-3.

3 Brown and Butcher, 1991: 6-7; see, however, Robertson, 1980: 403, 415-16, 416 n. 1; Myles, 1994: 126-9; Wurtele, 1984: 89; Patterson, 1987: 5; Besserman, 1988: 24.

4 Kiser, 1991: 7. Patristic criticism could also be seen as a pioneering instance of Foucault's emphasis on the historically specific nature of human subjectivity or as an illustration of the rejection of 'identity theory', in which difference and opposition are reduced to sameness, championed by the Frankfurt School. See Patterson, 1987: 34, 72.

5 Muscatine, 1972: 6; Aers, 1980: 207; Aers, 1986c: 58; Brown and Butcher, 1991: 6.

6 Minnis, Scott and Wallace, 1988: 13.

7 Miller, 1977: 75; Moffat, 1908; 40; Aers, 1975: 52-9.

8 Minnis, Scott and Wallace, 1989: 423; Allen, 1982: 6-11, 18, 217, 288, 293; Minnis, 1991b: 39, 55-6.

9 Robertson, 1984: 13; Makarewicz, 1953, 208, 225-6; Miller, 1977: 53; Dods, 1883: 90-1; Robertson, 1970: 4-5, Robertson, 1969: 22-3, 70-4; Smalley, 1981: 121-2.

10 Huppé, 1959: 9-10, 30-1; Robertson, 1984: 6, 13; Dods, 1883: 34, 37-8, 80-90, 126, 239, 164; Miller, 1977: 55; Evans, 1984: 3-4.

11 Miller, 1977: 42, 59-62; Huppé and Robertson, 1963: chapter 1; Robertson, 1969: 315-16.

12 Lubac, 1959a; Miller, 1977: 61, 63, 65 n. 1, 81; Robertson, 1969: 292; Allen, 1982: 212-13; Kolve, 1984: 301; Owst, 1966: 59-60; Howard, 1966: 17; Evans, 1984: 4, 114-18.

13 Minnis, Scott and Wallace, 1988, 203, 260, 267; Smalley, 1964: 246-8; Allen, 1971: 107-8; Minnis, 1988: 34; Forshall and Madden, 1850: 42-3.

14 Miller, 1977: 56; Dods, 1883: 46, 101-3; Miller, 1979: 328; Mâle, 1972: 32-3; Hardison *et al.*, 1974: 207; Allen, 1971: 58-9.

15 Dods, 1883: 101-2; Forshall and Madden, 1850: 45; Smalley, 1964: 44-65; Smith, 1966: 15; Fowler, 1977: chapter 2; Robertson, 1984: 12-13; Mâle, 1972: 2, 20; Evans, 1984: chapter 3. For editions of the *Glossa*, see *PL*, 113-14 or *BS*, I–VI.

16 Besserman, 1984: 66-7; Wurtele, 1984: 107.

17 Smalley, 1964: 87-108, 128-9, 187-8, 196, 216, 230-4, 240-61, 281-5, 299-305, 330; Lubac, 1961, II/I: 287-327; Robertson, 1969: 304-9; Evans, 1984: 8, 29, 67, 166-7; Minnis, 1988: 5, 39, 74, 85, 107.

18 Bloomfield, 1958: 87-8; Alford, 1984: 198; Kolve, 1984: 62-3, 83; Besserman, 1984: 68; Forshall and Madden, 1850: 43-5; Wurtele, 1984: 90, 92; Jeffrey, 1984b: xiv; Jeffrey, 1984c: 118, 122, 133-8; Aers, 1986c: 62; Evans, 1985: 39-47, 45, 51-2, 59-60; Smalley, 1960: 184; Smalley, 1981: 151-3, 179-81; Minnis, Scott and Wallace, 1988: 204 n. 24; Aers, 1975: 10, 22-4, 26-32.

19 Aers, 1975: 18; Curley, 1979: xiii–xiv; Minnis, Scott and Wallace, 1988: 72-3; Smalley, 1964: 88; Allen, 1982: 194; Evans, 1984: 32, 51-6; Evans, 1985: 10; Myles, 1994: 46, 55, 73-4.

20 Wenzel, 1989: 209; Mâle, 1972: 29, 42, 46; Barber, 1992: 142, 146-7, 169; Curley, 1979: 9-10, 71-2.

21 Huppé and Robertson, 1963: 7-8, 27-8; Seymour, 1975; Kaske, 1989.

22 Huppé, 1959: 29-30; Allen, 1971; Allen, 1982: 211, 215, 256; Minnis, 1988: 6.

23 Curtius, 1953: 215-26; Aers, 1975: 10, 55-7, 35; Allen, 1971: 11-12, 25; Baswell, 1985; Lord, 1992.

24 Minnis, Scott and Wallace, 1988: 318, 367, 371-2; Allen, 1971: 131.

25 Smalley, 1964: 281, 284, 299-301; Mâle, 1972: 32-3; McDermott, 1989: 3-4; Aers, 1975: 86-7; Allen, 1971: 49, 75-6, 81, 97-8; Wurtele, 1984: 90; Lord, 1992; Howard, 1966: 24; Delany, 1990: chapters 2, 3.

26 Howard, 1966: 20, 23; Miller, 1977: 82.

27 Miller, 1977: 138-9, 151.

28 Hardison *et al.*, 1974: 204-5.

29 Wenzel, 1967; Howard, 1966: chapter 2.

30 Robertson, 1984: 6, 20; Besserman, 1988: 174-8.

31 Knoepflmacher, 1970: 180-1; Andrew, 1989. The identifications of Biblical texts in Jacobs, 1980 seem rather more tenuous.

32 Kaske, 1959; Kaske, 1965; Wood, 1971: 270, 273; Wood, 1984: 39; Fleming, 1984: 184-5; Cooper, 1989: 57; Curry, 1960: 38-47; Braswell-Means, 1991.

33 Robertson, 1969: 151-6, 250-7.

34 Szittya, 1986: 232-46.

35 Belsey, 1980: 18-19, 21; Pearsall, 1986: 134-7; Patterson, 1987: 19-25; Patterson, 1991: 165.

36 Robertson, 1969: 287; Allen, 1982: 151-2; Jauss, 1978-9; Allen, 1971: vii.

37 Kittredge, 1911-12: 130; Kittredge, 1915: chapter 5; Lumiansky, 1980: 11, 13, 51; Broes, 1963; Kendrick, 1988: 37-8; Rooney, 1989: 29; Neuse, 1991: 89.

38 Neuse, 1991: 9, 14, 116-17; Hansen, 1992: 27; Kendrick, 1988: 133; Leicester, 1990: 89, 99; for criticisms of the dramatic approach, see Malone, 1951: 186-201, Shumaker, 1951, and Benson, 1986; for a critique of the psychoanalysis of fictional characters, see Walker, 1985.

39 Robertson, 1969: 190, 247, 249, 330; Baker, 1991: 243.

40 Howard, 1987: 525; Besserman, 1988: 25-6.

41 Caie, 1984: 78-88; Wurtele, 1984: 99-102.

42 Shallers, 1975: 324-6; Yates, 1983: 120.

43 Wirtjes, 1991: 11-12; Varty, 1967: 51, 54-9, 90-1; Bowden, 1954: 125; Robertson, 1985: 15-16.

44 Donovan, 1953: 501-2; *PL*, 15: 34; *PL*, 177: 33-5, 335-6.

45 Dahlberg, 1954; Casagrande and Kleinhenz, 1985: 312, 316; Salu, 1990: 36; Robertson, 1969: 252; Rowland, 1971: 55; Szittya, 1986: 231 n. 1; see also Scase, 1989: 211 n. 4. For the association of friars with the Devil, see Haskell, 1971: 220.

46 Smalley, 1964: 33, 95; Minnis, Scott and Wallace, 1988: 66-7, 81, 86.

47 Varty, 1967: 52-5, 58-9; Owst, 1966: 257; Bloomfield, 1952: 145.

48 Utley, 1965; Howard, 1966: 26-7, 33; Aers, 1975: 87, 94, 113-14, 119, 131; Besserman, 1988: 25-9; Kolve, 1984: 82, 83, 359-60; Marchalonis, 1974; Dean, 1984: 282; Patterson, 1987: 34.

49 *PL*, 177: 59; Varty, 1967: 90-1; Curley, 1979: 27-8; Barber, 1992: 65-6; Donovan: 1953.

50 Lumiansky, 1980: 114.

51 Huppé, 1967: 182-3.

52 Greenhill, 1954; Loomis, 1965, plate 148; Levy and Adams, 1967; Neuse, 1991: 93-4, 97; Hieatt, 1970.

53 Pearsall, 1984: 3, 11; Donaldson, 1977: 149; Coghill and Tolkien, 1959: 15; Bloomfield, 1979: 70; Muscatine, 1957: 242; Bishop, 1988: 160.

54 Howard, 1966: 26-7, 33; Brown and Butcher, 1991: 6; Pearsall, 1984: 11; Bloomfield, 1958: 86; Besserman, 1988: 25-9; Rogers, 1980; Donaldson, 1977: 135, emphasis added; Kolve, 1974: 317-18; Pearsall, 1986: 138; Patterson, 1987: 34, 37; Coghill and Tolkien, 1959: 29.

55 Donovan, 1953: 507; Donaldson, 1977: 148.

56 Donaldson, 1977: 147.

57 Gallo, 1971: 43-7.

58 Gallo, 1971: 154, 159.

59 Utley, 1965; Donaldson, 1977: 149; Knight, 1973; Coghill and Tolkien, 1959: 46-50; Gallo, 1971: 25-51.

60 Donaldson, 1977: 149; Pearsall, 1984: 3, 11, 12; Pearsall, 1985: 238; Pearsall, 1992: 239; Manning, 1960: 416; Burrow, 1992: 90; David, 1976: 229; Ebin, 1979: 325; Fyler, 1979: 158-62; Kolve, 1984: 78; Sklute, 1984: 134-5; Aers, 1986: 8-13; Rogers, 1986: 102-9; Cooper, 1983: 187; Cooper, 1989: 359; Mann, 1991a: 189-94; Brody, 1979: 43. Leicester finds a very similar moral in the Pardoner's Tale, see Leicester, 1982: 47-50.

61 Wright, 1872: 3-145; Mann, 1975: 277-8; Muscatine, 1957: 238, 241-3; Shallers, 1975: 328-9, 335.

62 Pearsall, 1984: 3, 12; Allen, 1969; Hussey, 1965: 39-40; Scheps, 1970; David, 1976: 229; Aers, 1986: 11-13; Bishop, 1988: 164; Smalley, 1960: 43; Dods, 1883: 68, 124, 164-5.

63 Shallers, 1975: 320.

64 Power, 1922: 446-7, 506, 544-5; Pearcy, 1968.

65 David, 1976: 223; Craik, 1964: 81; Broes, 1963: 158; Hussey, 1965: 8-10; Friedman, 1973: 262-3; Elbow, 1975: 100; Bishop, 1988: 162; Oerlemans, 1992: 320.

66 Robertson, 1984: 20; Peck, 1984: 143.

67 Donovan, 1953: 502-4; Dahlberg, 1954: 283-4; Dods, 1883: 167.

68 Pearsall, 1992: 239-40; Myles, 1994: 52-3, 68, 75, 127-9.

69 In other words, both exegetical and humanist critics could offer 'dramatic' read-

ings of the tales but the kinds of meanings and lessons which they would draw from the tales would still tend to be mutually exclusive.

70 Minnis, 1982: 15. A third alternative is that Chaucer saw exegetical allegorising as a legitimate mode of literature but did not himself choose to adopt it. See Gradon 1971: 7.

71 Donaldson, 1977: 137.

72 Donaldson, 1977: 146.

73 Spiegel, 1987: 169-70.

74 *CT*, VII: 3179; Howard, 1966: 26. For lions, however, see Allen, 1969: 29 on Proverbs 30: 29-32.

75 Marchalonis, 1974; Aers, 1975: 17-25; Cooper, 1983: 11; Allen, 1971: 87-91; Neuse, 1991: 101-2; Baswell, 1985: 187.

76 Miller, 1977: 56; Miller, 1979: 328; Hardison *et al.*, 1974: 207; Mâle, 1972: 32-3; Allen, 1982: 102-3.

77 Robertson, 1969: 317-18, 332; Howard, 1966: 26-7, 33.

78 Dods, 1883: 9.

79 Psalm 144: 9; Robertson, 1969: 128, 130, 132, 133, 482; Kolve, 1984: 67-8, 71-2, 75-7, 83, 357, 360; Boening, 1983: 3-4; Howard, 1987: 404; Stephens, 1989: 42; Neuse, 1991: 136. Given their context, it *does* seem reasonable to see the Miller's bagpipes as having a symbolic significance.

80 Wood, 1984: 35-6, 44; Coletti, 1981: 244; Levy and Adams, 1967: 183.

81 Reiss, 1984: 47; Besserman, 1988: 4; Coghill, 1967: 8.

82 Donaldson, 1977: 149; Coghill and Tolkien, 1959: 29; Pearsall, 1984: 3, 11; Pearsall, 1985: 230-8; Howard, 1976: 283.

83 Coghill and Tolkien, 1959: 28-9.

84 Marchalonis, 1974.

85 Knowles, 1972: 649-53.

86 Aers, 1975: 17-23.

87 Pearsall, 1985: 231; Hill, 1991: 145; Oerlemans, 1992: 319, 325-6.

88 Lenaghan, 1963: 305-7; Watson, 1964: 281; Shallers, 1975: 321; Howard, 1976: 283; Howard, 1987: 447, 498; Payne, 1981: 159, 181; Cooper, 1983: 183-4.

89 Cooper, 1983: 48.

90 *Bo*: 426; Jefferson, 1917: 49; Watson, 1964; Fyler, 1979: 157; Aers, 1980: 186-7; Hill, 1991: 127; Zatta, 1994: 115-17, 124.

91 Muscatine, 1972: 113; Elliott, 1965: 20-5.

92 Manly, 1926a: 283; Ellis, 1986: 275.

93 Payne, 1973: 57.

94 Bfrch, 1982: 22.

95 Myles, 1994: 19, 23, 26; Reiss, 1979: 69-70; Jordan, 1987: 169-73.

96 See Kiser, 1991: 1-9.

97 Allen, 1971: chapter 4.

98 Robertson, 1969: 85; Beicher, 1950; Kaske, 1962: Kolve, 1984: 159, 164, 172-4, 185, 213-15; *CT*, I: 3248, 3260, 3263, 3346-7; Smith, 1990: 210. For the 'Miller's Tale' as a parody of the annunciation, see Rowland, 1970.

99 Finlayson, 1971: 95-6; Pearsall, 1992: 264.

100 Olson, 1982: 19-23, 48, 89. 91-2, 97, 128, 141.
101 See Armstrong, 1991 for texts by these writers.
102 Miller, 1955: 235-40.
103 Kolve, 1984: 302-3, 308, 316, 325-30, 340 and 349.
104 Allen, 1969; Allen, 1971: 132; Tachau, 1991: 337-8.
105 Scase, 1989: 82; Robertson, 1969: 332; Cooper, 1983: 173; Alford, 1984; Reiss, 1984: 58; Edwards, 1991: 62.
106 Calin, 1980: 35-8.
107 Allen, 1969; Allen, 1971: 128-9.

4

Misogynist versus feminist
Chaucer

Diverse men diversely hym tolde
Of mariage manye ensamples olde.
Somme blamed it, somme preysed it, certeyn.
('The Merchant's Tale', *CT*, III: 1469-71)

ALL of the critical debates we have examined so far come together in the final issue we have to consider: Chaucer's representation of women. For the Wife of Bath, anti-feminism (meaning, in a medieval context, the criticism of women rather than of feminists!), was the dominant tendency in the clerical teachings about women current in her day: 'no womman of no clerk is preysed'. Her opinion is supported by the numerous misogynist *exempla* and authorities compiled in the 'book of wicked wives', real-life examples of which survive in large numbers, which Jankyn, her fifth husband, insists on reading to her (*CT*, III: 685, 688-91, 706). Even the Clerk, the representative of the estate attacked by the Wife of Bath, admits that 'clerkes preise wommen but a lite' despite the fact that no man can be as humble or even half as true as woman can (*CT*, IV: 935-8). As Christine de Pizan put it in her *Book of the City of Ladies* (1405), a comprehensive rejoinder to the misogyny of her day, the philosophers, poets and orators 'all concur in one conclusion: that the behaviour of women is inclined to and full of every vice'.[1] As we shall see, whether outright misogyny *was* the most common attitude to women in medieval society as a whole is debatable. Nevertheless, anti-feminism was undoubtedly one of the loudest voices amongst the competing opinions about women in the later Middle Ages, one which often drowned out other views which, precisely because they were taken for granted rather than being explicitly expressed, bore a rather closer relation to the reality of women's social position than did misogynist abuse. How then did Chaucer's work address such issues? Did Chaucer's representation of women rehearse and buttress the misogyny common to so much medieval literature or did Chaucer himself supply a critique of such misogyny, being, as Gavin Douglas put it in 1513, ever 'womanis frend'?[2]

Interest in Chaucer's representation of women has intensified in recent years as the issue of gender has come to the fore in medieval studies under the impact of feminist scholarship. Feminist approaches to literature are based on two fundamental assumptions. Firstly, that although there are unchanging biological differences between the sexes, these differences are always construed in socially and historically specific ways so that what seems 'natural' and 'obvious' about the sexes in one society will seem totally alien and mistaken in another. Through such social interpretation, biological differences between male and female become the socially constructed categories of masculine and feminine: sex becomes gender. Secondly, in a patriarchal society in which women enjoy a lesser degree of wealth, status and power than the men of their own class, the construction of gender involves not just the creation of social difference but also the reaffirmation of a fundamental inequality between the sexes, as sexual differences come to be presented as a justification for sexual inequality.[3] Feminist literary critics thus tend to explore how works of literature participate in the construction of gender differences and ask to what extent they embody or challenge the dominant gender ideology of their day.

However, just as patristic critics need not agree on the allegorical meaning of any particular tale told by Chaucer's pilgrims, so there is no reason why feminist critics should agree on the nature of Chaucer's sexual politics. For instance, Delany, though herself a feminist, adopts the view of the patristic critics that we as readers are intended to take the 'Nun's Priest's Tale' seriously and that the voice of the Nun's Priest can be equated with that of Chaucer. She thus sees the misogyny of this tale, its blaming of women for man's downfall and its treatment of marriage, as a rehearsal by Chaucer of the male supremacism characteristic of medieval intellectual orthodoxy. Indeed, she sees Chaucer's 'Nun's Priest's Tale' as reactionary not just in our terms but even by the standards of earlier medieval versions of the story which, in having Chauntecleer's wife as the one who correctly interprets his dream, had shown women to be superior to men in perception and foresight. Mann, by contrast, refuses to equate the voice of Chaucer with that of the misogynist Nun's Priest and instead sees Chaucer as satirising the latter's views. For Mann, the 'Nun's Priest's Tale' by no means reproduces the misogyny typical of medieval thought. Instead, by transferring traditional gender roles on to a cock and a hen, it reveals the arbitrary and superfluous nature of human sexual conventions and thus undermines the power-structures upon which they rest. Far from Chaucer being reactionary by the standards of the fourteenth century, he is up-to-date by the standards of the late twentieth century. Thus, whereas a critic such as Hansen sees Chaucer's poetry as bringing Woman to life only 'in order that she may be killed off, lost, silenced and erased', Mann is happy to describe Chaucer as a 'feminist' writer.[4]

As we have seen (Chapter 1), medieval literature cannot be used directly to read off the reality of medieval social life since literature actively interprets social reality in the light of its own conventions of character, narrative and genre and of the broader ideological conceptions and values of its time. Literary and generic convention is certainly crucial for the representation of women in the *Canterbury Tales*. There is a world of difference between the portrayal of women in a bawdy *fabliau* such as the 'Miller's Tale' (woman as lustful, deceitful wife), in the Knight's chivalric romance-cum-epic (woman as a romantic ideal to be worshipped and as a means of cementing political alliances) or in the saint's life told by the Second Nun (woman as virgin martyr).[5] Inevitably, medieval literature also incorporated broader cultural stereotypes and ideological assumptions about the sexes so that women in literary narratives were presented in the light of a variety of non-literary discourses, particularly those expounded in medieval scientific treatises and theological works. Thus the register or topos of misogyny is to be found in a wide variety of medieval genres. Conversely, one genre, such as the romance, could be used to express a variety of opinions about women.[6] In examining Chaucer's construction of gender and representation of women, it would, therefore, be wrong to see the *Canterbury Tales* as simply reproducing *the* late medieval conception of women since there was no single medieval conception of women for Chaucer's works to reproduce in the first place. Rather, the *Canterbury Tales* comprise an arena in which virtually every medieval discourse about women clashes and competes for our attention, providing in the process an encyclopedia of medieval views about women and the inevitably related issues of love and marriage. This chapter outlines some of the major medieval discourses about sexual difference which inform Chaucer's depiction of women in the *Canterbury Tales*, in particular, the tendency of medieval writers to polarise their views of women, condemning them to the pit or elevating them to the pedestal (section i). It then asks whether any of these views can be equated with Chaucer's own position by examining the Wife of Bath's rejection of the pedestal (section ii) and, finally, by exploring the alternative to both the pit and the pedestal offered in the 'Tale of Melibee' and the 'Parson's Tale' (section iii).

(i) Women in medieval literature: the pit and the pedestal

That there was no single medieval view about the nature of women, love or marriage, issues which were invariably raised in association with one another by medieval writers, can be seen in the tendency for conflicting views to be pitted against each other in formal debate. For example, in the famous letters between Abelard and Heloise, Abelard praises women's piety and Heloise replies by attacking her own sex as the cause of the downfall of mankind, her letters being one of the works included in Jankyn's 'book of wicked wives' (*CT*, III: 677-8).[7] In the late thirteenth-century poem *The Thrush and the Nightingale*, a male and a female bird discuss whether women are noble and gentle or fickle and dishonest whilst in Sir John Clanvowe's *The Book of Cupid*, a cuckoo and a nightingale debate the merits of love.[8] *Dives and Pauper* (1405-10), an early fifteenth-century exposition of the Ten Commandments, includes a dialogue in which Pauper defends women from Dives's stock accusations about feminine vice.[9] Women and relationships between the sexes have been seen as Chaucer's own favourite subject and his literary career viewed as a 'lifelong engagement with the woman question'. Indeed, critics have regarded such issues as central to the *Canterbury Tales* ever since Kittredge identified a 'marriage debate' between the pilgrims, a debate supposedly initiated by the Wife of Bath when she claimed that men should be governed by their wives. Kittredge saw a number of the other pilgrims as responding to the Wife's comments: the Clerk, who tells a tale of the patient Griselda which defends the orthodox view of female submissiveness within marriage; the Merchant, whose shrewish wife is the opposite of Griselda and who tells a tale of feminine deceit; the Host, who also complains of his wife; and the Franklin, who offers a view of marriage as based on mutual love, respect and forbearance which Kittredge identified as that of Chaucer himself. In fact, views about marriage pervade even more of the tales than Kittredge suggested. If, as Neuse argues, the tales are like a philosophical symposium in which, rather than following logically one after another, the speakers discuss a number of related topics, women, love and marriage are central to the themes which the pilgrims address.[10]

Thus, paying attention to gender and gender ideology is by no means to bring an anachronistic, twentieth-century perspective to bear on Chaucer's work. On the contrary, the Middle Ages had a very clear conception of gender difference and a clearly formulated theory of sexual inequality. However, given that the male was taken as the norm and woman as the 'marked case', medieval attitudes to gender tended to be most explicitly formulated in discussions of women's nature. Certainly, Lawler found very few generalisations about men in the *Canterbury Tales*, apart from those made to contrast them with general claims about woman's nature, whereas the tales are littered with over 140 generalisations about women, a point which is nowhere more apparent than in the 'Wife of Bath's Tale', in which a knight, in order to save his life, has to discover 'What thyng is it that wommen moost desiren?' (*CT*, III: 905).[11] Whilst men are defined in terms of their estate or occupation, women in the *Canterbury Tales*, as in other contemporary estates literature, are defined in relation to men, sex and marriage: as virgins (for instance, Virginia in the 'Physician's Tale'), married women, whether faithful (Griselda in the 'Clerk's Tale') or unfaithful (as in the 'Manciple's Tale'), mothers (in the 'Prioress's Tale' and the 'Man of Law's Tale'), prostitutes (perhaps the merchant's wife who sells her body to a monk in the 'Shipman's Tale'), or widows (as in the 'Wife of Bath's Prologue'). Typically, the magical mirror brought to the court of Cambyuskan in the 'Squire's Tale' allows the king to see any threats to his kingdom whereas it enables women see if their lovers are unfaithful (*CT*, V: 132-40).[12]

That man was the norm against which woman was defined as inferior or deformed was certainly the assumption underlying the scientific thought about women which the Middle Ages inherited from the ancient world. Aristotle, for instance, assumed that male domination was the rule in *all* natural species. Men were morally, intellectually and physically superior to women; to attempt to counter such natural superiority would, therefore, damage the entire community, including women. To the Aristotelian tradition was added the influence of Galen (fl. second century A.D.) who advanced a case for female inferiority based on the doctrine that everything within the sublunary world is composed of the four basic elements: earth, fire, water and air, each of which has related quality: coldness, heat, wetness and dryness (see above, p. 7). For Galen, it was women who were dominated by the cold and wet qualities, men by the hot and the dry. Since heat is nature's primary instrument it follows that 'within mankind the man is more perfect than the woman'.[13] Such views passed into medieval scientific orthodoxy. For Albertus Magnus, a thirteenth-century Aristotelian, female children were the product of weak semen: women were, in a sense, deficient or imperfect men. Aquinas rejected the claim that women, as God's creation, were misbegotten, but he accepted Aristotle's view that in conception it is the male force which is active in giving form to the material passively provided by the female. Since 'the active cause is always more honourable than the passive', it followed that 'it is the father who should be loved more than the mother'. This notion of women's bodily imperfection was associated with the idea of their mental inferiority. For Aquinas, 'the power of rational discernment is by nature stronger in man' than in woman who is 'by nature of lower capacity and quality than man'. Man's superior reason explained why 'woman is naturally subject to man'. God had given the task of reproduction to women in order to free men for other tasks, including the intellectual work to which their superior reason suited them. Since, in a human family, good order was the product of the rule of the wisest, women should naturally be subject to men. For the author of *Dives and Pauper*, sin was more serious in man than in woman since 'by nature man has greater strength and greater intelligence and reason' with which to withstand the Devil's guile. Chaucer's Wife of Bath even twists man's supposed greater reason to her own advantage, citing it as a reason why her husband should bow to her will: 'Oon of us two moste bowen, / doutelees, / And sith a man is moore resonable / Than womman is, ye must been more suffrable' (*CT*, III: 440-2).[14]

If the idea of women as physically, mentally and socially inferior was inherited by the Middle Ages from the ancient world, there is no doubt that it was buttressed by the account of the creation and the fall given in the book of Genesis. Here, on being expelled from paradise, Eve is told by God: 'thou shalt be under thy husband's power and he shall have dominion over thee' (Genesis 3: 16). As St Paul says in justifying man's authority over woman, 'Adam was first formed, then Eve. And Adam was not seduced; but the woman being seduced, was in the transgression' (1 Timothy 2: 13-14). Adam and Eve might be the mother and father of us all but, nevertheless, it was, as Innocent III pointed out, women who suffered in childbirth as a reminder to them of their kinship with Eve. That the fall was primarily the result of Eve's disobedience, rather than of Adam's, was a frequent refrain of medieval authors. In the early thirteenth-century *Ancrene Riwle*, St Paul's requirement that women, unlike men, should cover their heads when praying or prophesying (1 Corinthians 11: 5-13) was interpreted as a commandment to each woman to 'cover her shame, as a sinful daughter of Eve, in remembrance of the sin which brought shame upon all of us in the beginning, and not use the covering as a means of adorning herself, as a matter of pride'. Aquinas had argued that the superior rationality of men meant that the subjection of woman must have obtained even before the fall, but for the author of *Dives and Pauper* it was only when Eve sinned that 'woman was made subject to man'.[15]

Woman's responsibility for the fall is certainly taken for granted by a number of the Canterbury pilgrims. For instance, in the 'Man of Law's

Tale', when the Sultan of Syria's evil mother opposes her son's intention to convert to Christianity on his proposed marriage to Custance and murders the Christians who accompany Custance to Syria, the Man of Law says that Satan knows of old the way to women and it was he who 'madest Eva brynge us in servage': when he seeks to beguile us, he makes woman into his instrument. Even Custance, the heroine of the tale, takes for granted in her prayer to the Virgin that it was through woman's instigation that 'Mankynde was lorn, and damned ay to dye', Christ's suffering on the Cross being needed to overcome the effects of Eve's actions (*CT*, II: 323, 365-71, 841-4). This charge is repeated in Jankyn's 'book of wicked wives': it was woman that was 'the los of all mankynde' (*CT*, III: 685, 715-20). Similarly, the 'Nun's Priest's Tale' reminds us that '*In principio / Mulier est hominis confusio*': it was 'Wommanes conseil broghte us first to wo / And made Adam fro paradys to go', although the Nun's Priest himself denies any responsibility for this opinion and Chauntecleer manages to interpret the phrase to mean that 'Womman is mannes joye and al his blis' (*CT*, VII: 3163-6, 3257-66). It is the Parson who stresses that Adam was not free of guilt in the fall, citing St Paul (Romans 5: 12) to argue that sin and death entered the world by a single man: 'And this man was Adam'. Even though it was Eve who sinned first in being tempted into tasting of the forbidden fruit, Adam remained in a state of innocence until he too consented to eating the fruit so that it was Adam from whom we took original sin 'for of hym flesshly descended be we alle' (*CT*, X: 321-4, 330-3).

The events of the fall were frequently interpreted allegorically, with Adam representing the superior aspect of our nature, reason, and Eve signifying our lower nature, the flesh. This hierarchy, with Eve, woman, the flesh and the carnal appetites of our lower nature on the one hand, and Adam, man, the spirit and our superior, rational nature on the other, was a commonplace of Christian theology from the patristic period to the end of the medieval period. Even when Augustine used the serpent to represent the flesh, Eve still figured as lower reason and Adam as the higher wisdom: the latter should dominate the former as the husband does the wife. Duns Scotus similarly saw paradise as an allegory of human nature in which the man represents the interior region of the spirit, truth, goodness and reason, and the woman represents the exterior region of the corporeal senses, falsity and vain fantasies. All error begins in the exterior region which may then corrupt the inner region, just as Eve tempted Adam.[16] It is this standard allegorical reading of the fall that is expounded by Chaucer's Parson when he interprets the temptation of Adam and Eve and the events of the fall to mean that 'deedly synne hath, first, suggestion of the feend, as

shewth heere by the naddre; and afterward the delit of the flessh, as
sheweth heere by Eve; and after that, by the consentynge of resoun, as
sheweth here by Adam'. Although it was the flesh – 'that is to seyn Eve' –
which first took delight in the forbidden fruit, it was reason – 'that is to
seyn Adam' – which consented to it (*CT*, X: 330-1).

Since sin was the result of a delight in the things of this world, the temptations of power, riches and of the flesh, it followed that the highest human
condition was to renounce the transitory glories of this world and to live a
life of poverty, chastity and obedience, vows of which were required from
those regular clergy who had, supposedly, withdrawn from the pursuit of
the things of this world. Virginity in particular was presented by theologians as the highest spiritual state. As St Paul said, 'It is good for a man not
to touch a woman'. 'I say to the unmarried and the widows, it is good for
them if they so continue, even as I'. 'The unmarried woman and the virgin
thinketh on the things of the Lord, that she may be holy both in body and
in spirit. But she that is married thinketh on the things of the world, how
she may please her husband' (1 Corinthians 7: 1, 8-9, 34). From Tertullian
(*c.* A.D. 160–*c.* A.D. 225) onwards, theologians argued that 'abstinence
from sex was the most effective technique with which to achieve clarity of
soul'. Sexual sin was, Aquinas argued, 'more disgraceful than other im-
moderate action', partly because during sex 'our reason gets submerged'.
Abstaining from such bodily pleasure allows us to 'seek the soul's good in
a life of contemplation mindful of the things of God'.[17] Perhaps the most
famous statement of this view, one which, inevitably, was included in
Jankyn's compilation of misogamous texts alongside the work of Tertullian (*CT*, III: 673-6), was *Adversus Jovinianum* (*c.* A.D. 393), in which St
Jerome attacked the belief that, once baptised, the single, married and
widowed could all attain equal spiritual merit. Against this belief, he cited
the work of the pagan philosopher Theophrastus to support his argument
that the wise man should not marry: even the pagan Greeks and Romans
had recognised the superior virtue of virginity. According to Jerome, the
reward of the hundredfold fruit is ascribed to virginity, that of the sixtyfold
fruit to widowhood, and that of the thirtyfold fruit to those who are
married. It is true that, as Paul said, virginity is a counsel to us rather than
a command (1 Corinthians, 7: 6-9) but nevertheless, this still means that
'Christ loves virgins more than others', since they willingly give what was
not commanded of them. For Jerome, the difficulties involved in married
life were a 'rhetorical commonplace' which could be invoked to dissuade
both men and women from marriage or remarriage.[18]

In the *Canterbury Tales*, the Parson defends this view of virginity as superior even to chastity in marriage or widowhood: the virgin is spouse to Christ, beloved of the angels, and the equal of the martyrs; Christ was born of a virgin and was a virgin himself (*CT*, X: 915, 943, 947-50). Similarly, the 'Second Nun's Tale' tells of the heroic life of a woman, St Cecilia, who was both virgin and martyr, retaining her chastity even in marriage, converting her husband and brother-in-law to the true faith, and defying the male authorities of the Roman Empire who demanded that she should renounce her Christian beliefs. Thus, whilst the Wife of Bath claims that clergymen cannot speak well of any woman unless she is a 'holy saint', it is actually one of the other women amongst the pilgrims, the Second Nun, who sings the praises of a woman who is a virgin martyr (*CT*, III: 688-91; VIII: 87-8). The 'Physician's Tale' also sings the praises of a virgin, Virginia, who 'floured in virginitee / With alle attemperaunce and pacience, / With mesure eek of beryng and array', whose father kills her rather than surrender her to Apius, as he is ordered to do, 'in lecherie to lyven' (*CT*, VI: 44-6, 206).

Inevitably, given the churchman's obligation to celibacy, the works which attacked women most virulently were those addressed to monastic and clerical audiences and whose generic conventions, designed to strenghten clerics in their vow of chastity, portrayed women as the gateway leading to sin and damnation. Similar texts, vividly depicting women's misery in marriage and their pain in childbirth, could be produced for female recluses or to dissuade women from marriage or remarriage. The problem was that attacks on women intended for clerical ears could be cited outside their original context and came to be presented as expressions of general truths about womankind. Thus in Walter Map's 'Letter of Valerius to Ruffinus, Against Marriage' (*c.* 1180), another work included in Jankyn's book (*CT*, III: 671), it is claimed that even the very best woman, 'who is rarer than the phoenix', cannot be loved 'without the bitterness of fear, anxiety and frequent misfortune', let alone the wicked women who devote themselves to tormenting men. In such cases, misogamy, opposition to marriage, came to be justified in terms of misogyny, the abuse of women.[19]

It was this misogamous tradition which provided the raw materials for much of the portrait of the Wife of Bath which emerges in the unusually lengthy 'Prologue' to her tale. The vivid speech and disarming frankness of the Wife's of Bath's lengthy autobiography, in which she recounts the way in which she mastered her first three husbands by deceit and trickery, seem when we first encounter them, to provide us with a rare glimpse of domestic life of the kind which medieval sources rarely allow us, an account based on the 'experience' to which the Wife appeals in support of her views and which thus seems to be drawn straight from life. In fact, long passages of the Wife's tirade, as when when she accuses her husbands of saying things when they were drunk of which they were entirely innocent ('Thou seist that oxen, asses, hors and houndes, / They been assayed at diverse stoundes; ... But folk of wyves make noon assay, / Til they be wedded' etc. etc.), are lifted almost verbatim from Theophrastus's *Liber de Nuptiis* as passed on to the Middle Ages by Jerome's *Adversus Jovinianum*. Far from being drawn from real life, the Wife here is rehearsing lines attacking women by a pagan philosopher of the fourth century B.C. as preserved for us by a Church Father of the late fourth century A.D. (*CT*, III: 1-6, 235-302, 669-72).[20] The *Lamentations of Matheolus* of Matthieu of Boulogne (*c.* 1295; translated from Latin into French *c.* 1371 by Jehan le Fèvre), in which, just as in the Wife's 'Prologue', a clerk marries a widow but then bemoans his fate, depicting his marriage to a deceitful, nagging, disobedient woman as a purgatory on earth, was obviously also a major source for the Wife's 'Prologue'.[21] Her speech is equally indebted to the 'sermon' by *La Vieille* in Jean de Meun's continuation of the *Roman de la Rose*, a lengthy monologue in which the old woman gives cynical advice on the ruses which allow love to be used to obtain money and power. Indeed, the Wife often repeats verbaim the words of *La Vieille*, regretting her lost youth, advising women to be like the mouse that always has a hole to run to and claiming that even Argos with his hundred eyes could not do anything to stop a wife intent on adultery. In addition, the Wife's confession owes much to the words of Dipsas, the old woman who gives cynical advice on how to turn a girl's sexual attractions to her advantage in Ovid's *Amores*.[22]

Inevitably, the association of man with humanity's rational and intellectual faculties and the affiliation of women with the carnal and the worldly was particularly pronounced in those texts which warned the male philosopher against the servitude of love and the worldly distractions of marriage. In Abelard's *Historia Calamitatum*, for instance, Heloise tries to dissuade him from marriage by echoing the warnings in *Adversus Jovinianum* about the 'burden', 'base servitude', 'unbearable annoyances' and 'endless anxieties' of marriage and quotes Jerome's example of Cicero who refused a second marriage on the grounds that 'he could not devote himself to a wife and philosophy alike': 'What harmony can there be between pupils and nursemaids, desks and cradles, books or tablets and distaffs, pen or stylus and spindles?' As Seneca said, 'Philosophy is not a subject for idle moments. We must neglect everything else and concentrate on this, for no time is long enough for it'.[23] The Wife of Bath characterises this opposition in terms of the astrological influences of Mercury and Venus, i.e., 'wysdam and science' versus 'ryot and dispence': 'ech falleth in otheres exaltacioun' (*CT*, III: 607-705). Thus, in addition to the equation of the masculine with the superior, with reason, spirit, the active, heat and dryness and the feminine with the inferior, the flesh, body, the passive, coldness and wetness, went a whole series of associated binary oppositions which are personified by Chauntecleer and Pertelote in the 'Nun's Priest's Tale' and by Alisoun and Jankyn in the 'Wife of Bath's Prologue':

masculinity	femininity
Chauntecleer	Pertelote
Jankyn	Alisoun
the thinker	the wife
Mercury	Venus
the public	the domestic
the intellect	the body
the abstract	the practical
the universal	the particular
the other-worldly	the mundane
bookish authority	everyday experience
the ideal	the material

Typically, when Chauntecleer has a nightmare warning him of the danger ahead, he mounts a lengthy and learned defence of the view that dreams presage the future, buttressing it with *exempla* and authorities, whereas the down-to-earth Pertelote tells him that it is simply the product of overeating and recommends a laxative (*CT*, VII: 2923, 2943, 2970-3156). Equally typically, Chauntecleer then ignores his own fine words and is lured into forgetfulness by his lustful delight in Pertelote's sensual charms, just as all of Jankyn's book-learning about the wiles of women is useless when it comes up against the wordly cunning of his wife. Like Jerome's Gorgias the Rhetorician, who preached an excellent sermon on concord to the Greeks yet could not keep peace between himself, his wife and his maid, all of Chauntecleer's and Jankyn's learning is of no avail when confronted with the seductive might of woman and the power of their own lower natures. One of the most popular secular images in all medieval art, that of Aristotle being ridden by Phyllis, Alexander's palace courtesan, epitomised this opposition between the flesh and the intellect and the weakness of the latter when confronted with the power of the former. In this story, Alexander is berated by Aristotle, his tutor, for abandoning all reason and becoming like a dumb beast because of his infatuation for the beautiful Phyllis. Phyllis and Alexander then teach the philosopher a lesson when she seduces Aristotle but agrees to make love to him only on the condition that she can saddle him and mount him and Alexander then appears to confront his tutor with the evidence of his inability to follow his own teachings.[24] The familiar image of the flesh as the horse and reason as its rider is thus inverted, an inversion alluded to by the Wife of Bath when she refers to herself as the 'whippe' for her husbands and as having the bridle of marriage in her hand (*CT*, III: 175, 813).

However, despite the tradition of misogamy which flourished in literature, in reality the vast majority of medieval men and women did marry. As St Paul said, those who cannot commit themselves to virginity should marry: 'it is better to marry than to be burnt' (1 Corinthians 7: 9; *LB*: 18). Indeed, whether medieval writers presented women as members of their husband's estate or whether women were presented as an estate in their own right, with their own internal sub-divisions into lay and religious, single, married and widowed, marriage was central to a woman's social identity in a way that it was not for men, since men's legal and property rights remained unaffected by it. Thus, although the 'General Prologue' tells us that the Wife of Bath was a cloth-maker whose abilities exceeded those of Ypres and of Ghent, cloth-making is, in this context, a traditional gendered trait rather than a profession or the focus of Chaucer's interest.[25] It is her expertise as a wife which is emphasised in the lengthy autobiographical 'Prologue' to her tale, her skills in the arts of marriage having been perfected on the five husbands which she has had since the age of twelve, skills which have allowed her to win control of each of them, whether through sex, trickery, lying or jealousy. The 'Wife of Bath's Tale' itself reinforces this association of women and marriage when the knight, given the task of finding out what women most desire, eventually learns that the answer is that 'wommen desiren to have sovereynetee / As wel over hir housbond as hir love, / And for to been in maistrie hym above' (*CT*, I: 447-8; III: 1-6, 155, 173-4, 488, 813-22, 905, 1038-40).

In the realm of marriage, as everywhere else, the message of the theologians was that of man's superior reason and woman's inferiority. As St Paul said, it was wrong for women to usurp authority over men since 'Adam was first formed, then Eve. And Adam was not deceived, but the woman being seduced was in the transgression'. Since women were 'commanded to be under obedience' by God, it followed that if women sought to learn anything they should 'ask their husbands at home, for it is a shame for women to speak in the church' (Genesis 3: 16; 1 Corinthians 14: 34-5; 1 Timothy 2: 11-14). It is true that St Paul had said that, once united in

Christ, 'There is neither Jew nor Greek, there is neither bond nor free, there is neither male nor female' (Galatians 3: 28). But just as this did not mean that there should be *social* equality between freeman and bond, neither did it entail the earthly equality of men and women. On the contrary, 'The head of every man is Christ; and the head of woman is the man; and the head of Christ is God'. Man was created as the 'image and glory of God but the woman is the glory of the man'. 'Neither was the man created for the woman; but the woman for the man' (Genesis 1: 26-7; 1 Corinthians 11: 3, 7-9). Just as Christ is the head of the Church so 'the husband is the head of the wife'. Just as Christ loves the Church, so 'ought men to love their wives as their own bodies' (Ephesians 5: 22-33). St Paul's arguments were rehearsed by Chaucer's Parson: a man should love his wife as much as Christ did the Church, for which he was prepared to die. Man is the head of the woman, so a woman should have only one husband so that she did not have more than one head, 'an horrible thing biforn God' (*CT*, X: 920-30).

Since medieval preachers took for granted the superiority of the husband within marriage, they were frequently obliged to denounce women who failed to respect such superiority. They thus invoked the harlot of the Book of Proverbs (7: 10-12) and the wicked woman of the Book of Ecclesiasticus (25: 23-36) to criticise women for wandering about when they should remain at home and for exhibiting the supposed female faults of impatience, foolishness and inconstancy. Of course, it is the function of sermons to denounce sin and preachers were just as likely to denounce sinners who were male as they were to criticise women. The difference was that whilst male sin was presented either as an example of general human frailty or as related to particular occupations and estates (the avarice of the merchant, the pride of the knight), women's faults were seen as specifically female, as arising from the weaknesses of their sex *per se*. In particular, lust was seen as the female sin *par excellence*. There was a familiar double standard at work: when women fall prey to lust, this was because they were prone to such weakness by their nature; when men submitted to their own carnal desires, this was often said to be because they had been tempted by women or by demons in female form. It was, said the preachers, wise for men to abstain from 'the dawnsynge of wommen and other open syghtes that draweth men to synne', to reject the company of 'folyes women' and, in general, to avoid excessive familiarity with any member of the female sex. After all, who was stronger than Samson, wiser than Solomon, holier than David? And yet they were all overcome 'by the queyntise and whiles of women'. Closely associated with misogynist accusations of *luxuria* was the charge of female vanity. In particular, in a tradition going back to St Paul (1 Timothy 2: 9) and Tertullian, woman's pride in her appearance, her love of adornment, expensive clothing and head-dresses, were attacked as the occasion of sin in both men and women. With their long tail-like gowns and 'horned' heads, women reduce themselves to the level of beasts and become the 'Devil's nets, with which he fishes in God's fish-pond, seeking to transfer His fish to the lake of Hell'.[26]

Garrulity was also seen by the preachers as a particularly feminine fault, perhaps because it was measured not by the standards of male talkative-ness or misogynist loquacity but by that of female silence, as is shown by the *Speculum Laicorum*, a thirteenth-century sermon collection, which advises women to be like the well-bred dog, silent and free of guile, rather than the ill-bred dog which is noisy and ill-tempered. Similarly, both the London preacher William Lichfield and the author of the *Ancrene Riwle* named the Virgin Mary as 'a model for all women' on the grounds that she 'spoke so little that we find her words recorded in Holy Scripture only four times'. Above all, women were urged to be obedient. That feminine disobedience would be punished was the constant lesson of such sermons. As John Bromyard, a fourteenth-century preacher, pointed out, all intend-ing husbands faced the risk of a contrary wife. As a warning against such contrariness, he cited the story of a man with such a wife who, knowing a ladder to be rotten, told her not to climb it 'because he knew that she would do the very reverse of what he said'. Predictably, she disobeyed him and as a result broke both her legs.[27]

Women are advised to eschew such feminine vices by Chaucer's Parson: women should please their husbands by being 'mesurable in lookynge and in beryinge and in lawghynge' and 'discreet in alle hir wordes and hire dedes' rather than 'by hire queyntise of array': 'It is a greet folye, a womman to have a fair array outward and in hirself be foul inward' (*CT*, X: 929-36). Again, this literary tradition fed into the image of the Wife of Bath which emerges from both the 'General Prologue' and the Wife's own 'Prologue'. She embodies all of the stock traits which anti-feminist authors and preachers such as Robert Rypon, William Lichfield, John Bromyard and Nicholas Bozon habitually ascribed to women: their lustful-ness and contrariness, their vanity and delight in fashionable clothes, their talkativeness and disobedience. Even the accusation that the Wife in her fine array is like a cat whose fur has not been singed and so loves to wander from home was a 'hoary commonplace' of the pulpit (*CT*, III: 348-54). Her first-person monologue, with its length, roundabout style and tendency to wander off the point, is itself a classic illustration of the stock charge of feminine garrulity, of her tendency to verbal, as well as to sexual, 'wandering by the way'.[28]

Given the currency of misogyny within medieval thought, even the apparent praise of women and of marriage by medieval writers was often meant ironically – or at least was read as such. A fifteenth-century lyric, 'What women are not', begins 'Of all creatures women be best' but, before going on to list women's virtues (their patience, ability to keep a secret, their refusal to spend their husbands' money at the alehouse), adds *'Cuius contrarium verum est'*: 'the contrary of which is true'. Likewise, Lydgate's praise of women in his 'Beware of Doubleness' should, a manuscript gloss tells us, be read *'per antifrasim'*, i.e., to mean the opposite of what it explicitly says.[29] Chaucer's 'Merchant's Tale', perhaps drawing on Eustache Deschamps's *Miroir de Mariage* in which 'Free Will' is urged to marry by his false friends, Desire, Folly, Servility and Hypocrisy, whilst 'Storehouse of Knowledge' puts the case against,[30] contains such mock-praise of women and marriage. Here the elderly Januarie, after a life of lust, decides that marriage will provide him with a paradise on earth. Since the Merchant has already told us that married men live a life of 'sorwe and care' and that his own wife is so cruel and malicious that she could outmatch the Devil himself, his subsequent lengthy approval of Januarie's self-delusions ('How myghte a man han any adversitee/That hath a wyf?' etc. etc.,) and urging of his audience to ignore Theophrastus come across as rather heavy-handed sarcasm. The ironic praise of marriage continues when Januarie's two friends, Placebo ('I shall please') and Justinus ('the just one') debate his plans. Placebo, the flattering courtier, does not dare to disagree with Januarie and urges him to go ahead with his marriage. Justinus warns him – to no avail – that a married man's life is one of 'cost and care', full of duties 'of alle blisses bare', a truth he knows from experience even though his own wife has the reputation for being loyal and mild-mannered (*CT*, IV: 1213-28, 1264-1392, 1478-1575).[31]

Yet, despite the common misogyny of the age, a number of medieval writers did attempt a defence of the female sex and there were a variety of more sympathetic views of women available. If the story of Eve's role in the Fall provided the archetypal symbol of female evil then, as hardly needs saying, it was the Virgin Mary, the 'Quene of Paradis, of Hevene, of erthe, of all that is', who represented female virtue. All of the evidence available to us, from church, chapel and parish-guild dedications to the ballads of Robin Hood, points to the genuine popularity of her cult. It has been claimed that the cult of Mary and of the other virgin saints, in creating an ideal which was impossible to emulate, tended to bolster the medieval view of women as inferior. After all, unlike the Virgin, other women do not bear children whilst remaining, in the words of the Prioress and the Second Nun, a 'Virgine wemmelees' and a 'mayden pure' (*CT*, VII: 462; VIII: 47-8). Margery Kempe, for example, doubted her own salvation because she was not a virgin and had to be reassured that God loved her 'as much as any maiden in the world'. Thus it has been claimed that only with the Protestant Reformation did the role of wives as mothers come to be celebrated by Chritian theologians.[32]

Nevertheless, despite the uniqueness of her 'singular grace', the Virgin Mary *was* regularly cited by those who wished to defend *all* women, as in *The Thrush and the Nightingale*, in which the nightingale finally overcomes the thrush's misogyny by invoking the Virgin's name.[33] Her exaltation in heaven above all the choirs of angels (the *ex exaltacione* topos) was one of the five arguments commonly used to show why woman was preferred to man (the others being the *e materia* topos: Adam was made from clay, Eve from Adam's rib; *e loco*: Adam was made outside paradise, Eve inside it; *e conceptione*: a woman conceived Christ not a man; *ex apparicione*: Christ appeared first to a woman after the resurrection).[34] Similarly, 'Women are worthy', a carol from the fifteenth or early sixteenth century, argues that 'Our Blessed Lady bereth the name / Of *all* women wher that they go'. In 'The Mother and Her Son on the Cross', a lyric of *c.* 1300, Mary asks for help from her son for all those who cry out to her whether they be maidens, wives or 'fol wimmon' (prostitutes). The virgin saints could be recommended as models for all women, maidens, wives and widows, and one of them, St Margaret, was even the patron saint of childbirth. In general, the virgin saints did not so much serve as examples to be followed as reservoirs of particularly effective intercessory power which was available to be tapped by the faithful. In much medieval poetry, it was the Virgin Mary's motherhood, her tender love for her child, rather than a purity which was impossible to emulate, which led people to worship her and seek her intercession. That a high regard for motherhood did not arrive only with the Reformation can be seen in the frequent medieval descriptions of the Church as our 'spiritual mother' which carries and gives birth to us, washes, bathes, clothes, nurses and feeds us, and lays us down to rest. Thus, despite the frequent claim that good mothering is a modern invention and that pre-modern societies regarded the welfare of infants and children with indifference, medieval writers did present motherhood as a particularly honoured female role. If medieval writings assigned fathers the role of educating and disciplining their children, it was mothers who were expected to nurture and care for them. As 'Women are worthy' says, it is shameful to abuse women because women are the mothers to us all.[35]

It is as the merciful intercessor who intervenes to avert our Father's wrath that the Virgin is portrayed in Chaucer's 'An ABC' in praise of the Virgin (*ABC*: 49-56) and the '*Invocacio ad Mariam*' in the 'Second Nun's Prologue' (*CT*, VIII: 39-84). But it is as the caring mother that the Virgin appears most prominently in the *Canterbury Tales*, as when Custance in the 'Man of Law's Tale' prays to the Virgin, the 'glorie of wommanhede' who suffered by seeing her own son die in torment, to take pity on her child when they are placed in the rudderless ship in which they are cast adrift from Northumbria (*CT*, II: 841-54). In the 'Prioress's Tale', an example of the popular genre of the 'Miracles of the Virgin', the nurturing qualities of the Virgin and of earthly mothers are combined in the tale of a seven-year-old boy who is murdered by the Jews and his body thrown into a cesspit in a Christian city in Asia for singing the song '*O Alma redemptoris*' in the Virgin's honour as he passes through the Jewish ghetto on the way to and from school. His widowed mother, 'With moodres pitee in her brest enclosed', searches frantically for her missing son until she finally discovers his body when she hears it singing '*O Alma redemptoris*', the Virgin having come to him and promised that he should continue to sing the song until a seed which she places on his tongue is removed. Only when the abbot removes the seed does the boy 'yaf up the goost ful softely' to be united through his death with the Virgin (*CT*, VII: 551-71, 593-4, 658-69, 672, 691). The Virgin's role as merciful intercessor could also be ascribed to earthly women. In the 'Knight's Tale', it is the tears of Ypolita, Emelye and the ladies of Theseus's court which win mercy for Palamon and Arcite when Theseus has condemned them to death; in the 'Wife of Bath's Tale', it is Queen Guinevere and her ladies who beg for mercy and obtain a reprieve for the knight sentenced to death for rape; in the 'Tale of Melibee', Melibeus's enemies beseech his wife Prudence to sway Melibeus with her 'wommanly pitee' when they submit themselves to his judgement. Far from the Virgin being a reproach to all other women, who necessarily failed to emulate her perfection, her virtues inform many of the heroines and worthy women of the *Canterbury Tales* (*CT*, I: 1748-71; III: 894-905; VII: 1749-50).[36]

If the religious cult of the Virgin offered the possibility of a more sympathetic treatment of women, the conventions of 'courtly love' have traditionally been seen as a secular challenge to clerical misogyny. Indeed, women themsleves were frequently presented as the readers of chivalric romances, as when the Nun's Priest says that it is women who 'holde in ful greet reverence' the 'book of Launcelot de Lake' (*CT*, VII: 3212-13).[37] 'Courtly love' is often rejected by scholars as far too embracing or inaccurate a term to be useful. Certainly, C. S. Lewis's famous claim that adultery was a necessary part of such love finds little support in medieval English literature. None the less, whilst never constituting a clearly defined code of conduct, courtly love is useful as a portmanteau term with which to refer to a group of loosely related literary concerns and conventions.[38] Love in this conception is the 'unrestrained adoration of a lady', a love caused by her beauty, charm, wit and character. Such love ennobles and improves the lover himself, both as a warrior, who might be inspired to fight to bring honour to his lady or to win the renown needed to gain her approval, and as a courtier, who is expected to display the refinement needed to win a lady's heart such as the ability to compose love-songs, or at least to sing them, to dance, and to engage in witty and charming conversation. Along with these qualities went specific forms of stock behaviour (such as falling in love at first sight, frequent sighing, an inability to sleep and thinking only of one's lady) and of literary expression, particularly those relating to feudal service, with the lover cast in the role of the faithful vassal who must perform a love-service for his lady. In particular, the literature of romance emphasised the obstacles to love's realisation, such as absence or marriage, and consequently presents love as suffering, as an 'inquietude' of heart. For instance, Marie de France told the story of Guigemar who falls in love with an (unnamed) lady already married to another lord and so suffers extreme pain and anguish, fearing that he will die of grief if she does not grant him her mercy: 'love is an invisible wound within the body'.[39] Such romantic love need not be mutual or consummated although it was more likely to be presented as reciprocal in the later, northern European romances, where it was seen as compatible with, or even desirable for, marriage, than it was in the lyrics of the early troubadours of courtly love of twelfth-century Languedoc.[40]

The patristic critics have argued that many of the works supposedly illustrative of 'courtly love' are in fact satires of a lecherous 'idolatrous passion' which was seen as destructive of chivalry rather than as the inspiration for it. Nevertheless, even Robertson has space for the concept of a 'courteous love' in which a knight is inspired to courtesy and bravery by love of his lady.[41] For instance, in the romance *Guy of Warwick* (composed in Anglo-Norman *c.* 1232-42, translated into English *c.* 1300), Guy, the son of the Earl of Warwick's steward, falls in love with the inaccessible Felice, daughter of the earl. He grows sick and laments his fate, calling on death to end his suffering but eventually wins her love when his deeds of arms prove that he is the best knight in all the world.[42] The conventions of such *fin amour*, or 'fyn lovynge' (*LGW*, F: 544), are to be found in the works of Chaucer himself, particularly his shorter poems and lyrics such as 'A Complaint to his Lady', where the despairing sleepless lover, 'slayn with Loves fyry dart', who values his lady above all earthly things, pledges that he will be her true and obedient servant and begs her to take pity on his suffering (*CL*: 1-7, 32, 36, 61, 91-3, 110-11, 118, 124-7).

Such conventions are also put to work in the *Canterbury Tales* themselves, most notably in the 'Squire's Tale' which describes the tercelet, the male falcon, who through his apparent humility, truth, years of love-service and outward observance of all 'That sownen into gentilesse of love', wins the love of the peregrine falcon (*CT*, 514-35). Similarly, in the 'Franklin's Tale', Arveragus, in order to win the love of Dorigen, performs 'many a labour, many a greet emprise', finally telling her of 'his wo, his peyne and his distresse' so that she, 'for his worthynesses', takes pity on him and agrees to marry him. In turn, Aurelius the squire, whose dancing and singing exceeds every other man's, falls in love with Dorigen, keeps his love to himself for two years and, though tormented and despairing, expresses his feelings only in the 'layes, songes, compleintes, roundels [and] virelayes' which he composes, before he too reveals his suffering to her (*CT*, V: 729-42, 925-59). Love as adulterous longing appears also in the 'Miller's Tale', where Absolon serenades Alison, his loved one, beneath her window (*CT*, I: 3352-63) and in the 'Merchant's Tale', where Damyan, the young squire, undergoes a now-familiar suffering because of his love for May, the wife of January, his master. He weeps, sighs and complains, burning in the flames of Venus's fire so that 'he dyeth for desyr' until he can win her 'pitee' and her 'verray grace' (*CT*, IV: 1774-82, 1875-84, 1940, 1995-7).

Yet courtly love is far from being celebrated in these tales. In the 'Squire's Tale', the tercelet, having finally won the heart of the falcon, betrays her, his love having been won by a kite, and leaves her alone to bemoan her fate (*CT*, V: 504-631). Similarly, in the 'Franklin's Tale', Aurelius's love poses a threat to the happiness of Dorigen's marriage to Arveragus and the narrative problem which has to be resolved is how Dorigen can avoid giving herself to Aurelius, as her promise obliges her to do once Aurelius appears to have removed the rocks upon which she feared the returning Arveragus would be shipwrecked (*CT*, V: 993-7). In the cynical 'Merchant's Tale, romantic love is as much of a self-delusion as any other idealisation of human relationships.[43] Finally, in the satirical 'Miller's Tale', courtly love is simply held up as a piece of ridiculous affectation. Lewis's four criteria of courtly love (Humility, Courtesy, Adultery and the Religion of Love) nowhere appear more clearly in the *Canterbury Tales* than when they are parodied in the figure of Absolon, the parish clerk, who cannot sleep for love, sings like a nightingale as all lovers should, and swears to be his loved one's page, wooing her with the words of the Song of Songs (*CT*, I: 3371-77, 3695-707).

Romantic love appears as an ideal within the tales only in the context of marriage, as at the end of the 'Knight's Tale' when Emily loves Palamon so tenderly and Palamon serves her 'so gentilly' that there was never a cross word between them. Yet, as we have seen (above, p. 39), marriage here is only permitted after Palamon has been made to wait for the 'lengthe of certeyn yeres' and has overcome the irrational power of his love for Emily. Before this, the love which strikes Palamon and Arcite on their first sight of Emily is presented as a destructive force, one which exceeds the bounds of reason and divides the two beloved kinsmen and friends from one another with fatal results, depriving them of their rationality and turning the whole world into their prison, even when they escape their captivity. Such love is the emotion whose suffering and disastrous effects are depicted on the walls of the Temple of Venus at which Palamon worships, where can be seen the tears and lamentations of lovers and the fate of those such as Solomon and Hercules who were trapped and destroyed by the snares of love (*CT*, I: 1077-9, 1918-54, 2967, 3101-6). In all of these cases, courtly love is presented by Chaucer either as a form of dangerous and ineffective posturing when indulged in by noble youths or as an affectation and a sham when adopted by their inferiors.[44]

If the misogynist tradition within medieval thought consigned woman to the pit, the conventions of courtly love, like those of the cult of the Virgin Mary, have often been seen as elevating woman to the pedestal but, in the process, as rendering women passive, restricting them to the role of beautiful objects whose function is to inspire action in others. When women do take on an active role in love, it is often that of the predatory temptress, like the lovely lady who attempts to seduce Sir Gawain in *Sir Gawain and the Green Knight*.[45] In those cases when we *are* presented with events from the woman's viewpoint, it is frequently when the woman, like the falcon in the 'Squire's Tale', is the victim of male duplicity, bewailing the treachery of the lover who deserts her once she has given him her heart. Chaucer's *Legend of Good Women* is a collection of such tales of 'goode wymmen, maydenes and wyves', such as Dido and Ariadne, 'that weren trewe in lovyng al hire lyves', and of the false men, such as Aeneas and Theseus, who betrayed them (*LGW*: F: 484-5, 1254-89, 2170-92).

More recently, literary critics have challenged the view that romances simply confine women to the pedestal as a passive idol who is there to be worshipped. Instead, they argue that medieval French romances *do* allow the interrogation of the power dynamic of male–female relations, offering forceful alternative responses and resistance to traditional notions of femininity. Whilst female characters in the romance are often 'displaced from the centre of narrative action', losing their autonomy and agency, romances could also offer the potential for a more active critical response and a questioning of the power relations between men and women.[46] Thus, despite the characteristic presentation of the male lover as the unworthy vassal performing his love-service to win his reward from his lady, romantic love could also be expressed in the language of *mutual* love, service and obedience: 'love is not honourable unless it is based on equality', as King Equitan's lady tells him in Marie de France's Breton *lai*.[47]

In Chaucer's 'Franklin's Tale', itself introduced by its narrator as a Breton *lai* (although no direct Breton source is known for this tale),[48] Arveragus, in order 'to lede the moore in blisse hir lyves', swears to his wife Dorigen that he will never 'take no maistrie / Agayn her wyl' but instead will obey and follow her in all things whilst, in return, she promises to be his 'humble trewe wyf'. When the Franklin asks 'Who koude telle, but he hadde wedded be, / The joye, the ese, and the prosperitee / That is bitwixe an housbounde and his wyf?', we are meant to take his praise of marital bliss seriously rather than reading it as irony, as we do in the case of the Merchant's almost identical eulogy of married life. As the Franklin says, repeating the words of the *Roman de la Rose*, 'When maistrie comth, the God of Love anon / Betheth his wynges and farewel, he is gon'. Both men and women by their natures 'desiren libertee, / And nat to been constreyned as a thral' so that those who want their love to endure, 'everych other moot obeye' (*CT*, IV: 1338-41; V: 709-15, 744-806).[49] By these means, we are told, Arveragus achieves a blissful life, although, as Crane argues, the actual plot of the 'Franklin's Tale' tends to undermine this impression: equality and mutuality are more successful when they bring events to a close, as they do in the 'Wife of Bath's Tale', rather than when, as here, they function as a premise of the narrative.[50] Even the Goodman of Paris, whose book of guidance (*c.* 1395) to his young wife constantly urges her to be unquestioningly obedient to his commands, says that in love husband and wife desire 'to do pleasure and obedience unto each other ... if they love each other, they care naught for obedience and reverence'.[51] Courtly romances have often been seen by feminist critics as an ideological mystification of patriarchy which, through their idealisa-

tion of love and marriage, invite the female reader's complicity with traditional gender ideology. Nevertheless, such idealisations of male–female
relations do provide a genuine contrast with the Nun's Priest's misogyny,
the Parson's insistence on female subordination and the Merchant's misogamy. The *Canterbury Tales* thus provide us with an encyclopedia of
medieval discourses about love and marriage and of medieval representations of women. But is it possible to equate any of its multiple views with
those of Chaucer himself? It is to this issue that we now turn.

(ii) The Wife of Bath: the pedestal rejected

In attempting to establish Chaucer's own view of women and of marriage,
the Wife of Bath, a figure whose opposition to clerical misogyny has
caught the imagination of century after century of readers, must necessarily have a central role. Critics are, however, divided in their interpretations
of the Wife into two main camps. On the one hand, many critics reject the
idea that Chaucer's voice can be equated with the Wife's or that the reader
is intended to sympathise with her views. For such critics, Chaucer is
satirising the Wife by having her condemn herself out of her own mouth in
her attempts to become a preacher and a scriptural exegete, thus substanti-
ating all that the theologians had ever said against women. This interpretation is particularly favoured by the patristic critics who read the
Wife's 'Prologue' as a warning of the dangers of misunderstanding texts by
ignoring their spiritual meaning and reading them only for their carnal or
literal sense.[52] Those who adopt this view are often accused themselves of
joining in the clerical castigation of women. Certainly, Robertson himself
made the astonishing claim that if the Wife of Bath's carnal character still
seems feminine to us today, this 'is a tribute to the justness of the ideas
which produced her'.[53] Nevertheless, it is perfectly possible and legitimate
for modern critics to argue that *Chaucer* intended us to interpret the Wife
as a corroboration of misogynist attitudes even though they themselves
may reject such attitudes.

On the other hand, many critics believe that, far from there being a gap
between the voice of Chaucer the author and that of the Wife of Bath, it is
'quite certain' that the Wife's views are those of Chaucer himself. Critics
who adopt this approach believe that we as readers are supposed to identify with the Wife of Bath's opinions, to agree with her shrewd attacks on
clerical misogynists, and to accept her arguments for the male surrender of
sovereignty within marriage as a means of establishing the relations of the
sexes on a new basis of mutual accommodation. As Hansen says, there is

now a 'general consensus' that the Wife of Bath is an 'authentic female speaker' (although Hansen herself rejects this view), one who illustrates Chaucer's 'radical criticism of the anti-feminist tradition'. The Wife's portrait thus reveals Chaucer as open-minded and sympathetic to women in his questioning of the inevitability of the gender hierarchy, which he shows to be an unstable social construct.[54] Even Evans and Johnson, who warn us that to celebrate the Wife as a modern feminist 'simplifies both history and textuality', accept that the Wife can be seen as a 'point of resistance' to the clerical anti-feminism and anti-matrimonialism which she 'wittily debunks'. Similarly, for Patterson, the Wife's rhetoric offers not just delectation 'but the higher pleasures of ethical understanding'. In offering a rhetoric that is 'at once carnal *and* moral', she 'ameliorates the harsh polarisations of Augustinian theory'.[55]

Above all, it is the Wife's defence of women against clerical misogyny which – understandably – draws the approval of modern critics. In particular, critics have praised the 'reflexivity' of the Wife's discourse, i.e., its tendency to uncover the speaking subject of misogynist discourse, a figure whom that discourse, in seeking to pass itself off as an impersonal authority, tries to render invisible. Medieval misogyny was typically a 'citational mode' of discourse, one epitomised by Jankyn's anthology of antifeminist *auctores*, 'whose rhetorical thrust is to displace its own source away from anything that might be construed as personal', emphasising instead the sacred authorities which legitimate its hostility to women. The Wife, by contrast, shows us that such discourses are grounded in particular individuals; they are not abstract or eternal verities but rather the words of particular men with their own particular agendas and interests. She thus 'desublimates a reified discourse', exposing the motivations which lie behind it and subjectivising and subverting a supposedly objective patriarchal wisdom. In both her 'Prologue' and her tale, it is claimed, she reveals and recovers 'those things necessarily excluded by patriarchal discourse'.[56] Unusually, her performance does not merely personify or illustrate the traditional clerical view of women's nature, rather 'she has an attitude to it, just as it has an attitude to her'.[57] In the Wife's case we do not just see the anti-feminist stereotype from the outside; here the stock type speaks back and defends herself. She is not the ignorant sinner awaiting enlightenment from her betters. On the contrary, she is familiar with the clerics' arguments and seeks to counter them, rejecting clerical denunciations of women as the work of embittered, impotent old men, personalising their supposedly impersonal authority and accusing *them* of the viciousness with which they tax wives (*CT*: III: 707-10). Her first-person

'Prologue' requires us to see events from her standpoint; for the viewpoint of a man who has been in the same position as one of the Wife of Bath's first three husbands we have to await the testimony of the 'Merchant's Prologue' and 'Tale'. For a number of critics, 'mimicry' is central to the reflexive nature of the Wife's speech. This idea is taken from the work of Luce Irigaray who says that in mimicry, 'one must assume the feminine role deliberately. Which means already to convert a form of subordination into an affirmation and thus to begin to thwart it.' By an act of 'playful repetition' mimicry makes visible what was supposed to remain invisible. In this perspective, the Wife's actions are not simply a corroboration of the patriarchal discourse of misogyny. Rather, like other female characters in the tales, 'she *mimics* the operations of patriarchal discourse' and, in so doing, exposes those operations to view. By consciously acting out and reproducing the discourse of others, she offers a witty parody which undermines the authority of the original.[58]

There are two classic instances where the Wife's 'Prologue' explicitly exposes the subjective interests underlying the supposed objective truth of patriarchal discourse. The first is where she explains the fact that 'no womman of no clerk is preysed' on the grounds that misogynist clerks are frustrated old men: 'The clerk, whan he is oold, and may nogt do / Of Venus werkes worth his olde sho, / Thanne sit he doun, and writ in his dotage / That wommen kan nat kepe hir mariage!' (*CT*, III: 707-10). For those who sympathise with her argument, one which Chaucer may have taken from Le Fèvre's *Livre de Leësce* and which was to be employed by Christine de Pizan, the Wife is able to judge the anti-feminist tradition 'so accurately as the outpourings of psychically crippled' males.[59] The second instance of the Wife's subjectivising of misogynist authority is in her allusion to the fable (which Chaucer perhaps knew from the work of Marie de France)[60] in which a peasant shows a lion a picture of a peasant killing a lion, to which the lion replies 'Who peyntede the leon, tel me who?' In other words, why should we trust tales about women told by men: 'By God, if wommen hadde writen stories, / As clerkes han withinne hire oratories, / They wolde han writen of men more wikkednesse / Than al the mark of Adam may redresse' (*CT*, III: 693-6). The Wife thus demonstrates that 'the truth of any picture often has more to do with the prejudices and predilections of the painter than with the "reality" of the subject' and anticipates the modern feminist insistence that no criticism is value-free: we all speak from some position.[61]

Besides this general subjectivising of misogynist authority, many critics have been impressed by the Wife's mastery of 'scole matere' (*CT*, III: 1270-3), believing that the Wife takes on the misogynist expositors of the Bible and beats them at their own game. Such critics approve of the 'good points' in the Wife's case, as when she questions the clerical criticism of sex by pointing out that without sex there would be no virgins in the first place (*CT*, III: 71-2).[62] Whilst Alisoun accepts the superiority of virginity over marriage, her use of the metaphor of the different vessels in a lord's household, some of which are of gold and some of wood (*CT*, III: 99-104), seems to show the equal serviceableness of both and to offer a convincing justification for her 'cheerful renunciation of spiritual ambition'. Indeed, Mann argues that whilst there is no evidence that the Wife's first three husbands ever did make the accusations against her which she claims they came out with when they were drunk, 'by the same token, there is no evidence that the Wife actually did the things that are alleged of women'.[63] The experience of teaching the Wife of Bath also suggests that many modern readers are impressed by her views. After all, isn't it 'common sense' that we should 'increase and multiply', as the Lord bade us (Genesis 1: 28), a text which the Wife says she can 'wel understonde' (*CT*, III: 28-9)? Why shouldn't the Wife of Bath cite the wise King Solomon, who had seven hundred wives and three hundred concubines, to support her case for multiple marriage (3 Kings 11: 3; *CT*, III: 35-43)? If the sixth 'husband' of the Samaritan woman whom Jesus met was not really her husband (John 4: 18), how many times *was* it lawful to marry? Does the fact that Jesus only attended one marriage, that at Cana, *really* mean that we can only marry once (*CT*, III: 10-13, 17-18)? In citing such texts for her own purposes, the Wife has been seen as simply doing what more orthodox Biblical exegetes did to their texts, pulverising and fragmenting them so as to impose their own predetermined meanings on them. In turning the scholastic method against itself, the Wife seems to confirm that, as Alanus de Insulis sagely observed: 'Authority has a waxen nose; that is, it can be turned in either direction'. Thus, in so far as Chaucer was mocking the Wife's arguments, he was, 'however discreetly', mocking the official tradition from which she learned her methods of interpretation.[64]

This positive assessment of the Wife of Bath's achievement tends to be qualified by those who adopt it only by a New Historicist pessimism about the possibility of our ever entirely throwing off the thought-patterns of society's dominant ideological discourses. In contrast to those liberal or radical critical approaches which stress the power of art and literature to question or challenge existing social relations and dominant world-views, New Historicists have often argued that acts of social opposition tend to use the very tools they condemn and thus risk falling prey to the very practices they oppose. In its most extreme form, this approach can become a belief that social opposition merely confirms the original power structure of society or even, as in Orwell's *1984*, that such opposition is one of that structure's delusive political effects.[65] Chaucer's portrait of the Wife of Bath in the *Canterbury Tales* has certainly been read in this way. Aers, for instance, argues that Chaucer presents the Wife of Bath' rebellion against conventional controls and attitudes as 'real' while simultaneously showing how subordinate groups 'may so internalise the assumptions and practices of their oppressors that not only daily strategies of survival but their very acts of rebellion may perpetuate the outlook against which they rebel', thus producing 'a significant conformity with the established values which they are opposing'. For instance, the Wife does not reject the economic attitude to marriage of her time, she simply seeks to turn it to her own advantage. Similarly, in depersonalising sex and separating it from 'any constant and total human love', she reproduces rather than undermines the orthodox ecclesiastical tradition. Defining herself against the image of women constructed by clerical anti-feminism, she becomes that discourse's own mirror-image. As Patterson puts it, try as she might to articulate feminist truths, Alisoun 'remains confined within a prison house of masculine language'. She is dependent upon her voice for those she attacks. As a result, 'her performance is a kind of transvestism'.[66]

Here, in contrast to those critics who argue that Chaucer intends us to sympathise with the Wife's reflexive exposure of clerical misogyny, I will argue that Chaucer himself satirises her performance. Even though Alisoun relies on familiar clerical and scholastic modes of argument, such as appealing to traditional authorities, citing stock *exempla* and glossing Biblical passages to her own advantage, much of the humour of the 'Prologue' depends upon the Wife's misuse and 'gross misunderstandings' (by medieval standards) of such modes of argument to support her own unorthodox and (again, by medieval standards) wilfully perverse conclusions.[67] In the Wife of Bath, Chaucer could simply have personified all of the faults of which medieval authors accused women, thus showing the 'truth' of such accusations. Alternatively, he could have rejected such accusations by having the Wife refute them one by one. In practice, Chaucer does neither. Instead, for comic literary effect, he has the Wife substantiate the clerical accusations of garrulity, lust and disobedience in the very act of attempting to refute them. In other words, the Wife's defence of women is to be read ironically. We today often associate irony with radicalism, with uncertainty, scepticism and the subversion of established authority.[68] In the Middle Ages, by contrast, much literary irony was grounded in certainty: it is because we are assumed to know the opinion which is morally correct (and to share the author's view about this) that it is possible to see the 'ridiculousness' of those voices which diverge from it, as when the Monk tells us that he does not give an oyster for the rules of his order (*CT*, I: 189-82). Similarly, an appreciation of the humour of the 'Wife of Bath's Prologue' depends upon a recognition that her arguments are intended to justify a position which is the opposite of the accepted medieval norm and that, by medieval standards, it is a rather inadequate refutation of that norm. Medieval misogyny associated woman with sophistry, with persuasion and deception by means of false logic. As the *Lamentations of Matheolus* says, 'a woman can lead her man to false conclusions by means of five different types of sophism', a sophistry which was also associated with Epicurean voluptuousness. The Wife of Bath, with her face that is 'reed of hewe' (*CT*, I: 458), is one of those ruddy-faced Epicureans denounced by Jerome who find scriptural justification for their own incontinence.[69] It is this sophistic mode of argument which the Wife of Bath personifies, a comic sophistry which we tend to overlook because we ourselves agree with her conclusions. Whilst patristic critics are often accused of taking Chaucer too seriously in imposing a moral message on to his poetry, in the case of the Wife of Bath it is the patristic critics who can argue that it is those who take the Wife's arguments seriously who are missing a large part of the joke, a joke which, whether we like it or not, is made at the Wife's expense. To avoid inevitable misunderstandings, I cannot emphasise too strongly that I myself am *not* criticising the Wife's attempt to refute medieval misogyny; I am claiming that it was *Chaucer* who was satirising the Wife's reasoning and mode of speech. It is regrettable to have to go through the Wife of Bath's arguments in order to show why, in medieval terms, they are inadequate but the number of scholars who now believe that we are supposed to find the Wife's case convincing requires us to perform this task.

Why should we see the Wife's mode of argumentation in her 'Prologue' as being satirised and ridiculed by Chaucer? What are the textual cues and markers which indicate the presence of irony within the text? A good example of such irony is provided by the Wife's use of the metaphor of the need for vessels of both gold and silver and of wood and earth in a lord's household to justify why she will not be a virgin (i.e., a gold vessel): people can serve God in different ways; not all are called to be virgins (*CT*, III: 99-104). The Wife takes this metaphor from St Paul (2 Timothy 2: 20-1) whom the *Glossa Ordinaria* interpreted to mean that 'Just as wooden and earthen vessels are of value for cleansing gold and silver vessels, in the same way, the evil are of profit for the improvement of the good' since they provide the good with a lesson in what to avoid. With this gloss in mind, identifying one's self with the wooden vessels would seem to be a rather double-edged form of defence.[70] Significantly, perhaps, the passage from St Paul to which she draws our attention continues: 'Flee thou youthful desires and pursue justice, faith, charity and peace'. By contrast, the Wife, it will be remembered, regrets the passing of her youthful beauty and vigour (*CT*, III: 469-78). In particular, St Paul advises those who would be honoured vessels to 'avoid foolish and unlearned questions' which engender strife. The servant of the Lord should not wrangle but should rather be meek to all men (2 Timothy 2: 22-4). In setting herself up as a Biblical exegete, the Wife also draws our attention to biblical passages and glosses which undermine her own case and point out her own faults, condemning herself out of her own mouth even though she herself does not realise it.[71]

However, even if we ignore the Biblical glosses explaining the meaning of the different vessels in the lord's household and take this passage of scripture in its immediate sense, as St Jerome himself did, to mean simply that we can all serve God in different ways,[72] many of the Wife's arguments against the clerics' exaltation of virginity are beside the point. The orthodox teaching of the Church was *not* that everyone had to strive for the perfection of virginity since, as the Wife reminds us, St Paul only counselled virginity but could not command it for all (1 Corinthians 7: 6-8; *CT*, III: 73-86). Jerome himself went out of his way to deny that in praising virginity he therefore condemned marriage, a position which he ascribed to the Manichean heresy. 'All' that Jerome argued was that although marriage was an honourable and lawful state, a gift of God, it was still inferior to virginity and that the heavenly reward for virginity would exceed that of widowhood, just as that for widowhood would exceed that for marriage: to praise virginity is not to disparage marriage. They represent not the polarity of bad versus good but the hierarchy of good versus better. Thus, although Jerome argued that by going only once to a marriage Christ taught that men and women '*should* only marry once', he did *not* prohibit second, third or even eighth marriages. People 'should' only marry once in the same sense that they 'should' be virgins rather than married: it is the superior of the two states. In his letter to Ageruchia, Jerome *did* argue that those women who (like Alisoun) married five times identified themselves with harlots, rioting in every kind of excess. However, just as it is better to marry than to burn in lust, so it is better to remarry than to be guilty of fornication, even though the chastity of widowhood is a superior state. It is permitted for widows to remarry (1

Corinthians 7: 39) but all that is permitted is not necessarily expedient: that remarriage is not condemned does not mean that is positively commended.[73]

More importantly, what the Wife ignores is that if few can attain the most perfect state, all (according to medieval theologians) can attempt to attain perfection within their own state.[74] A wife, for instance, can be saved 'through childbearing; if she continue in faith, and love, and sanctification with sobriety' (1 Timothy 2: 15); 'the woman that feareth the lord, she shall be praised' (Proverbs 31: 30). Yet leading a life of sobriety and living in the fear of the Lord is just what the Wife has not done. Mann says that there is no evidence that the Wife was ever guilty of the things of which her first three husbands supposedly accused her. In fact, the Wife herself confesses to faults at least as bad as the charges made against women which she puts into her husbands' mouths. She herself tells us that she has been her husbands' 'whippe'; that, since they had given her control of their wealth, she did not need 'to winne hir love, or doon hem reverence'; that she 'chidde hem spitously'; that she could lie so well that she made them believe that black was white; that she deceived her husbands and conspired against them with others even when her husbands were innocent of what she accused them of; that she had the better of them 'by sleigthe, by force' and by 'continueel murmur or grucching'; that she refused to have sex with them until they gave her control of their property; that she was drunken and lecherous; that she could not keep her husbands' secrets; and that she lied to Jankyn in order to win his love while her fourth husband was still alive (*CT*, III: 175, 204-6, 223, 228-32, 382-3, 405-6, 419, 464, 531-42, 582). It *was* open to a wife such as Prudence, the wise wife in the 'Tale of Melibee', to reject misogynist denunciations of woman's evil: 'by youre leve, that am nat I' (*CT*, VII: 1087; see also below, p. 157). Such a rejection of clerical criticism of women was, in medieval terms, less convincing when it came from the mouth of a woman who has already pleaded guilty to the clerical charges made against her sex. Not aspiring to the pedestal of virginity did not, for medieval writers, justify wallowing in the pit of self-confessed sin.

The Wife of Bath's sophistry can be seen in the use she makes of many of the other Biblical texts to which she alludes. For instance, she quotes St Paul who 'bade our housbondes for to love us weel. / Al this sentence me liketh every deel' (*CT*, III: 161-2). In fact, what St Paul actually says in these passages is that whilst each man should love his wife as Christ does the Church, so, just as Christ is the head of the Church, the husband 'is the head of the wife' and she should submit herself to him as to the Lord, as a child should to its parent, or as a servant to his master (Ephesians 5: 22-33;

Colossians 3: 18-22). The Wife is on slighter safer ground when, following St Paul, she refers to her husband as her 'dettour' and her 'thrall' (*CT*, III: 129-30, 153-60), since Paul said that, in marriage, husband and wife should render their marital 'debt' to each other, so that each had power over the other's body (1 Corinthians 7: 3-4), a text to which the Wife refers eight times.[75] However, in refusing to have sex with her husbands until they submit to her (*CT*, III: 409-11), she is happy to ignore St Paul's teaching that if the wife has power over her husband's body then she 'hath not power over her own body, but the husband'. Furthermore, even though Paul wrote that the husband 'hath not power over his own body', he still said 'Let women be subject to their husbands' (Ephesians 5: 22). This remained the standard argument of theologians such as Peter Lombard and Jacques de Vitry who argued that 'however much a married couple is equal as regards the carnal debt, in other things the husband is his wife's head, to rule her, correct her (if she strays) and restrain her (so she does not fall headlong)', a teaching which was to be repeated by Chaucer's Parson (see below, pp. 154-5).[76]

What of the Wife's argument that without sex there would be no virgins in the first place and that God made the sexual organs to be used for sexual purposes (*CT*, III: 71-2, 115-28)? Powerful though this argument is to the modern reader, Jerome had anticipated it a thousand years previously when Jovinian, someone with all the status for a late medieval audience that a flat-earther has for a modern one, had used it to bolster his claim that marriage was not inferior to virginity. As Jerome said, the fact that we had sexual organs did not compel us to use them, otherwise virginity would not have a superiority over marriage, a superiority which the Wife of Bath herself accepts (*CT*, III: 105). Should Christ have made use of his sexual organs, simply because God had given them to him, rather than remaining a virgin? We will still possess our sexual organs after the resurrection of the body at the Last Judgement but will we be then required to use them? Jerome thus argued that if marriage replenishes the earth then 'virginity fills Paradise'. Besides, he added, urging people to replenish the earth was not really a priority in an age when lust was raging and rampant.[77]

Nor is the Wife's argument in favour of multiple marriages enhanced by her appeal to King Solomon's seven hundred wives and three hundred concubines since, according to the Old Testament, these women, who came from foreign nations forbidden to the Jews, turned away his heart to the idolatrous worship of strange gods, a sin for which God promised to divide and rend his kingdom out of the hand of his son (Exodus 34: 16; 3 Kings 11: 1-12). For Jerome, in *Adversus Jovinianum*, Solomon's experience meant that 'no one can know better than he, who suffered through them, what a wife or woman is'.[78] Solomon's parables, which claim that 'it is better to dwell in the wilderness than with a quarrelsome and passionate woman' (Proverbs 21: 19) and that 'it is better to sit in the corner of the housetop than with a brawling woman' (Proverbs 25: 24) are thus included in Jankyn's compilation of misogynist texts (*CT*, III: 679). Their description of the woman in 'harlot's attire ... talkative and wandering. Not able to be quiet, not able to abide still at home' (Proverbs 7: 10-11) may have a particular relevance for the portrait of the Wife of Bath. Solomon himself was a stock figure, along with Samson and David, cited for century after century as a demonstration that even the best of men could be brought low by a woman. As Jerome said, if Solomon is to be cited as evidence that it is acceptable to have many wives, is he also to be taken as a proof that it is fine to have three hundred concubines?[79]

What of the Wife's claim that she can 'wel understonde' the Lord's commandment that we should 'increase and multiply' (Genesis 1: 28; *CT*, III: 28-9)? Jerome's response to this argument was that under the Old Law of the Old Testament, humanity *was* enjoined to go forth and multiply and that even multiple marriages were then permitted, but that now another command applied to the people of an age whose duty was to act as though the end of the world were imminent: as Abraham, with his three wives, once 'pleased God in wedlock, so virgins now please him in perpetual virginity'. In a similar vein, the author of *Dives and Pauper* argued that the command to go forth and multiply no longer applied once humanity had propagated itself and that husbands and wives were now free to choose, by mutual consent, to be chaste.[80] Furthermore, whilst the Lord's command to the beasts to multiply (Genesis 1: 22) was interpreted literally, his instruction to humanity to multiply was traditionally also given a spiritual interpretation. Tropologically, it meant that we should multiply our virtues; allegorically, it meant that we should multiply the congregation of the faithful in the Church.[81] The Wife's interpretation, however, is restricted to the literal sense, to the letter of the Old Law, although she interprets even this sense to her own advantage by using it as a justification for her own lust and wandering by the way.

In her failure to understand the spiritual meaning of this passage and her twisting of the literal meaning to justify her own sin, the patristic critics see the Wife as 'dominated by the senses or the flesh rather than by the understanding or the spirit, by oldness rather than by newness. In short, the Wife of Bath is a literary personification of rampant femininity or carnality and her exegesis, in consequence, is rigorously carnal and literal.' Femininity here should be seen as 'a philosophical rather than a psychological concept'. As St Ambrose said, 'She is "woman" to the extent that she does not believe, because a woman who believes hastens "unto the perfect manhood, unto the measure of the age of the fullness of Christ" (Ephesians, 4: 13), lacking then her temporal name, her bodily sex, the wantonness of youth, the garrulity of old age'. The feminine is associated here, as it is in the 'Parson's Tale' (above, pp. 122-3), with the flesh and with the transitory, the masculine with the reason which grasps the eternal and the spiritual.[82] As St Paul said, 'the flesh lusteth against the spirit: and the spirit against the flesh'. He went on to identify the works of the flesh as 'fornication, uncleanness, immodesty, luxury, idolatry, witchcrafts, enmities, contentions, emulations, wraths, quarrels, dissensions, sects ["*sectae*": significantly, the Clerk refers to the Wife of Bath and "al hire secte" (*CT*, IV: 1170)], envies, murders, drunkenness, revelings and such like'. Opposed to these are the works of the spirit: charity, joy, peace, patience, benignity, goodness, forbearance, mildness, faith, modesty and chastity (Galatians 5: 16-23). If it is possible for a woman to aspire to the 'perfect manhood' of Christ, it is equally possible for a man to be characterised by the supposedly 'feminine' trait of carnality. Thus the (male) summoner of the 'Friar's Tale' is characterised by Robertson as 'hopelessly "carnal"' in his blindness to the spiritual aspects of reality whilst Fleming sees the Wife's carnality as relatively moderate when compared to that of the (male) Pardoner.[83]

The equation between the Wife and the flesh is also suggested by the parallels hinted at in the 'General Prologue' and the 'Prologue' to her tale between the Wife and the Samaritan woman whom Jesus met 'biside a welle' at Sychar (John 4: 5-30). The Wife herself invokes the example of the Samaritan woman and, like her, Alisoun has been married five times (*CT*, III: 6, 15-25). That the Wife herself comes from 'biside Bathe' (*CT*, I: 445) may thus be a joking allusion to the name 'Bath and Wells', one of the two double sees in medieval England, although the humour of her name also depends upon the common classical and medieval association of bath-houses with prostitution and illicit sex: the bath-house as temple of Venus.[84] In John's gospel, Jesus arrives at the well 'about the sixth hour' and asks the Samaritan woman for water. When she refuses on the grounds that he is a Jew, Jesus replies that he could give her 'living water': he who drinks water of the well will be thirsty again but he that drinks of Jesus's living water will never thirst again since it is the water of life everlasting. When Jesus tells her to call her husband, she says 'I have no husband', to which Jesus replies 'Thou hast said well ... For thou hast had five husbands and he whom thou now hast is not thy husband. This thou hast said truly.' When the woman answers, 'Sir, I perceive thou art a prophet', Jesus reveals to her that he is the Messiah, and she then brings many others to hear his teachings. For the *Glossa Ordinaria*, the water of the well represents sensual delight which offers no permanent satisfaction and is thus opposed to the grace which Christ's living water provides. Jesus arrives at the sixth hour, i.e., allegorically, in the sixth age of human history. According to Augustine, just as the world was created in six days and there are six phases in the life of man (infancy, boyhood, adolescence, youth, maturity and old age), so world history is divided into six ages. The first five (from Adam, from Noah, from Abraham, from David, and from the Babylonian captivity) represent the Old Law (see above, pp. 80-1). The sixth age, from the coming of Jesus until the end of the world, sees the decline of the exterior man but the possibility of his inner renewal under the promise of the New Law which offers the eternal rest of the sabbath.[85] Allegorically, the wife's five husbands represent the five ages of the Old Law. When Jesus says 'he whom thou now hast is not thy husband', this means that she should turn from the letter of the Old Law to join herself with the spirit of the New Law. Tropologically, her five husbands represent her five senses which have formerly ruled her but which should now be replaced with spiritual understanding. The equation of the Wife with the Samaritan woman thus associates her once more with the Old Law, with the flesh and with literal understanding.[86]

As we have seen, those who believe that we are supposed to accept the Wife of Bath's arguments often claim that, in citing Biblical texts for her own purposes, the Wife is simply turning the traditional methods of scholastic exegesis against itself and twisting the waxen nose of authority to her own advantage. Certainly, as *Dives and Pauper* shows, Biblical citations could be used for contradictory purposes, proving either that 'Solomon said much about the evil of woman' or, alternatively, that 'Solomon said much about the good of women'.[87] Nevertheless, despite the flexibility of scriptural authority, the Wife of Bath can still be seen as an unreliable exegete, one who is unable, for instance, even to ascribe the Gospel reference to 'barley-breed' to the correct evangelist (*CT*, III: 145; John 6: 9; compare with Mark 6: 38), just as later she mistakenly refers to Sulpicius Gallus as 'Symplicius Gallus' (*CT*, III: 643). Indeed, when confronted with Jesus's words to the Samaritan woman, all the Wife can retort is 'What that he mente therby, I kan nat seyn' – thus inviting us to consider what he *did* mean (or, more significantly, what Biblical exegetes said he meant). Similarly, when faced with St Paul's command that women should adopt 'decent apparel: adorning themselves with modesty and sobriety, not with plaited hair or gold or pearls or costly attire' (1 Timothy 2: 9), she simply says that for this text 'I wol nat wirche as muchel as a gnat' (*CT*, III: 20, 327-47). Again, it may be significant that St Paul's text continues: 'Let the woman learn in silence, with all subjection. But I suffer not a woman to teach, nor to use authority over man; but to be in silence' (1 Timothy 2: 11-12). In short, the Wife of Bath's arguments do not so much twist the waxen nose of authority one way as pull it off altogether by using it to support an opinion of 'wilful heterodoxy'. Jerome could almost have been describing Alisoun in his letter urging the pious widow Ageruchia not to remarry but implicitly addressing his words, as he puts it, to those who are 'idle, inquisitive and given to gossip. They wander from house to house … Of the scriptures they know nothing except the texts which favour second marriages but they love to quote the example of others to justify their own self-indulgence.'[88]

Does the Wife's confession of the faults supposedly typical of her sex ('kan ther no man / Swere and lyen as a womman kan' etc. (*CT*, III: 237-8) actually constitute a subversive mimicking of patriarchal discourse rather than a humorous confirmation of it? Undoubtedly, the Wife does show an amusing ability to mimic the stock misogynist accusations against women, most notably in those passages where she puts such accusations into the mouths of her first three husbands. As Leicester says, she seems to construct her life-story from the discourses about women contained in Jankyn's book of wicked wives.[89] Nevertheless, in general, the Wife seems to lack the ironic distance and deliberation which would make mimicry subversive of misogynist notions of feminine nature. The view of femininity and of feminine language which she embodies seems best expressed by the digression in the Wife's tale where she tells an adapted version of the story of King Midas. In Ovid's original, it is the king's barber who cannot keep the secret of Midas's ass-like ears. In the Wife's version, it is the king's wife who swears that she will never reveal his secret but who thinks that she will die if she has to keep it to herself: 'Hir thoughte it swal so soore about hire herte / That nedely som word hire moste asterte'. She runs to a marsh where she burbles the secret into the water, only for the whispering reeds to betray it to all (*CT*, III: 945-82).[90] Similarly, in her 'Prologue' the Wife tells us that she could not have kept one of her husband's secrets from her 'gossib', even if it was a thing which would have cost him his life (*CT*, III: 530-42). Rather than ironically mimicking notions of femininity from the outside, the Wife seems helpless in the face of the compulsion to act, and above all to speak, in line with the demands of her inner nature.

Should we see the Wife's arguments in favour of female sovereignty as really being an argument for the renunciation by men of their supremacy within marriage which is the precondition of a new and more equal relationship between the sexes? Certainly, the Wife tells us that once her fifth husband surrendered 'the governance of hous and lond, / And of his tonge, and of his hond also', she was then 'to hym as kynde / As any wyf from Denmark unto Ynde, / And also trewe, and so was he to me'. Her tale also ends with the knight surrendering 'maistrie' to the old hag he has been forced to marry, putting himself in her 'wise governance' whilst she then swears to be 'good and trewe / As evere was wyf', obeying him in all things so that the two of them lived 'in parfit joye' (*CT*, III: 811-25, 1230-56). The reader might at this point ask, in the Wife's own words, 'Yes, but who painted the lion?' After all, one of the Wife's favourite themes in her 'Prologue' is 'her skill at manipulating others with false speech'. Certainly, the Wife's picture of the marital bliss which results from female sovereignty tends to be undermined by her closing prayer at the end of her tale for Christ to send women 'Housbondes meeke, yonge, and fresh abedde' and to shorten the lives of those husbands 'that noght wel be governed by hir wyves' and for God to send a pestilence on those husbands who are miserly (*CT*, III: 1258-64). That the Wife was intended to depict the 'sorwe and wo' characteristic of the thraldom of marriage would certainly seem to be implied by Chaucer's 'Lenvoy de Chaucer a Bukton' where Chaucer prays his addressee to read the Wife of Bath if he would know of the bondage of wedlock (*LB*: 5, 20, 29-32).[91]

Thus, in the figure of the Wife of Bath, Chaucer did not just personify the faults ascribed to women by contemporary preachers but neither did he simply negate them by having her refute such accusations. Instead, for satirical literary purposes, he negated this negation by having her personify such faults in the very act of refuting them, producing a defence of women which was intended to be read ironically so as implicitly to undermine the very position it explicitly expounds. Explaining Chaucer's humour at length, as I have done here, inevitably tends to ruin Chaucer's joke, but perhaps this is preferable to not getting the joke in the first place. In other words, for all the Wife's explicit desire to defend women, the controlling viewpoint of the her 'Prologue' remains 'unmistakably anti-feminist'.[92] This is not because, as the New Historicists argue, the Wife is genuinely struggling but failing to express feminist truths, but rather because she herself is an embodiment of the anti-feminist 'truths' of medieval culture. In this perspective the 'Wife of Bath's Prologue' is not a failed attempt to break out of the prison-house of masculine language – it is another brick in the prison wall. In offering a defence of women which was actually meant to be read ironically, Chaucer may have been influenced by Jehan Le Fèvre's *Livre de Leësce* which, though seemingly a reply to the accusations made against women in the *Lamentations of Matheolus* (which Jehan himself had translated into French) may actually have been intended as a mock-defence, as when it argues that Solomon's sensual delight in his wives and concubines at least helped to propagate the species and meant that he eschewed homosexuality. Whether the *Livre de Leësce was* originally intended to be read ironically is unclear, although it does seem that it was received in this way in the later Middle Ages.[93] Similarly, it has been argued that Hoccleve's translation and reception of Christine de Pizan's *Epistre au Dieu d'Amours* undermined the sense of Christine's pro-feminist original, allowing him to 'laugh at women whilst ostensibly defending them'.[94]

If we read the 'Wife of Bath's Prologue' as a *fabliau*, as the story of a series of tricks played by a clever wife to gain mastery over her husbands, we will suspend our moral judgement and simply enjoy the humour and comic frankness of Alisoun's speech. Yet, her story is more than a *fabliau*, much though it owes to the conventions of that genre. As the Pardoner says, the Wife speaks to us as a 'preacher' who seeks to persuade us of a particular viewpoint (*CT*, III: 165). The Wife invites us to judge her arguments and, in so doing, draws our attention to a whole series of Biblical texts which, even if we do not accept the patristic interpretation of her as the carnal reader, undermine her own arguments and suggest an alternative standard by which to judge the faults to which she herself so readily admits. Reading her words in the light of such Biblical passages is not to impose some arcane sense on to Chaucer's text nor does it transform the critic into a cryptographer with access to some hidden level of connotation. On the contrary, the manuscript versions of her 'Prologue' are amongst the most heavily annotated sections of the *Canterbury Tales* with copious references to Chaucer's sources in the scriptures and in Jerome.[95] In short, the 'Wife of Bath's Prologue' is not, by medieval standards at least, a very convincing defence of women but rather has the effect of exonerating the anti-feminist position.[96] For Chaucer's critique of anti-feminism, we have to turn elsewhere in the *Canterbury Tales*.

(iii) Between the pit and the pedestal: woman as help-meet

Despite the widespread currency in the Middle Ages of the misogynist views which inform Chaucer's portrait of the Wife of Bath, it would be wrong to see the social identity of late medieval women as having been constituted only through the medium of misogynist discourse or to expect women's actual social position to have been be congruent with women's literary representation.[97] It is undoubtedly true that the women of late medieval England experienced a systematic social inferiority to men in terms of their wealth, status and power, of their inheritance and property rights, and in their access to formal education, political power, clerical office, a structured inferiority which justifies the description of late medieval England as a patriarchal society. Nevertheless, despite such inferiority, women's real social position was far superior to that which we might have predicted from a reading of the texts produced by clerical misogynists. As Eileen Power once said, 'The position of women is one thing in theory, another in legal position, yet another in everyday life'.[98] In the everyday life of late medieval England, it was the assumption that woman was both man's inferior *and* his companion, his fellow and his help-meet, rather than the ritual misogynist denunciation of woman as the snare of the Devil or her elevation into an ideal to be worshipped, which formed the basis of the reality of women's lives. There was thus a marked disparity between the claims of much medieval gender ideology on the one hand and the actual social practice of the time on the other, a gap between discourse and reality which usually worked to women's benefit. A classic instance of this divergence of theory and practice is that between the view expressed by Sir John Fortescue (*c.* 1390-1476), that women, with their inferior reason, were incapable of exercising the powers of concentration needed for business and the actual reality of medieval urban life in which women could function as entrepreneurs in their own right, renting shops and houses from which they ran their own businesses, trading on their own accord, and employing servants and apprentices, a role which was even given legal recognition in some towns where married women were allowed to sue and be sued as though they were single ('*femmes soles*'). Misogynists may have portrayed woman as an irrational creature who should respect her husband as her lord but a noblewoman such as Isabel, wife of Lord Berkeley, could write to her husband about the legal business which she was conducting on his behalf in London: 'treat not without me, and then all things shall be well'. Given the central role of the household in economic production, politics and piety, medieval women enjoyed the potential for a degree of economic power, political influence and personal status (albeit, it should be emphasised, one which was always inferior to that accorded to the men of their own class) which ill accords with more modern notions of the 'housewife' who inhabits a private realm divorced from public life.[99]

This social reality was addressed by a strand of medieval thought which was characterised neither by the stentorian hyperbole of contemporary misogyny nor by the elevation of woman to the status of a passive goddess but instead recognised that women could achieve a certain degree of status, responsibility and respect in their own domain. In such thought, women occupied neither the pit nor the pedestal but were assigned – or were simply assumed to hold – the position of respected inferior. Wives, it was argued, should be 'subject to their husbands' but, in return, husbands should 'give honour to the female as to the weaker vessel' (1 Peter 3: 1-7). As *Dives and Pauper* puts it, Eve was created by God from Adam's rib in order that he might have a help-meet (Genesis 2: 22-4) and woman was created as man's 'companion in love, helper in difficulty and closest comfort in distress'. Even though 'woman was made subject to man' because of Eve's sin and 'should be ruled by her husband and be in awe of him and serve him', the husband should 'respect and esteem his wife in that they are both one flesh and blood'. Thus, even though *Dives and Pauper* claimed that 'there are more wicked men than women', argued that the more malicious sins were more typically committed by men than by women and criticised those men who irrationally defamed the female sex in general for the faults of a few, its author continued to see male superiority as inevitable. Although Eve was made from Adam's rib as a symbol that she should be his companion whom he esteemed and respected, the woman should still 'love man as her origin' and 'respect man as her perfection, her principal who preceded her in the order of perfection'. In this perspective, woman may be man's inferior but she is also his respected companion, not a serf or slave to be held in base subjection.[100] Similarly, whilst misogamous writers might condemn marriage as a form of purgatory, others, such as Robert Mannyng, pointed out that marriage was a perfectly respectable institution: it was a sacrament which had been ordained by God in paradise and it was at a marriage (that at Cana) that Christ had performed his first miracle. As the *Sarum Missal* said, it was God who had consecrated the state of matrimony, which was a sacrament considered worthy enough to signify the union between Christ and the Church.[101]

It is this conventional view of woman as man's respected inferior within marriage which would seem to be the view which Chaucer himself puts forward in the two didactic prose works which appear in the *Canterbury Tales*. The first of these is the 'Tale of Melibee' told by Chaucer the pilgrim which is a translation from Reynaud de Louen's French version of Albertanus of Brescia's *Liber Consolationis et Consilii* (1246); the second is the 'Parson's Tale' which, as we have seen, enjoys an authoritative position at the end of the tales (see above, pp. 68-9). Against the misogamous tradition, the Parson repeats Robert Mannyng's defence of marriage as a sacrament, 'so noble and so digne', which had been ordained by God in paradise (unlike other human institutions such as the state and private property which were the consequence of the fall). Marriage had been legitimised by God, the 'auctor of matrimoyne', when he said 'A man shall lete fader and mooder and taken hym to his wif, and they shullen be two in o flessh' (Genesis 2: 24; Matthew 10: 7-9; Ephesians 5: 31). It was a state into which God, as Christ, had 'hymself be born' and which he had shown as blessed when he performed his first miracle at the marriage of Cana. For the Parson, sex between man and woman, which would otherwise be the deadly sin of lust, is changed through marriage into a mere venial sin. The sexual act is justified within marriage for three reasons: for the meritorious motive of producing children; so that husband and wife can render to each other 'the dette of hire bodies' to which St Paul refers, a motive which is also meritorious since it does not necessarily undermine the possibility of chastity within marriage; and as a means by which 'to echewe leccherye and vileynye', a motive which does involve venial sin, although such venial sin can scarcely be avoided in sexual pleasure. It is, however, wrong for husband and wife to indulge in sex 'oonly for amorous love', to experience the pleasure of 'brennynge delit, they rekke nevere how ofte'. Despite January's claim in the 'Merchant's Tale' that 'A manne may do no synne with his wyf', sex as an end in itself turns the sexual act into a deadly sin, in effect into a form of adultery, even when it takes place between husband and wife. For a husband to believe that he does not sin with that 'likerousnesse that he dooth with his wyf', is as mistaken as believing that a man cannot be killed with his own knife. Against the all-consuming passion admired in romances of courtly love, the Parson urges that 'Man sholde loven hys wyf by discrecioun, paciently and atemprely', as though she were his sister, rather than setting her up as an idol 'that he loveth biforn God' (CT, IV: 1835-40; X: 841-2, 858-60, 881-2, 903-5, 915-20, 938-42).

Within marriage, the Parson, like the author of *Dives and Pauper*, takes for granted the subordination of the wife to the husband.[102] Just as marriage figures the marriage of Christ to the Church of which he is the head, so 'man is heved of womman; algate, by ordinaunce it sholde be so' (Ephesians 5: 23-5). In other words, 'a womman sholde be subget to hire housbonde' (1 Peter 3: 1) so that she 'hath noon auctoritee to swere ne to bere witnesse withoute leve of hir housbonde that is hire lord'. (This was, in fact, the case in medieval English law where, for instance, a married woman could not make a will without her husband's permission.) 'She sholde eek serven hym in alle honestee' and 'above alle worldly thyng she sholde loven hire housbonde, and to hym be trewe of hir body' (*CT*, X: 921, 929-36). Neverthless, despite his assumption of woman's inferiority, the Parson also emphasises that she was made by God to be a 'felawe unto man'. Like the author of *Dives and Pauper*,[103] the Parson argues that God did not make Eve out of Adam's head for that would have signified a claim to female mastery and, as daily experience showed, 'ther as the womman hath the maistrie, she maketh to muche desray'. Yet neither had God made Eve out of Adam's foot, signifying that she should be his thrall: 'for she ne sholde nat been holden to lowe; for she kan nat paciently suffre'. Unlike the Wife of Bath, the Parson, who assumes that wives should be obedient to their husbands, is not inclined to cite man's supposed superior reason and patience as a justification for wives to have their own way (*CT*, III: 436-42), but he does conclude that since God made Eve out of Adam's rib (Genesis 2: 21-3), this signified that 'womman sholde be felawe unto man' and that he should treat her with 'suffraunce and reverence'. If a woman should love her husband with all her heart and be faithful to him, 'so sholde an housbonde eek be to his wyf'. Since the wife's body is her husband's, so should her heart be, or else there is 'no parfit mariage' between them (*CT*, X: 924-30, 936-8). The Parson's presentation of woman as both the companion and the inferior of her husband was a patriarchal ideal but, as an ideal to aspire to, it was one which was rather closer to the everyday reality of women's lives than the vicious misogyny of many clerical texts.

Similar views of women and marriage are expressed in the 'Tale of Melibee' through the figure of Dame Prudence. In the 'Nun's Priest's Tale', as we have seen, the narrator, or at least Chauntecleer his surrogate, expresses the view that 'Wommanes conseils been ful ofte colde' (i.e., fatal) and that it was a woman's counsel that 'made Adam fro Paradys to go' (*CT*, VII: 3256-66). The 'Tale of Melibee' told by Chaucer the pilgrim makes exactly the opposite case by showing how Melibeus benefits from the advice of his wife, Prudence, after three of his enemies have assaulted Prudence and his daughter Sophie. In order to decide whether he should take revenge on his foes, Melibeus calls a 'greet congregacion of folk', a council which ignores the wise advice of those who urge caution and urges him on to vengeance (*CT*, VII: 1004, 1008, 1027, 1034-5, 1049). When his wife cautions him against hasty action, Melibeus gives five reasons why he intends to ignore her advice (*CT*, VII: 1053-62). Dame Prudence listens patiently to her husband, asks permission from him to speak and then, gracefully, refutes his points one by one (*CT*, VII: 1063-82, 1083-113).

Whilst most of Chaucer's heroines, such as Custance, Prudence and Cecile, suffer for their virtue, Prudence instead teaches it to her husband.[104]

Firstly, Melibeus argues that people would hold him a fool if, by reason of her advice alone, he changed what had been affirmed by the advice of many. To this Prudence replies that it is no folly to change one's mind for the better once things appear differently from the way they had previously and that it is better to listen to the 'fewe folk that been wise and ful of resoun' rather than the 'greet multitude' amongst which 'every man crieth and clatereth what that hym liketh. Soothly swich multitude is nat honest.' Whereas for a modern audience the problem is knowing what is to count as wisdom in the first place, Dame Prudence identifies an *a priori* wisdom possessed by a favoured few, not the opinion of the many, as the basis of authority. As Aquinas put it, 'it does not befit a wise man that he should be induced to act by someone else but that he should use his knowledge to induce others to act'.[105]

Secondly, Melibeus says that he will ignore her advice on the misogynist grounds that 'alle wommen be wikke and noon good of hem alle' and that, as Solomon said, in a thousand men he had found one good one, but among women 'good womman foond I nevere' (Ecclesiastes 7: 29). Prudence replies to this argument with classical wisdom and Biblical *exempla*. As Seneca said, he who would have wisdom should not be ashamed to learn 'of lasse folk than hymself'. Far from all women being wicked, 'ther hath been many a good womman', including the Virgin Mary, to whom Christ himself was born, and Mary Magdalene, to whom, 'for the grete bountee that is in wommen', Christ first appeared following the Resurrection. Even if Solomon said that he had never found a good woman, many other men have done so. Besides, Solomon's words that he had only found one good man may simply have meant that 'ther is no wight that hath soveryn bountee save God allone' (as Prosperyna, queen of 'Fayerye', also argues in her defence of women in the 'Merchant's Tale' (*CT*, IV: 2287-90)) since 'ther nys no creature so good that hym ne wanteth somwhat of the perfeccioun of God' (*PL*, 113: 1124). By invoking wisdom and moral worth as the key issues in whether one should take someone's counsel, Prudence is therefore able to argue that it is honourable to be advised by lesser folk while simultaneously dismissing the views of the foolish multitude. If in the figure of the Wife of Bath, Chaucer parodies woman as the carnal exegete, in the case of Prudence he shows us a woman who *can* read allegorically in order to provide her husband with the discretion he lacks and to correct *his* literal-mindedness. The example of Prudence would thus seem to indicate that, unlike Hoccleve, Chaucer does not simply urge women to leave arguments about holy writ to 'clerks grete' and to 'cackle' about some other subject while getting on with their spinning.[106]

Thirdly, Melibee claims that to take Prudence's counsel would be to admit her 'maistrie' over him and 'if the wyf have maistrie, she is contrarious to hir housbonde'. Here, Prudence argues that if men were only counselled by their superiors they would not so frequently receive the advice of others. Listening to the advice of one's inferiors is not to grant them mastery: one is not constrained by their advice but still has a free choice whether to act on it or not.

Fourthly, Melibeus claims that, if he worked by her advice, his counsel would never be secret 'as the chattering of woman can hide nothing'. Prudence replies that such sayings apply only to those women 'that been jangleresses and wikked', of whom Solomon rightly said 'it were bettre dwelle in desert than with a womman that is riotous' (Proverbs 21: 19). However, if some other women are riotous, he should know that she herself is not 'for ye han ful often assayed my grete silence and my grete pacience, and eek how wel that I kan hyde and hele thynges that men oghte secreely to hyde'. Like Christine de Pizan, who argued that to condemn all women for the faults of some was tantamount to labelling all of God's angels bad because of the evil of a few, Prudence asks Melibeus to judge her by individual worth rather than by her sex. Like the words of many of the other virtuous women of the *Canterbury Tales*, such as the Man of Law's Custance and the Second Nun's Cecilia, Prudence's speech is persuasive because she herself embodies the values, such as patience and forgiveness, of which she is attempting to convince her husband. Lacking any *a priori* power or status, Chaucer's women have to establish an authority for their speech by the persuasiveness of their morality and their deeds.[107]

Finally, Melibeus quotes Aristotle's saying that 'through evil counsel, women conquer men'. Prudence, however, reinterprets this claim to mean that it is the man who is prevented from doing wicked deeds by the 'reson and good conseil' of his wife who is restrained or vanquished by her and that such a wife deserves praise, not blame, for doing so. Again, Prudence argues that all women should not be blamed for the faults of some, citing the Biblical examples of Rebecca, Judith, Abigail and Hester, along with many other good women, to show how often men have benefited from female counsel. Furthermore, God had made Eve to be Adam's help-meet: 'if that wommen were nat goode, and hir conseils goode and profitable, / oure Lord God of hevene wolde nevere have wroghte hem, ne called hem help of man, but rather confusioun of man' – as indeed the Nun's Priest later labels them. Prudence concludes with a series of proverbial questions and answers: 'What is better than gold? Jasper. What is better than jasper? Wisdom. What is better than wisdom? Woman. What is better than a good woman? Nothing.' Whilst wicked women undoubtedly do exist, 'manye wommen been goode amd hir conseils goode and profitable'.

Melibeus is convinced by his wife's arguments and decides to be ruled by her counsel in all things. Prudence here represents an aspect of Melibeus's own intellect, that higher mental faculty 'which disposes reason to issue good commands' and which teaches us how to live well and to distinguish good from evil. As Aquinas says, citing Aristotle, 'a prudent man is a well-advised one'.[108] Prudence counsels her husband against vengeance, urging him to be reconciled with his enemies and securing mercy for them once she has persuaded them to submit to her husband's judgement. Metaphorically, as the virtue of prudence, Melibeus grants her governance over him but, as a wife, Prudence accepts that she is her husband's inferior and that her wisdom and advice are there for the benefit of her 'lord' (*CT*, VII: 1081-3, 1278-81, 1285-6, 1426, 1495, 1674, 1713, 1717, 1724 1727, 1744, 1765-6, 1772, 1834, 1852, 1871-2, 3163-4).[109]

The examples of *Dives and Pauper*, the 'Tale of Melibee' and the 'Parson's Tale' would seem to indicate that even those medieval authors who were sympathetic towards women also took for granted their social inferiority and subservience to men; their works tended to be anti-misogynist rather than pro-equality. Significantly, even when Christine de Pizan sought to defend of women against misogynist slander in *The Book of the City of Ladies* by citing examples of women who were skilled rulers or learned in philosophy, who invented new arts and crafts and who were Christian teachers and martyrs, she still accepted that God had 'ordained man and woman to serve Him in different offices', giving to each sex 'a fitting and appropriate nature and inclination'. Women should, therefore, be assiduous 'in those duties assigned to them to perform', i.e., governing their households and in providing everything for them. At the end of her book, she still calls on married women not to 'scorn being subject to your husbands'. Women should prove their worth by their individual moral conduct (being humble, modest in their dress etc.), making liars of the misogynists by showing forth their virtue and fleeing vice. Those women with good husbands should thank God for this boon, those with husbands who are not completely bad should seek to moderate the latter's vices (exactly as Dame Prudence does to Melibeus), whilst those who have cruel, mean and savage husbands who cannot be reformed should 'strive to endure them' so that they 'will acquire great merit for their souls through the virtue of patience'.[110] Both here and in her practical guidance to women in *The Book of the Three Virtues*, the sequel to *The City of Ladies*, Christine takes as given the constraints imposed on women in her contemporary society and so concentrates, in her defence of her sisters, on women's exercise of their intellectual qualities and practical skills as governors of their households. Above all, as in 'The Tale of Melibee', the necessity of replying to misogynist attacks on women's moral worth meant that the medieval defence of women became a justification of women's potential as moral agents with souls and free will, rather than a call for social equality.[111] Significantly, it is 'Worldly Prudence' who teaches the wise princess how to order her life and to conduct herself honourably in *The Book of the Three Virtues*, prudence itself frequently being presented by medieval writers as one of the feminine virtues. Indeed, the dialogue of Melibeus and Prudence was actually included alongside Christine's *The City of Ladies* and her *Book of the Three Virtues* in a de luxe manuscript compiled at the Burgundian court *c.* 1450-82 whilst, at one time, the French translation of Albertanus of Brescia's work was even erroneously ascribed to Christine.[112] In its rejection of misogyny, the Wife of Bath's 'Prologue' has sometimes been equated with Christine's defence of women; in fact, it is the discourse of Chaucer's Dame Prudence which is rather closer to the spirit of Christine's medieval feminist project.

As the 'Tale of Melibee' suggests, it was not that medieval writers did not have a good word to say about women or even that, as the Wife of Bath claims, they only praised women who were holy virgins. The important point is that, following the 'valiant woman' of Proverbs 10-31 and Ecclesiasticus 1-4, 16-24, the qualities of the 'good woman' in everyday life were defined in terms of how she could benefit her husband.[113] As Bartholomaeus Anglicus put it, the husband should care and protect his wife and undertake all perils for her sake but, in return, the good wife ('*Ecclesia*') will be 'busy and devout in God's service, meek and obedient to her husband'. 'Such a wife is worthy of praise who studies to please her husband more with her good behaviour than with her curled hair, more with her virtue than with rich clothing.' She should not be like the evil wife ('*Synagoga*') 'who cries and quarrels, is drunk, lecherous, changeable, contrary, costly, inquisitive, envious, lazy, wearisome, wandering, bitter, suspicious and hateful'. 'No man is happier than he who has a good wife. And no man is unhappier than he who has an evil wife.' It was this view which was put forward in medieval courtesy books addressed to women such as that of *The Goodman of Paris* who taught his young wife that her main priorities should be the salvation of her soul and the comfort of her husband, followed by the good governance of her household in her role as its 'sovereign mistress' and, finally, by her own amusement.[114] Chaucer's Parson agreed: wives should be obedient to their husbands and 'setten hire entente to plesen hir housbondes' by loving them 'aboven alle worldly thyng' (*CT*, X: 929-36). Thus, whilst the 'Tale of Melibee' uses woman to personify man's higher faculties, the patience and the prudence which temper his masculine desire for violent revenge, and the 'Parson's Tale' interprets woman as the flesh which first succumbs to temptation before overcoming reason, both tales arrive at a similar conclusion about the ideal relationship between the sexes. Each casts woman as the companion and help-meet of her husband who, by her behaviour, can prove herself worthy of her husband's respect.

(iv) Conclusion

As we have seen, medieval views of women were frequently polarised between extremes of praise and condemnation, between the position of, as Chauntecleer put it, '*hominis confusio*' and that of 'mannes joye and al his blis' (*CT*, VII: 3164-6). As John Gower said, the good woman is 'one whose praise is above all things' whereas the bad woman is 'a subtle snare for the destruction of men' (*VC*, V: 6). Nevertheless, this straightforward opposition between invective and panegyric needs to be qualified in a number of respects. Firstly, we should not read such opinions of women too literally, since how women were presented in any specific text was determined by its particular rhetorical purposes. In the 'Man of Law's Tale', for instance, the narrator's purpose is to establish the evil nature of the Sultan's treacherous mother who murders Custance's Christian companions and sets Custance herself adrift in a rudderless ship. To achieve this goal he is quite happy to see her, like Eve, as an archetypal female instrument of the Devil while simultaneously describing her as a 'feyned womman', invoking the ideal image of woman as nurturing mother to criticise the Sultaness's treachery towards her own son. In a like manner, he first, refers to Donegild, Custance's Northumbrian mother-in-law, as 'mannysh' (i.e., unwomanly) in her evil, before going on to denounce her treachery as inhuman and diabolical (*CT*, II: 358-71, 781-4). Similarly, whilst the Man of Law blames Eve for the Fall because of his purposes, the Monk, whose generic purpose in his tale is to tell us the tragic tales of men of 'heigh degree' who fell into adversity, argues that it was Adam's own 'mysgovernaunce' which had led to his expulsion from Eden (*CT*, VII: 2012-14). In this mode of thought, an argument or *exemplum* exists for the sake of a conclusion which is already given, rather than the conclusion flowing from the argument or the illustrations which buttress it. As a result, according to his generic purposes, Chaucer was able to interpret the figure of Theseus *in malo* in the context of the *Legend of Good Women* where he features in a catalogue of masculine treachery (*LGW*, F: 2174), but *in bono* in the context of a chivalric epic such as the 'Knight's Tale' where he becomes the wise ruler. The meaning of a medieval image, including that of woman, can be understood only from its role in specific generic and rhetorical contexts.

Secondly, misogynist texts were not necessarily meant to be taken literally but rather exhibited the medieval love of adopting a stance for the purposes of debate and then taking it to its extreme, demonstrating learning and ingenuity with the support of any possible argument, evidence or authority, purposes to which the 'citational mode' of misogyny, with its reliance on traditional authorities, was particularly well suited.[115] An instance of the extremes to which this literary game could lead is provided by the *Lamentations of Matheolus* in which Matheolus's desire to push his case to its 'logical, if extreme conclusion' at one point even leads him to argue the heretical case that it is impossible for a woman's soul to be saved and that, at the Last Judgement, when Adam is made whole by the return of the rib from which woman was made, 'woman will be no more'.[116]

This point needs particularly to be borne in mind when medieval writers says that 'Woman is this' or 'Woman or that'. Beneath such rhetorical exaggeration, what is frequently meant in such cases is 'Some women are this', or 'Women can be that', or 'For the purposes of moral admonition it is useful to see woman as this', or 'Women can metaphorically be seen as that, which is the subject I am actually interested in'. A classic instance is the *Liber Decem Capitulorum* of Marbod of Rennes (d. 1123), which contains one of the most vituperative pieces of medieval misogyny in which we are told that 'woman' is a dire monster to be avoided, 'woman' is the greatest snare of the Devil, 'woman' is envious, capricious, irascible etc. etc. etc. Yet, in the very next chapter, this blanket condemnation of women's viciousness is replaced by the claim that virtue has not 'often been found to be lesser in the inferior sex, nor has wrong-doing been found to be greater', as is illustrated by the Virgin Mary and by Judas.[117] Thus, even if we accept that Chaucer uses woman metaphorically to represent sophistry and carnality in the 'Wife of Bath's Prologue', we should also note that he uses women in other tales to personify each of the four cardinal virtues: the fortitude of Custance in the 'Man of Law's Tale', the eponymous virtue of Dame Prudence in the 'Tale of Melibee', the temperance of Virginia in the 'Physician's Tale', and the justice of Griselda, who renders to others what is their due, in the 'Clerk's Tale'. Indeed, male writers of the Middle Ages seem to have had a particular preference for using femininity as a symbol of the virtues of the meek.[118] But women who rejected such meekness were likely to be depicted as monstrous, as in the case of the Sultaness, or comic, as with the Wife of Bath: the theological opposition between the rebelliousness of Eve and the humility of the Virgin was reproduced in literary form.[119] Thus, if Griselda and Prudence seem to be opposites to the modern reader, with Griselda's absolute submissiveness to Walter contrasting with Prudence's willingness to 'maken semblant of wratthe' in order to correct her husband (*CT*, VII: 1696-710), the two women are united in each personifying what, for medieval thought, was a particular virtue or attitude needed in life. If Prudence represents the mental faculty which prompts reason to good acts, then Griselda does not, in medieval terms, simply represent passive suffering but is rather a model of active co-operation with God's will, proving her faith by her works, like Abraham and Job, as we are urged to do in the epistle of St James which the Clerk recommends as the end of his tale (James 1: 2-4; 2: 14-26) (*CT*, IV: 1154-5).[120] Thus the Goodman of Paris was able to cite both of these women as role-models whose example his wife should follow: Griselda for her humble obedience to her husband; Prudence for 'wisely and humbly' dissuading her husband from acting foolishly. In this perspective, the moral Dame Prudence is not so much the 'follow up' to the pro-feminist Alisoun of Bath as her exact opposite.[121]

The dominant medieval view of women, one that was often taken for granted rather than explicitly formulated, was that which saw woman as man's help-meet and companion, the *mulier economica* who exercised power within the household so long as it did not bring her into conflict with her husband's wishes.[122] It is this role which we see in the 'Shipman's Tale' when the merchant of St Denis sets off for Bruges and beseeches his wife that in his absence she will 'be to every wight buxom and make. / And for to kepe oure gode be curious, / And honestly governe wel oure hous. / Thou hast ynough, in every maner wise, / That to a thrifty houshold may suffise. / Thee lakketh noon array ne no vitaille; / Of silver in thy purs shaltow nat faille' (*CT*, VII: 242-8). It would, therefore, be wrong to portray medieval views of women as universally or straight forwardly misogynist or to see the idealisation of women as the only medieval alternative to such misogyny. On the contrary, in the sphere of gender relations as in that of class inequalities, the underlying assumption of the dominant social theory of the day was that order and harmony depended upon stable social hierarchies and that through each person fulfilling his or her role, all would benefit, even the socially inferior. The scientific, religious and social philosophy of the Middle Ages justified sexual inequality by portraying women's inferiority as natural, inevitable, divinely sanctioned and socially beneficial. Whilst extreme views of woman as the inhabitant of the pit or the pedestal made for exciting literature and provided the preacher with dramatic moral examples, the role which woman was assumed to hold elsewhere in medieval thought, that of respected inferior and helpmeet, which informed much actual medieval social practice lay at neither of these poles. It was this view, the one set out in the 'Tale of Melibee' and 'Parson's Tale', which, if we are to identify any of the multiplicity of opinions about women expressed in the *Canterbury Tales* with that of its author, would seem to be that of Chaucer himself. In the sense that he presented women as rational creatures with the potential to offer moral guidance to their husbands and who had a worthy respected part to play in society, it *is* possible to describe Chaucer as a 'feminist' writer, at least when his views are contrasted with the stentorian voice of medieval misogyny. It is simply that this 'feminism', one in which women are confined to the role of respected inferior, was of a kind which – understandably – is unlikely to appeal to modern feminists.

Notes

1 Ferrante, 1975: 1-2; Richards, 1983: 4; Bloch, 1987: 1; Fiero *et al.*, 1989: 5.

2 Brewer, 1978: 86.

3 Greene and Kahn, 1985a: 3; Crane, 1994: 4-5, 14.

4 Delany, 1990: 143-50; Mann, 1991a: xi–xii, 186-94; Hansen, 1992: 56. In 1914, Hadow claimed that 'it must be evident even to the most superficial observer, that Chaucer had an innate reverence for womanhood' even though he was well aware that not all women 'were angels' (Hadow, 1914: 124-41, quotations from 124-5).

5 Evans and Johnson, 1994b: 16.

6 Bloch, 1987: 1.

7 Radice, 1974: 70, 120-5, 130-1.

8 Blamires, 1992: 224-8; Scattergood, 1975.

9 Barnum, 1980: 66-71, 79-93.

10 Hansen, 1992: 10-12; Pearsall, 1992: 138; Kittredge, 1911-12: 133-58; Neuse, 1991: 87.

11 Hansen, 1992: 51; Walker, 1992: 167; Lawler, 1980: 58-64.

12 Lawler, 1980: 55-8; Maclean, 1980: 57; Martin, 1990: 30; Crane, 1994: 97-8, 134.

13 Bullough, 1973; Wood, 1981: 715-7; Cadden, 1993: 14-34.

14 Bullough, 1973; Wood, 1981: 723-4; Rowland, 1981: 59; Blamires, 1992: 38-42, 46-7, 92-3, 261-2, 270; Barnum, 1980: 67-8; Cadden, 1993: 121, 192-3.

15 Salu, 1990: 186; Blamires, 1992: 81, 92-3, 262, 265; Barnum, 1980: 66.

16 Bullough, 1973; Blamires, 1992: 59-63; Robertson, 1969: 22-3, 70-4; Ferrante, 1975: 18-21.

17 McDermott, 1989: 429-31

18 Fremantle, 1892: 346-416.

19 Colker, 1984: 163-5; Fiero *et al.*, 1989: 120-47; Millett and Wogan-Browne, 1992: 6, 21-35; Swanson, 1989: 114-18, 125-6; Blamires, 1992: 106; Wilson and Makowski, 1990.

20 Bowden, 1954: 214, 226-7; Fremantle, 1892: 383-4; Brown and Butcher, 1991: 22-7.

21 Blamires, 1992: 177-97; Van Hamel, 1892; Thundy, 1979.

22 Matthews, 1974; Dahlberg, 1983: 221-4; Blamires, 1992: 21-3.

23 Radice, 1974: 70-4.

24 Kolve, 1984: 246-7, *CA*, VIII: 2705-13; Van Hamel, 1905: 21, 26-9.

25 Rigby, 1995: 245; Lawler, 1980: 58; Crane, 1994: 98.

26 Blamires, 1992: 51-8; Karras, 1992; Owst, 1966: 375-404; Elliott, 1991.

27 Salu, 1990: 33; Owst, 1966: 375-404; Miller, 1977: 403-6.

28 Owst, 1966: 375-404; Patterson, 1983: 656-7.

29 Davies, 1963: 221-2; MacCracken, 1934: 438-42; Mann, 1991a: 2.

30 Miller, 1977: 387-90; see, however, Cooper, 1989: 244-5.

31 Brown, 1974: 387-8.

32 Davies, 1963: 103; Power, 1975: 31; 79; Roberts, 1985: 103-18; Warner, 1985: 73; Newlyn, 1989: 124; Blamires, 1992: 11-12; *PPB*, XVI: 68-72; Meech and Allen, 1940: 48-53; Ross, 1940: 246-9, 260, 318-19, 329, 332-3; Bennett, 1987: 54, 140.

33 Blamires, 1992: 227-8.

34 Meyer, 1877: 499-503; Meyer, 1886: 321; Power, 1975: 14.

35 Ross, 1940: 319; Davies, 1963: 86-8, 210, 283; Salu, 1990, 33; Sisam, 1962: 167-8; Richards, 1983: 254-5; Millett and Wogan-Browne, 1992: xxii, 45, 79; Duffy, 1990; Wenzel, 1989: 81, 89; Anderson, 1980: 59-61; Karras, 1992; Shahar, 1992: 1-4, 115-16, 205, 252.

36 Clasby, 1979: 225, 230; Martin, 1990: 19; Dinshaw, 1989: 108-9.

37 Painter, 1964: 95, 143-7; Krueger, 1993: xi–xii, 1-3.

38 Lewis, 1977: 2; Donaldson, 1977: 156; Calin, 1980: 34, 43.

39 Patterson, 1987: 125; Burgess and Busby, 1986: 46-7.

40 Painter, 1964: 112-14, 134-5; O'Donoghue, 1982: 5; Kane, 1982; Barron, 1990: 33; Duby, 1984: 224-5; McCash, 1990.

41 Robertson, 1970: 260-4; Robertson, 1969: 454-7.

42 Zupitza, 1883; Barron, 1987: 75-80.

43 Cooper, 1989: 211.

44 Patterson, 1987: 125; Mandel, 1985: 288.

45 Barron, 1974: 115-27.

46 Burns, 1993: 3-4, 241-2; Krueger, 1993: xiii, 10-11, 14, 247, 251.

47 Burgess and Busby, 1986: 49, 58.

48 See Rosenberg, 1980: 344; Cooper, 1989: 232-3.

49 Dahlberg, 1983: 154-70.

50 Crane, 1994: 109; Martin, 1990: 62.

51 Power, 1928: 110, 145, 147-8.

52 Cooper, 1990; Jordan, 1967: 216-26; Reid, 1970; Wilson, 1985: 249; Robertson, 1969: 317-31; Huppé, 1967: 107-29; Allen and Gallacher, 1970; Olson, 1986: 235-47.

53 Robertson, 1969: 331.

54 Oberembt, 1976; Spisak, 1980: 152; Van, 1994: 180, 191; Knapp, 1989: 50-1; Hansen, 1992: 11, 13, 27, 40, 42.

55 Evans and Johnson, 1994b: 1, 2, 8, 15; Patterson, 1991: 316, emphasis added.

56 Bloch, 1987: 6; Aers, 1980: 82-8; Gottfried, 1985: 206-7; Dinshaw, 1989: 126; Martin, 1990: 212-16; Hamel, 1979: 138; Hanna, 1989.

57 Mann, 1991a: 79-80; Root, 1994: 260.

58 Dinshaw, 1989, 115-16, 118-20; Martin, 1990: 31-2; Crane, 1994: 59, 62, 116; Moi, 1985: 139-43; Millard, 1989: 170, 175-6.

59 Pratt, 1994: 62; Fenster and Erler, 1990: 50-1; Aers, 1986: 80.

60 Spiegel, 1987: 123-5.

61 Carruthers, 1979: 22; Moi, 1985: 43, 84.

62 Brown and Butcher, 1991: 31; 37-8; Knapp, 1990: 121.

63 Crane, 1994: 119; Mann, 1991a: 72-3, 78.

64 Speirs, 1951: 137-8; Justman, 1976: 109; Mann, 1991a: 72; Mann, 1991b: 8; Spisak, 1980: 151-2, 156-7, 160; Aers, 1980: 86; Shoaf, 1983: 176; Schibanoff, 1986: 226-7; Bishop, 1988: 121-2.

65 Veeser, 1989b: xi; Gallagher, 1989: 38-9; Graff, 1989: 169-70, 174-8; Patterson, 1987: 63-5; Lentricchia, 1989: 235, 237, 239; Pecora, 1989: 267.

66 Aers, 1980: 147-50; Patterson, 1983: 682; Shoaf, 1983: 182-3.

67 Muscatine, 1972: 115; Jordan, 1967: 216-26; Crane, 1987: 21.

68 Sklute, 1984: 5; Moi, 1985: 35, 40.

69 Reiss, 1979: 81; Bloch, 1987: 17; Blamires, 1992: 179; Van Hamel, 1892: 26; Olson, 1986: 238, 243; Fremantle, 1892: 238, 377-8, 415-16.

70 Robertson, 1969: 327; *BS*, VI: 742.

71 Huppé, 1967: 108.

72 Fremantle, 1892: 67-71; Kaske, 1963: 183.

73 Fremantle, 1892: 23, 66-71, 76-8, 230-3, 344, 347-8, 351-2, 375, 379; Cook, 1978: 53.

74 Fremantle, 1892: 373; Huppé, 1967: 115-18.

75 Fremantle, 1892: 351; Patterson, 1983: 677.

76 Cook, 1978: 56; Blamires, 1992: 146; Morgan, 1970: 136.

77 Fremantle, 1892: 353, 360, 373-4.

78 Fremantle, 1892: 367.

79 Boren, 1975; Blamires, 1992: 75, 81, 90, 101, 106, 116, 180, 194, 264, 280; Smith, 1990: 208-10; Minnis, 1991b: 57-9; Fremantle, 1892: 364.

80 Fremantle, 1892: 234-5, 344, 356, 360, 364, 390; Barnum, 1980: 79.

81 Robertson, 1969: 322-3; Miller, 1955: 226-7; *BS*, I: 35.

82 Robertson, 1969: 321, 330-1; Walker, 1992: 178.

83 Robertson, 1969: 268-9; Fleming, 1985: 159; Myles, 1994: 126-9.

84 Weissman, 1980: 12-23; Dahlberg, 1983: 245-6; Fremantle, 1892: 378.

85 Burrow, 1986: 80-92, 199-200.

86 *BS*, V: 1075-9; Robertson, 1969: 321-2; Olson, 1986: 246-7.

87 Barnum, 1980: 80-1, 89-90; Blamires, 1992: 268.

88 Cook, 1978: 54; Fremantle, 1892: 238, see also 403, 415.

89 Leicester, 1990: 137; Hanna, 1989: 2; Owen, 1991: 42.

90 Innes, 1973: 250-1; Patterson, 1983: 657.

91 Crane, 1994: 117; Pearsall, 1992: 184, 259-60: Hamel, 1979: 138; Patterson, 1983: 683-4; Benson, 1986: 13; Rowland, 1986: 145-6.

92 Jordan, 1967: 216.

93 Van Hamel, 1905: 21, 26-7; Pratt, 1994.

94 Bornstein, 1981-2; Pearsall, 1992: 184; see, however, Fenster and Erler, 1990: 165-7.

95 Manly and Rickert, 1940, III: 496-502.

96 Jordan, 1967: 226.

97 Diamond, 1977: 61; Walker, 1992: 152; Crane, 1994: 7, 58-9.

98 Power, 1975: 9.

99 Barron, 1989: 45-7; Rigby, 1995: 268-78.

100 Fremantle, 1892: 351; Blamires, 1992: 261-270; Barnum, 1980: 66-71, 79-92; Fenster and Erler, 1990: 185.

101 Furnivall, 1901: 345; Miller, 1977: 381.

102 Barnum, 1980: 67-8.

103 Barnum, 1980: 66-7.

104 Owen, 1973: 270.

105 Olsson, 1992: 19 n. 11.

106 Ellis, 1986: 105; Seymour, 1981: 64-5.

107 Fenster and Erler, 1990: 42, 184; Cowgill, 1990: 174-6, 182-3.

108 Knowles, 1972: 854; McDermott, 1989: 55, 233, 235, 236, 237, 239, 376-82.

109 Pearsall, 1992: 254.

110 Richards, 1983: 31, 88-9, 255-7.

111 Lawson, 1985, 62-5, 145-9; Brown-Grant, 1994: 310; Gottlieb, 1985: 353-6.

112 Lawson, 1985: 55-98; Cadden, 1993: 205, 209; Curnow, 1975: 408-9, 423.

113 For the Wife of Bath as the anti-type of the *mulier fortis* of Proverbs 31: 10, see Boren, 1975.

114 Furnivall, 1901: 68; Miller, 1977: 385-7; Seymour, 1975: 307-9; Power, 1928: 43-6.

115 Gottlieb, 1985: 357; Bloch, 1987: 6.

116 Blamires, 1992: 193, 196-7; Van Hamel, 1892: 199-200.

117 Blamires, 1992: 100-3, 228-32.

118 Baker, 1991; Walker, 1992: 165-6, 175.

119 Utley, 1972: 218-21; Delany, 1974.

120 Martin, 1990: 219-20; McNamara, 1973.

121 Like Chaucer's Clerk, the Goodman recognised that husbands would be foolish to test their wives wife as Walter did Griselda. Power, 1928: 44-5, 112-38, 188-91, 320 n.; Daileader, 1994: 26, 38.

122 Maclean, 1980: 57-60.

Chaucer:
validity in interpretation

Chalcidius's 'admitted principle of interpretation was one which makes an author more liable to be misrepresented the more he is revered. In hard places, he holds, we must always attribute to Plato whatever sense appears "worthiest the wisdom of so great an authority"; which inevitably means that all the dominant ideas of the commentator's own age will be read into him.' (Lewis, 1971: 52)

IT would seem that on virtually every aspect of Chaucer's work, his readers are currently assailed by a host of mutually exclusive interpretations and critical approaches. On the one hand, Chaucer's poetry offers a conservative defence of traditional social hierarchies. On the other, the dialogic nature of his work undermines any notion of harmonious social order. On the one hand, Chaucer is an Augustinian allegorist; on the other, he is sceptical about exegesis as a mode of interpretation and satirises the excesses of moral allegorising. On the one hand, he is a misogynist; on the other, he a defender of women. That each critical school of thought constructs a Chaucer in its own image is nowhere clearer than in the competing interpretations of the Wife of Bath currently on offer to us. Alisoun is seen as at once a 'fully credible' late medieval figure and also a classic expression of Chaucer's adaptation of inherited literary forms. She is both an instance of Chaucer's monologic reaffirmation of established gender inequalities and a perfect illustration of the dialogic, unresolved, multiple perspectives which characterise his work. For some critics, the Wife is a convincing character who, in her own inimitable manner of speech, speaks not just for herself but also 'for many poets of all eras'. For others, her portrait is the product of a historically specific mode of allegorical writing by whose conventions she is not a character in the modern sense at all. It would thus seem that, as Cooper puts it, there is less critical consensus on what Chaucer was doing than for any other English writer.[1]

It is certainly possible to see why the *Canterbury Tales* have been susceptible to such a range of interpretations. Firstly, in rejecting an hortatory mode of writing, Chaucer tended to eliminate explicit sententiousness and didacticism and so, as Geoffrey of Vinsauf put it, left it to the discretion of the wise man to observe 'what is said through what is left unsaid'. As a result, Chaucer frequently allows us to interpret his characters *in bono* or *in malo* according to our own values, values which in the case of the modern reader are quite likely to differ from those of a court-poet of the late fourteenth century. Chaucer's portrait of the Wife of Bath can thus be read as a witty debunking of the official Church teaching of her day or, alternatively, as the supreme embodiment of such teaching.[2] Secondly, even when Chaucer *does* provide us with explicit judgements, we are always free to read them ironically or by 'antiphrasis' so that they come to mean 'the very opposite of what they say': when Chaucer tells us that the Monk's opinion was good, 'he certainly means that he thinks it was bad'. The variety of forms of irony to be found within the *Canterbury Tales* in general is now a critical commonplace. The difficulty is that the identification of any particular part of the text as ironic is extremely problematic. When Chaucer describes the Nun's Priest as brawny and vigorous, should we accept that 'the opposite is implied'? When Theseus is described as a noble ruler, does this mean that he is really a tyrant?[3] Thirdly, in literary criticism, as in history or the natural sciences, we never passively receive information and evidence but, inevitably, have to order it in line with our own particular theoretical interests and methodological presuppositions. As the Wife of Bath's lion said when presented with a picture of a man killing a lion: 'Who peyntede the leon, tel me who?' (*CT*, III: 692). The problem is that as a result of the (unavoidable) process of bringing our own conceptions and theories to bear on Chaucer's text, his work tends to become simply a mirror for its readers: when a patristic critic looks into it, he does not expect to see a humanist peering back at him.

If it is clear why Chaucer's work has been interpreted in such contradictory ways, it is far more difficult to decide whether we can prefer one reading of his work to another on any rational grounds. For some theorists, it would be foolish to seek such a consensus about any particular literary interpretation. For Stanley Fish, to set out conflicting opinions of the Wife of Bath as I have done here is profoundly misleading because it gives the impression that such disagreements could be resolved: 'such problems do not exist to be solved but to be experienced'. Conflicts of literary interpretation can never be settled: 'any procedure that attempts to determine which of a number of readings is correct will necessarily fail'.

Meaning is not something inherent in the words of the text which is then passed on to the reader. Readers do not simply discover pre-existing meanings but instead actively construct meanings out of the pliable raw material of the text. Such readings are not, however, based merely on individual whim but are the products of the methods and critical assumptions common to particular 'interpretive communities' of readers. Some people adopt the reading strategies of the interpretive community of patristic criticism, others adopt those of liberal humanism; each is simply doomed to talk past the other.[4] Christine de Pizan anticipated this view in the early fifteenth-century debate about the meaning of the *Roman de la Rose*: 'I don't know why we are debating these questions so fully, for I do not believe that we will be able to change each other's opinions'.[5] Some critics argue that it is this ability 'to explore propositions logically alternative to each other without having to make a choice between them' which is precisely what makes literature distinctive as a mode of discourse and as a means of knowing. Nevertheless, even if this is true of literature itself, any intellectual discipline with claims to producing knowledge of the world, and this includes the discipline of literary criticism, is obliged to make such choices between conflicting propositions. As Umberto Eco put it, 'I accept the statement that a text can have many senses. I refuse the statement that a text can have every sense.'[6]

Here, I have tried to show that the fact that there are innumerable plausible readings of Chaucer does not mean that there are no implausible ones and that, where specific readings are mutually exclusive, it *is* often possible to prefer one reading of Chaucer to another. In particular, I have tried to emphasise the ways in which seeing Chaucer in the context of the political issues, social values, generic conventions and literary theory of his own day can help us to understand the meaning of his work: how he could leave the text of the 'General Prologue' 'open' precisely because the response required of it was more closed than that expected from a modern novel; how the apparent contradictions which make Theseus a problematic figure for the twentieth-century reader may not have presented difficulties for a fourteenth-century audience; how the scepticism of the Nun's Priest has a rather different basis from that of modern scepticism; how the humour of the 'Wife of Bath's Prologue' lies in her unwitting confirmation of the criticisms levelled against women by clerical misogynists; and how the defence of women offered in the 'Tale of Melibee' is very different in nature from the feminist defences of women offered in our own day. Thus, even though Chaucer's poetry rarely addresses the political events of his day in any direct manner, his work still provides us with fascinating historical evidence about contemporary values, sensibilities and ideologies – and the conflicts between them.[7] Chaucer's poetry engages with a wide variety of ethical attitudes and thus (as medieval social theory itself emphasised) with a range of social and political outlooks, from the the Knight's Stoicism and the Parson's stern moralism to the Miller's love of discord and the Wife of Bath's Epicurean sophistry. In particular, Chaucer's work attempts to harmonise and balance outlooks and attitudes which we now are likely to find rather contradictory. In the 'Knight's Tale', he presents this world as a foul prison yet, eventually, is still able to find grounds for optimism and for rejecting despair (*CT*, I: 3061, 3068). In the 'Parson's Tale', he is able to recommend that wives should be humble and obedient whilst, in the 'Tale of Melibee', also urging that wives should correct their husbands' folly when necessary (*CT*, X: 927; VII: 1091-2).

Any historical criticism must attempt to steer steer a middle course between the Scylla of seeing Chaucer's work as conveying timeless truths about literature and humanity and the Charybdis of interpreting his poetry as a direct and immediate reflection of the particular social reality of his day. The tendency to see the Canterbury pilgrims as embodying eternal truths about human nature has a long pedigree in Chaucer studies, going back as far as Dryden's claim in 1700 that 'Mankind is ever the same' so that Chaucer's pilgrims were still to be found, albeit under different names, in the England of his own day. This tradition is continued by modern humanist criticism which sees Chaucer's pilgrims as the portraits of real individuals who are, nevertheless, eternal in their essentials.[8] Paradoxically, the recent rise of post-structuralist literary theory has not put an end to this timeless Chaucer but has simply created a new set of eternal essences which have to be identified within his work. Instead of the complex real-life characters beloved of humanism, we now have divided subjects; instead of seeing literary texts as works of imagination and emotion, we now view them as characterised by unlimited semiosis and the free play of the signifier.[9] But once we know *a priori* that humans are necessarily decentred and divided in their subjectivity, it requires little effort to show that Chaucer's subjects, such as the Wife of Bath, are divided. Once we know *a priori* that the free play of the signifier is an inherent part of textuality, it comes as no surprise to learn that Chaucer's texts are characterised by just this unlimited semiosis. In such cases, as Aers warns us, literary criticism runs the risk of becoming 'a monumentally egoistic and finally tedious projection of our own being onto every other human product, however alien'.[10] Thus, in recent years, Chaucer has been hailed by literary critics not just as the father of English literature but also as a thinker who managed to anticipate the social theory of Marx, the psychology of Freud and Lacan, and the linguistics of Derrida.

Here, by contrast, I have emphasised the alterity of medieval texts and of the presuppositions underlying Chaucer's world-view. In an age which demands 'relevance', an historical perspective suggests to us that the literature of the past may be interesting and relevant 'not because it is "modern", but for exactly the opposite reason: because it is different'.[11] Naturally, in stressing the medieval aspects of Chaucer's world-view, we must reject the 'fallacy of the homogenous past' in which the views of Chaucer can be syllogistically deduced from some uniform medieval mind: 'medieval man believed in social order; Chaucer was a medieval man; therefore Chaucer believed in social order'. We should also beware of the false logic whereby the *differences* between the medieval and the modern periods are reduced to a series of simple *oppositions*: 'modern literature involves psychologically complex characters; medieval literaure is different from modern literature; therefore medieval literature cannot involve psychologically complex characters'. Nevertheless, at the present moment, these fallacies seem to be far less of a danger than that of 'blind modernism', i.e., the belief in a homogeneity of past and present (in human nature, textuality etc.) which is shared by otherwise opposing critical positions.[12]

However, in rejecting a timeless Chaucer (whether in humanist or post-structuralist guise) and insisting on the need to see Chaucer in historically specific terms, we need to avoid the trap of regarding Chaucer's poetry as direct reportage of the social trends of his day. We do not, for instance, have to accept that his portrait of the poor widow in the 'Nun's Priest's Tale' was intended to leave us 'with a growing sense of unease' about her standard of living.[13] On the contrary, Chaucer's work was twice removed from historical reality, refracting the reality of contemporary social relations through a range of literary traditions and conventions and via a variety of ideological positions including, in the case of the Nun's Priest's widow, the virtues of patient poverty. The whole point of such representations of the world is precisely that they do *not* capture historical reality accurately but rather systematically distort and invert it, offering imaginary resolutions to real problems, reducing structural social inequalities to matters of personal morality, and presenting historically specific social arrangements as eternally valid. If it is impossible for literary texts to escape from historical reality, this is not because history, as represented by the Nun's Priest's allusions to the death of Richard I or to the Peasants' Revolt (*CT*, VII: 3348, 3394), constantly threatens to erupt into literature from the outside.[14] Rather, it is because the ideological outlook and literary strategies which constitute the meaning of any text are themselves always profoundly historical in nature. Attempts by literary texts to evacuate the sphere of concrete social relations and inequalities, whether by confining themselves to the domain of the personal on the one hand or by ascending to the realm of the eternal and the spiritual on the other, can never be anything but historically specific in their content and form. We began our survey of historical approaches to Chaucer's work by examining the search for specific historical references in his poetry. We end by concluding that what a contextual approach to Chaucer's work reveals, above all else, is that literary texts are nowhere more historical in their nature than when they seek to pass themselves off as timeless and dehistoricised.

Notes

1 Knight, 1986: 98; Patterson, 1983: 658; Olson, 1986: 235-47; Kiser, 1991: 137-142; Donaldson, 1977: 174; Patterson, 1987: 6-7; Shelley, 1968: 215-21; Burton, 1978: 34-5, 47; Robertson, 1969: 330; Cooper, 1983: 2.
2 Gallo, 1971: 51-3; Evans and Johnson, 1994b: 15; Robertson, 1969: 321-31.
3 Dods, 1883: 105; Fleming, 1984: 190-1; Birney, 1985; Shoaf, 1983: 172; Lumiansky, 1980: 108-9; Kendrick, 1988: 105; Webb, 1947: 296; Jones, 1980: 195.
4 Fish, 1980: 148-9; Freund, 1987: 104-11. Given such views, it is difficult to see why Fish rejects the characterisation of his views as relativist, see Fish, 1980: 174.
5 QR: 140.
6 Kolve, 1984: 155; Eco, 1992b: 141; Popper, 1989: 317.
7 Muscatine, 1972: 126-7; Coleman, 1981: 64-5; Crane, 1987: 20.
8 Brewer, 1978: 167; Parker, 1970; Pearsall, 1986: 132.
9 For the meaning of these phrases, see Sarup, 1988: 4, 14-16, 35-41. Post-structuralist approaches to Chaucer are worthy of a study of their own, one which I hope to offer in a future book.
10 Aers, 1986c: 59; Aers, 1986a: 6-7.
11 Robertson, 1969: viii; Jauss, 1978-9; Zumthor, 1972: 7, 19-20. Given this tendency to modernise Chaucer, the danger which once existed of overselling the strangeness of medieval culture is not now the main cause for critical concern. See Howard, 1972: 104.
12 Minnis, 1982: 9; Hirsch, 1976: 40-1; Dollimore, 1885: 4-5; Minnis, 1988: 7; Zumthor, 1979: 371.
13 Fehrenbacher, 1994: 138.
14 Fehrenbacher, 1994.

SELECT BIBLIOGRAPHY

Introductory works

P. Brown, *Chaucer at Work: the Making of the Canterbury Tales* (London, 1994) offers first-rate practical advice on how to begin reading and making sense of Chaucer's text. A. Blamires, *The Canterbury Tales* (Basingstoke, 1987) provides a brief but extremely useful survey of critical approaches to the tales. H. Cooper, *The Canterbury Tales* (Oxford, 1989) is an excellent companion and handbook to the tales which considers the date, text, genre, sources, structure and themes of each of the tales. The same author's *The Structure of the Canterbury Tales* (London, 1983) is an enthusiastic appreciation of the literary achievement of the *Canterbury Tales* which will inspire any reader to re-open Chaucer's works.

1 Chaucer: real-life observation versus literary convention

M. McKisack's *The Fourteenth Century* (Oxford, 1971) still provides a useful introduction to the period whose readability belies its textbook format. See also J. A. F. Thomson, *The Transformation of Medieval England, 1370-1529* (London, 1983). D. Pearsall, *The Life of Geoffrey Chaucer* (Oxford, 1992) is an excellent life of Chaucer which locates his works in their biographical context. J. M. Manly, *Some New Light on Chaucer* (New York, 1926) is the classic attempt to present Chaucer's work as referring to real-life characters; P. Brown and A. F. Butcher, *The Age of Saturn: Literature and History in the Canterbury Tales* (Oxford, 1991) is a more recent work which seeks to identify historical allusions in the *Canterbury Tales*. W. C. Curry, *Chaucer and the Medieval Sciences* (London, 1960; 2nd edition) is a good introduction to Chaucer's use of medieval science whilst J. Mann, *Chaucer and Medieval Estates Satire* (Cambridge, 1973) emphasises Chaucer's use – and adaptation – of traditional literary conventions.

2 Monologic versus dialogic Chaucer

There are now a number of introductions to the work of Mikhail Bakhtin although his discussions of the monologic and the dialogic text, carnival, Menippean satire and so on are easily accessible in Bakhtin's own works, particularly in his *Problems of Dostoevsky's Poetics* (Ann Arbor, 1973) and *Rabelais and his World* (Bloomington, 1984). On Gower, see the articles by Minnis and Porter in A. J. Minnis, ed., *Gower's Confessio Amantis: Responses and Reassessments* (Cambridge, 1983). For a portrayal of the *Canterbury Tales* as a monologic, conservative work, see P. A. Olson, *The Canterbury Tales and the Good Society* (Princeton, 1986). Dialogic readings of Chaucer are currently more popular, see W. E. Rogers, *Upon the Ways: the Structure of the Canterbury Tales* (English Literary Studies, 36; University of Victoria, Canada, 1986) and H. Cooper, *The Structure of the Canterbury Tales* (London, 1983). P. Knapp, *Chaucer and the Social Contest* (New York, 1990) and D. Aers, *Chaucer, Langland and the Creative Imagination* (London, 1980) emphasise the social and political implications of reading Chaucer dialogically. P. Strohm, 'Form and social statement in Confessio Amantis and the Canterbury Tales', in R. J. Pearcy, *Studies in the Age of Chaucer*, vol. 1 (Norman, 1979) contrasts the monologic Gower with the dialogic Chaucer.

3 Allegorical versus humanist Chaucer

Classic statements of the methods of 'patristic' or 'historical' criticism appear in D. W. Robertson's *A Preface to Chaucer* (Princeton, 1962) and his *Essays in Medieval Culture* (Princeton, 1970). B. F. Huppé, *A Reading of the Canterbury Tales* (New York, 1967) interprets the tales as a whole in terms of the Augustinian doctrine of charity. E. T. Donaldson, *Speaking of Chaucer* (London, 1977) offers a humanist perspective on Chaucer, a perspective which is brought to bear on the 'Nun's Priest's Tale' in D. Pearsall, *The Canterbury Tales* (London, 1985). D. Pearsall's Variorum edition of *The Nun's Priest's Tale* (Norman, 1984) includes an excellent survey of the critical debate on this tale. J. B. Allen *The Ethical Poetic of the Later Middle Ages* (Toronto, 1982) and G. Olson, *Literature as Recreation in the Later Middle Ages* (Ithaca, 1982) offer contrasting – but complementary – accounts of medieval views of the nature and function of literature.

4 Misogynist versus feminist Chaucer

For women's social position in medieval England, see S. H. Rigby, *English Society in the Later Middle Ages* (Basingstoke, 1995). A. Blamires (with K. Pratt, and C. W. Marx), *Woman Defamed and Woman Defended* (Oxford, 1992) is an invaluable anthology which illustrates the range of ways in which medieval writers could discuss feminine nature, whilst medieval views of women also figure prominently in the primary sources gathered together in R. P. Miller, *Chaucer: Sources and Backgrounds* (New York, 1977). Chaucer's views on women have been the subject of a number of books in recent years, each of which adopts rather a different approach. See, for instance, P. Martin, *Chaucer's Women: Nuns, Wives and Amazons* (Basingstoke, 1990), E. T. Hansen, *Chaucer and the Fictions of Gender* (Berkeley, 1992); J. Mann, *Geoffrey Chaucer* (London, 1991) and C. Dinshaw, *Chaucer's Sexual Poetics* (Madison, 1989).

Conclusion

The issue of validity in literary interpretation has been the subject of much debate amongst modern literary theorists. S. Fish, *Is There A Text In This Class?* (Cambridge, Mass., 1980) argues against the possibility of resolving such debates, E. D. Hirsch, *The Aims of Interpretation* (Chicago, 1976) offers a more traditional defence of the possibility of knowledge in interpretation, S. Collini, *Interpretation and Overinterpretation* (Cambridge, 1992) offers a variety of views on this issue, including those of Umberto Eco and Richard Rorty.

REFERENCES

(Original dates of publication are given only when this is particularly relevant for my discussion of the evolution of Chaucer criticism.)

Aers, D. (1975) *Piers Plowman and Christian Allegory* (London).
Aers, D. (1979) 'Criseyde: women in medieval society', *Chaucer Review*, 13.
Aers, D. (1980) *Chaucer, Langland and the Creative Imagination* (London).
Aers, D. (1986a) *Chaucer* (Brighton).
Aers, D., ed. (1986b) *Medieval Literature: Criticism, Ideology and History* (Brighton).
Aers, D. (1986c) 'Reflections on the "allegory of the theologians", ideology and Piers Plowman', in Aers (1986b).
Aers, D. (1988a) 'Introduction', in Aers (1988b).
Aers, D., ed. (1988b) *Community, Gender and Individual Identity: English Writing, 1360-1430* (London).
Aers, D. (1991) Review of Cooper (1989) in *Medium Aevum*, 60.
Alford, J. A. 'Scriptural testament in the Canterbury Tales: the letter takes its revenge', in Jeffrey (1984a).
Allen, J. B. (1969) 'The ironic fruyt: Chauntecleer as *figura*', *Studies in Philology*, 66.
Allen, J. B. (1971) *The Friar as Critic* (Nashville).
Allen, J. B. (1982) *The Ethical Poetic of the Later Middle Ages* (Toronto).
Allen, J. B. and Gallacher, P. (1970) 'Alisoun through the looking glass: or every man his own Midas', *Chaucer Review*, 4.
Althusser, L. (1971) *Lenin and Philosophy and Other Essays* (London).
Anderson, J. J., ed. (1974) *The Canterbury Tales: a Casebook* (London).
Anderson, M. (1980) *Approaches to the History of the Western Family, 1500-1914* (London).
Andreas, J. (1990) '"New science" from "olde bokes": a Bakhtinian approach to the Summoner's Tale', *Chaucer Review*, 25.
Andrew, M. (1989) 'Context and judgement in the General Prologue', *Chaucer Review*, 23.
Armstrong, K., ed. (1991) *The English Mystics of the Fourteenth Century* (London).
Aston, T. H., Coss, P. R., Dyer, C. and Thirsk, J., eds (1983) *Social Relations and Ideas: Essays in Honour of R. H. Hilton* (Cambridge).
Baker, D. N. (1991) 'Chaucer and moral philosophy: the virtuous women of the Canterbury Tales', *Medium Aevum*, 59.
Bakhtin, M. (1973) *Problems of Dostoevsky's Poetics* (Ann Arbor).
Bakhtin, M. (1984) *Rabelais and his World* (Bloomington).
Bakhtin, M. (1986) *Speech Genres and Other Late Essays* (Austin).

Bakhtin, M. (1992) *The Dialogic Imagination* (Austin).

Bakhtin, M. and Medvedev, P. N. (1985) *The Formal Method in Literary Scholarship* (Cambridge, Mass.).

Baldwin, R. (1955) 'The unity of the Canterbury Tales', in Schoeck and Taylor (1960).

Barber, C. L. (1959) *Shakespeare's Festive Comedy* (Princeton).

Barber, R., ed. (1992) *Bestiary: Being an English Version of Bodleian Library, Oxford MS Bodley 764* (London).

Barnum, P. H., ed. (1980) *Dives and Pauper*, vol. I, part 2 (EETS, 280).

Barrell, J. (1988) *Poetry, Language and Politics* (Manchester).

Barron, C. M. (1968) 'The tyranny of Richard II', *Bulletin of the Institute of Historical Research*, 41.

Barron, C. M. (1989) 'The "Golden Age" of women in medieval London', *Reading Medieval Studies*, 15.

Barron, W. R. J., ed. (1974) *Sir Gawain and the Green Knight* (Manchester).

Barron, W. R. J. (1990) *English Medieval Romance* (London).

Barthes, R. (1968) 'L'Effet de Réel', *Communications*, 11.

Bartholomew, B. (1966) *Fortuna and Natura: a Reading of Three Chaucer Narratives* (The Hague).

Baswell, C. (1985) 'The medieval allegorization of the Aeneid: MS Cambridge, Peterhouse 158', *Traditio*, 41.

Bean, J. M. W. (1972) '"Bacheler" and retainer', *Medievalia et Humanistica*, n.s. 3.

Beicher, P. E. (1950) 'Absolon's hair', *Mediaeval Studies*, 12.

Belsey, C. (1980) *Critical Practice* (London).

Bennett, J. A. W. (1966) 'Gower's "honest love"', in Nicholson, (1991).

Bennett, J. M. (1987) *Women in the Medieval English Countryside: Gender and House-hold in Brigstock Before the Plague* (Oxford).

Bennett, T. (1981) *Formalism and Marxism* (London).

Bennett, T. (1990) *Outside Literature* (London).

Benson, C. D. (1968) 'The Knight's Tale as history', *Chaucer Review*, 3.

Benson, L. David (1986) *Chaucer's Drama of Style: Poetic Variety and Contrast in the Canterbury Tales* (Chapel Hill).

Benson, L. D., ed. (1989) *The Riverside Chaucer* (Oxford).

Benson, L. David and Robertson, E., eds (1990) *Chaucer's Religious Tales* (Cambridge).

Besserman, L. (1984) '"Glosynge is a glorious thyng": Chaucer's biblical exegesis', in Jeffrey (1984a).

Besserman, L. (1988) *Chaucer and the Bible* (New York).

Betherum, D., ed. (1965) *Critical Approaches to Medieval Literature* (Columbia).

Birney, E. (1985) *Essays on Chaucerian Irony* (Toronto). Edited by B. Rowland.

Bishop, I. (1968) *Pearl in its Setting* (Oxford).

Bishop, I. (1983) 'Chaucer and the rhetoric of consolation', *Medium Aevum*, 52.

Bishop, I. (1988) *The Narrative Art of the Canterbury Tales* (London).

Blake, K. A. (1973) 'Order and the noble life in Chaucer's Knight's Tale', *Modern Language Quarterly*, 34.

Blake, N. F. (1979) *English Language in Medieval Literature* (London).

Blamires, A. (1987) *The Canterbury Tales* (Basingstoke).

Blamires, A. (1989) 'A Chaucer manifesto', *Chaucer Review*, 24.

Blamires, A., with Pratt, K. and Marx, C. W., eds (1992) *Woman Defamed and Woman Defended* (Oxford).

Blanch, R. J. and Wasserman, J. N. (1986) 'White and red in the Knight's Tale: Chaucer's manipulation of a convention', in Wasserman and Blanch (1986).

Bloch, R. Howard (1987) 'Medieval misogyny', *Representations*, 20.

Bloomfield, M. (1952) *The Seven Deadly Sins* (Michigan).

Bloomfield, M. (1958) 'Symbolism in medieval literature', in Bloomfield (1970).

Bloomfield, M. (1970) *Essays and Explorations: Studies in Ideas, Language and Literature* (Cambridge, Mass.).

Bloomfield, M. (1979) 'The wisdom of the Nun's Priest's Tale', in Vasta and Thundy (1979).

Blum, J. (1978) *The End of the Old Order in Rural Europe* (Princeton).

Boening, R. (1983) 'The Miller's bagpipes: a note on the Canterbury Tales A565-566', *English Language Notes*, 21.

Boitani, P. (1977) *Chaucer and Boccaccio* (Medium Aevum Monograph Series, n.s., 8).

Boitani, P. (1985a) 'Style, iconography and narrative: the lesson of the *Teseida*', in Boitani (1985b).

Boitani, P. (1985b) *Chaucer and the Italian Trecento* (Cambridge).

Boitani, P. (1986) 'Old books brought to life in dreams: The Book of the Duchess, The House of Fame and the Parliament of Fowls', in Boitani and Mann (1986).

Boitani, P and Mann, J., eds (1986) *The Cambridge Chaucer Companion* (Cambridge).

Boitani, P. and Torti, A., eds (1991) *Poetics: Theory and Practice in Medieval English Literature* (Cambridge).

Børch, M. N. (1982) *The Failure of Reason: Experience and Language in Chaucer* (Odense).

Boren, J. L. (1975) 'Alysoun of Bath and the Vulgate "Perfect Wife"', *Neuphilologische Mitteilungen*, 76.

Bornstein, D. (1981-2) 'Antifeminism in Thomas Hoccleve's translation of Christine de Pizan's *Epistre au Dieu d'Amours*', *English Language Notes*, 19.

Bowden, M. (1954) *A Commentary on the 'General Prologue' to the 'Canterbury Tales'* (New York). First published in 1948.

Boyd, B. (1973) *Chaucer and the Medieval Book* (San Marino).

Braddy, H. (1979) 'The French influence on Chaucer', in Rowland (1979).

Braswell-Means, L. (1991) 'A new look at an old patient: Chaucer's Summoner and medieval physiognomia', *Chaucer Review*, 25.

Brewer, D. (1973) *Chaucer* (London).

Brewer, D., ed. (1978) *Chaucer: the Critical Heritage. Volume I: 1385-1837* (London).

Brewer, D. (1979) 'The fabliaux', in Rowland (1979).

Brewer, D., ed. (1990) *Geoffrey Chaucer* (Woodbridge).

Britton, E. (1977) *The Community of the Vill* (Toronto).

Brody, S. N. (1979) 'Truth and fiction in the Nun's Priest's Tale', *Chaucer Review*, 14.

Broes, A. T. (1963) 'Chaucer's disgruntled cleric: the Nun's Priest's Tale', *Publications of the Modern Language Association of America*, 78.

Brown, E. (1974) 'Biblical women and the Merchant's Tale: feminism, anti-feminism and beyond', *Viator*, 5.

Brown, P. and Butcher, A. F. (1991) *The Age of Saturn: Literature and History in the Canterbury Tales* (Oxford).

Brown-Grant, R. (1994) 'Rhetoric and Authority: Christine de Pizan's Defence of Women' (University of Manchester Ph.D. thesis).

Bullough, V. L. (1973) 'Medieval medical and scientific views of women', *Viator*, 4.

Burgess, G. S. and Busby, K., trans. (1986) *The Lais of Marie de France* (Harmondsworth).

Burke, P. (1969) *The Renaissance Sense of the Past* (London).

Burnley, J. D. (1979) *Chaucer's Language and the Philosopher's Tradition* (Cambridge).

Burnley, J. D. (1983) *A Guide to Chaucer's Language* (Basingstoke).

Burns, E. Jane (1993) *Bodytalk: When Women Speak in Old French Literature* (Philadelphia).

Burrow, J. A., ed. (1969) *Geoffrey Chaucer: a Critical Anthology* (Harmondsworth).

Burrow, J. A. (1986) *The Ages of Man* (Oxford).

Burrow, J. A. (1992) *Ricardian Poetry: Chaucer, Gower, Langland and the Gawain Poet* (Harmondsworth).

Burton, T. L. (1978) 'The Wife of Bath's fourth and fifth husbands and her ideal sixth: the growth of a moral philosophy', *Chaucer Review*, 13.

Busby, K. and Kooper, E., eds (1990) *Courtly Literature: Culture and Context* (Amsterdam).

Cadden, J. (1993) *Meanings of Sex Difference in the Middle Ages: Medicine, Science and Culture* (Cambridge).

Caie, G. D. (1984) 'The significance of the marginal glosses in the earliest manuscripts of the Canterbury Tales', in Jeffrey (1984a).

Calin, W. (1980) 'Defense and illustration of *fin amor*: some polemical comments on the Robertsonian approach', in Smith and Snow (1980).

Callinicos, A. (1987) *Making History* (Cambridge).

Carr, E. H. (1970) *What is History?* (Harmondsworth).

Carruthers, M. (1979) 'The Wife of Bath and the painting of lions', in Evans and Johnson (1994a).

Carruthers, M. J. and Kirk, E. D., eds (1982) *Acts of Interpretation: the Text in its Contexts, 700-1600* (Norman).

Casagrande, C. and Kleinhenz, C. (1985) 'Literary and philosophical perspectives on the wheel of the five senses in Longthorpe Tower', *Traditio*, 41.

Chalmers, A. F. (1982) *What is this Thing Called Science?* (Milton Keynes).

Clark, R. P. (1976) 'Doubting Thomas in Chaucer's Summoner's tale', *Chaucer Review*, 11.

Clasby, E. (1979) 'Chaucer's Constance: womanly virtue and the heroic life', *Chaucer Review*, 13.

Clogan, P. M. (1992) 'The Knight's Tale and the ideology of the *roman antique*', *Medievalia et Humanistica*, n.s. 18.

Clopper, L. M. (1990) '*Miracula* and *The Treatise of Miraclis Pleyinge*', *Speculum*, 65.

Coffman, G. R. (1965) 'John Gower in his most significant role', in Vasta (1965).

Coghill, N. (1967) *The Poet Chaucer* (1967).

Coghill, N. and Tolkien, C., eds (1959) *The Nun's Priest's Tale* (London).

Cohen, R., ed. (1974) *New Directions in Literary History* (London).

Coleman, J. (1981) *English Literature in History, 1350-1400: Medieval Writers and Readers* (London).

Coletti, T. (1981) 'The *mulier fortis* and Chaucer's Shupman's Tale', *Chaucer Review*, 15.

Colker, M. L. (1984) 'The lure of hunting, women, chess and tennis', *Speculum*, 59.

Collette, C. P. (1989) 'Umberto Eco, semiotics and the "Merchant's Tale"', *Chaucer Review*, 24.

Collini, S., ed. (1992) *Interpretation and Overinterpretation* (Cambridge).

Cook, J. (1986) 'Carnival and the Canterbury Tales: "Only equals may laugh" (Herzen)', in Aers (1986b).

Cook, J. W. (1978) '"That she was all out of charitee": point and counterpoint in the Wife of Bath's Prologue and Tale', *Chaucer Review*, 13.

Cooper, H. (1983) *The Structure of the Canterbury Tales* (London).

Cooper, H. (1989) *The Canterbury Tales* (Oxford).

Cooper, H. (1990) 'The shape-shiftings of the Wife of Bath', in Morse and Windeatt (1990).

Coopland, G. W., ed. (1949) *The Tree of Battles of Honoré Bonet* (Liverpool).

Coopland, G. W., ed. (1975) *Letter to King Richard II: a Plea Made in 1395 for Peace between England and France* (Liverpool).

Cowgill, J. (1990) 'Patterns of feminine and masculine persuasion in the Melibee and Parson's Tale', in Benson and Robertson (1990).

Craik, T. W. (1964) *The Comic Tales of Chaucer* (London).

Crane, S. (1987) 'Alisoun's incapacity and poetic instability in the Wife of Bath's Tale', *Publications of the Modern Language Association of America*, 102 (1).

Crane, S. (1992) 'The writing lesson of 1381', in Hanawalt (1992).

Crane, S. (1994) *Gender and Romance in Chaucer's Canterbury Tales* (Princeton).

Crone, P. (1989) *Pre-Industrial Societies* (Oxford).

Crow, M. M. and Olson, C. C., eds (1966) *Chaucer Life-Records* (Oxford).

Curley, M. J., trans. (1979) *Physiologus* (Austin).

Curnow, M. C. (1975) 'The *Livre de la Cité des Dames* of Christine de Pisan: a Critical Edition' (Vanderbilt University Ph.D. thesis).

Curry, A. (1993) *The Hundred Years War* (Basingstoke).

Curry, W. C. (1960) *Chaucer and the Medieval Sciences* (2nd edition, London).

Curtius, E. R. (1953) *European Literature and the Latin Middle Ages* (London).

Dahlberg, C. (1954) 'Chaucer's cock and fox', *Journal of English and Germanic Philology*, 53.

Dahlberg, C. (1983) *The Romance of the Rose* (Hanover).

Daileader, C. R. (1994) 'The Thopas–Melibee sequence and the defeat of anti-feminism', *Chaucer Review*, 29.

Dane, J. A. (1980) 'The mechanics of comedy in Chaucer's Miller's Tale', *Chaucer Review*, 14.

David, A. (1976) *The Strumpet Muse: Art and Morals in Chaucer's Poetry* (Bloomington).

Davies, R. T., ed. (1963) *Medieval English Lyrics: a Critical Anthology* (London).

Dean, J. (1984) 'Spiritual allegory and Chaucer's narrative style: three test cases', *Chaucer Review*, 18.

Dean, J. (1989) 'Chaucer's repentance: a likely story', *Chaucer Review*, 24.

Delany, S. (1974) 'Womanliness in the Man of Law's Tale', *Chaucer Review*, 9.

Delany, S. (1990) *Medieval Literary Politics* (Manchester).

Diamond, A. (1977) 'Chaucer's women and women's Chaucer', in Diamond and Edwards (1977).

Diamond, A. and Edwards, L. R., eds (1977) *The Authority of Experience: Essays in Feminist Criticism* (Amherst).

Dinn, R. B. (1990) 'Popular Religion in Late Medieval Bury St Edmunds' (University of Manchester Ph.D. thesis, 2 vols).

Dinshaw, C. (1989) *Chaucer's Sexual Poetics* (Madison).

Dobson, R. B., ed. (1983) *The Peasants' Revolt of 1381* (Basingstoke).

Dods, M., ed. (1883) *The Works of St Augustine: a New Translation*, vol. IX (Edinburgh).

Dollimore, J. (1985) 'Introduction: Shakespeare, cultural materialism and the new historicism', in Dollimore and Sinfield (1985).

Dollimore, J. and Sinfield A., eds (1985) *Political Shakespeare: New Essays in Cultural Materialism* (Manchester).

Donaldson, E. T. (1977) *Speaking of Chaucer* (London).

Donovan, M. J. (1953) 'The moralite of the Nun's Priests's Sermon', *Journal of English and Germanic Philology*, 52.

DuBruck, E. E., ed. (1989) *New Images of Medieval Women* (Lewiston).

Duby, G. (1980) *The Three Orders: Feudal Society Imagined* (Chicago).

Duby, G. (1984) *The Knight, the Lady and the Priest: The Making of Modern Marriage in Medieval France* (London).

Duffy, E. (1990) 'Holy maydens, holy wyfes: the cult of women saints in fifteenth-century and sixteenth-century England', in Sheils and Wood (1990).

Duverger, M. (1972) *The Study of Politics* (London).

Dyer, C. (1981) 'A redistribution of incomes in fifteenth-century England?', in Hilton (1981).

Dyer, C. (1984) 'The social and economic background to the rural revolt of 1381', in Hilton and Aston (1984).

Eagleton. T. (1976) *Criticism and Ideology* (London).

Ebin, L. (1979) 'Chaucer, Lydgate and the "myrie tale"', *Chaucer Review*, 13.

Eco, U. (1984) 'The frames of comic "freedom"', in Sebeok and Erickson (1984).

Eco, U. (1992a) 'Interpretation and history', in Collini (1992).

Eco, U. (1992b) 'Reply', in Collini (1992).

Edwards, A. S. G. (1991) 'Chaucer and the poetics of utterance', in Boitani and Torti (1991).

Eilers, W. (1884) 'Dissertation on the Parson's Tale and the *Somme de Vices et Vertus* of Frère Lorens', *Essays on Chaucer*, Part V (*Chaucer Society*, 2nd series, vol. 19).

Elbow, P. (1975) *Oppositions in Chaucer* (Middletown).

Elliott, D. (1991) 'Dress as mediator between inner and outer self: the pious matron of the high and later middle ages', *Mediaeval Studies*, 53.

Elliott, R. W. (1965) *The Nun's Priest's Tale and the Pardoner's Tale* (Oxford).

Ellis, D. S. (1992) 'Chaucer's devilish Reeve', *Chaucer Review*, 27.

Ellis, R. (1986) *Patterns of Religious Narrative in the Canterbury Tales* (Beckenham).

Emerson, C. (1986) 'The outer word and inner speech: Bakhtin, Vygotsky and the internalisation of language', in Morson (1986a).

Evans, G. R. (1984) *The Language and Logic of the Bible: the Earlier Middle Ages* (Cambridge).

Evans, G. R. (1985) *The Language and Logic of the Bible: the Road to Reformation* (Cambridge).

Evans, R. and Johnson, L., eds (1994a) *Feminist Readings in Middle English Literature* (London).

Evans, R. and Johnson, L., (1994b) 'Introduction', in Evans and Johnson (1994a).

Fehrenbacher, R. W. (1994) '"A yeerd enclosed al aboute": literature and history in the Nun's Priest's tale', *Chaucer Review*, 29.

Fenster, T. S. and Erler, M. C., eds (1990) *Poems of Cupid, God of Love* (Leiden).

Ferrante, J. M. (1975) *Woman as Image in Medieval Literature: from the Twelfth Century to Dante* (New York).

Ferris, S. (1981) 'Chaucer at Lincoln (1387): the Prioress's Tale as a political poem', *Chaucer Review*, 15.

Ferster, J. (1985) *Chaucer on Interpretation* (Cambridge).

Fichte, J. O., ed. (1987) *Chaucer's Frame Tales* (Cambridge).

Fiero, G. K., Pfeffer, W. and Allain, M., eds (1989) *Three Medieval Views of Women* (New Haven).

Fifield. M. (1968) 'The Knight's tale: incident, idea and incorporation', *Chaucer Review*, 3.

Finlayson, J. (1971) 'The satiric mode and the Parson's Tale', *Chaucer Review*, 6.

Finlayson, J. (1992) 'The Knight's Tale: the dialogue of romance, epic and philosophy', *Chaucer Review*, 27.

Fish, S. (1980) *Is There A Text In This Class?* (Cambridge, Mass.).

Fisher, J. H. (1973) 'The three styles of Fragment I of the Canterbury Tales', *Chaucer Review*, 8.

Fleming, J. V. (1966) 'The antifraternalism of the Summoner's Tale', *Journal of English and Germanic Philology*, 65.

Fleming, J. V. (1984) 'Gospel asceticism: some Chaucerian images of perfection', in Jeffrey (1984a).

Fleming, J. V. (1985) 'Chaucer and Erasmus on the pilgrimage to Canterbury: an iconographical speculation', in Heffernan (1985).

Fletcher, A. J. (1983) 'Chaucer's Norfolk Reeve', *Medium Aevum*, 52.

Fletcher, A. J. (1991) '"The unity of the state exists in the agreement of its minds": a fifteenth-century sermon on the three estates', *Leeds Studies in English*, n.s. 22.

Forgacs, D. (1986) 'Marxist literary theories', in Jefferson and Robey (1986).

Forshall, J. and Madden, F., eds (1850) *The Holy Bible Containing the Old and New Testaments with the Apocryphal Books in the Earliest English Versions made from the Latin Vulgate by John Wycliffe and his Followers* (Oxford).

Fourquin, G. (1978) *The Anatomy of Popular Rebellion in the Later Middle Ages* (Amsterdam).

Fowler, D. C. (1977) *The Bible in Early English Literature* (London).

Fremantle, W. H., trans. (1892) *The Principal Works of St Jerome*, in P. Scaff and H. Wace, eds *A Select Library of Nicene and Post-Nicene Fathers of the Christian Church* (second series), VI (Grand Rapids, n.d.).

Freund, E. (1987) *The Return of the Reader* (London).

Friedman, J. B. (1973) 'The Nun's Priest's tale: the preacher and the mermaid's song', *Chaucer Review*, 7.

Friedman, J. B. (1981) 'Another look at Chaucer and the physiognomists', *Studies in Philology*, 78.

Frost, W. (1949) 'An interpretation of Chaucer's Knight's tale', in Anderson (1974).

Furnivall, F. J., ed. (1901) *Robert of Brunne's 'Handlyng Synne'* (EETS, 119).

Fyler, J. M. (1979) *Chaucer and Ovid* (New Haven).

Gallagher, C. (1989) 'Marxism and the New historicsm', in Veeser (1989a).

Gallo, E. (1971) *The Poetria Nova and Its Sources in Early Rhetorical Doctrine* (The Hague).

Ganim, J. M. (1990) *Chaucerian Theatricality* (Princeton).

Gash, A. (1986) 'Carnival against lent: the ambivalence of medieval drama', in Aers (1986c).

Gaylord, A. T. (1974) 'The role of Saturn in the Knight's Tale', *Chaucer Review*, 8.

Georgianna, L. (1990) 'The Protestant Chaucer', in Benson and Robertson (1990).

Giffin, M. (1956) *Studies in Chaucer and his Audience* (Quebec).

Given-Wilson, C., ed. (1993) *The Chronicles of the Revolution, 1397- 1400* (Manchester).

Gleason, M. J. 'Clearing the field: towards a reassessment of Chaucer's use of Trevet in the *Boece*', in Minnis (1987a).

Goodman, A. (1992) *John of Gaunt: the Exercise of Princely Power in Fourteenth-Century Europe* (London).

Gottfried, B. (1985) 'Conflict and relationship, sovereignty and survival: parables of power in the Wife of Bath's Prologue', *Chaucer Review*, 19.

Gottlieb, B. (1985) 'The problem of feminism in the fifteenth century', in Kirshner and Wemple (1985).

Gradon, P. (1971) *Form and Style in Early English Literature* (London).

Graff, G. (1989) 'Co-optation', in Veeser (1989a).

Greenblatt, S. (1992) *Shakespearean Negotiations* (Oxford).

Greene, G. and Kahn, C. (1985a) 'Feminist scholarship and the social construction of woman', in Greene and Kahn (1985b).

Greene, G. and Kahn, C., eds (1985b) *Making a Difference: Feminist Literary Criticism* (London).

Greenhill, E. S. (1954) 'The child in the tree: a study of the cosmological tree in Christian tradition', *Traditio*, 10.

Hadow, G. E. (1914) *Chaucer and his Times* (London).

Haidu, P. (1968) *Aesthetic Distance in Chrétien de Troyes: Irony and Comedy in Cligès and Perceval* (Geneva).

Haldane, J. B. S. (1968) *Science and Life: Essays of a Rationalist* (London).

Hamel, M. (1979) 'The Wife of Bath and a contemporary murder', *Chaucer Review*, 14.

Hamlin, B. F. (1974) 'Astrology and the Wife of Bath: a reinterpretation', *Chaucer Review*, 9.

Hanawalt, B. A., ed. (1992) *Chaucer's England: Literature in Historical Context* (Minneapolis).

Hanawalt, B. A. (1993) *Growing Up in Medieval London* (New York).

Hanna, R. (1989) '*Compilatio* and the Wife of Bath: Latin backgrounds, Ricardian texts', in Minnis (1989).

Hansen, E. T. (1992) *Chaucer and the Fictions of Gender* (Berkeley).

Hardison, O. B., Preminger, A., Kerrane, K. and Golden, L., eds (1974) *Medieval Literary Criticism* (New York).

Hargreaves, H. (1993) 'The Wycliffite *Glossed Gospels* as source: further evidence', *Traditio*, 48.

Haskell, A. S. (1971) 'St Simon in the Summoner's Tale', *Chaucer Review*, 5.

Hatton, T. J. (1968) 'Chaucer's crusading Knight: a slanted ideal', *Chaucer Review*, 3.

Haveley, N. (1979) 'Chaucer's Friar and Merchant', *Chaucer Review*, 13.

Havely, N. (1985) 'Chaucer, Boccaccio and the friars', in Boitani (1985b).

Heffernan, T. J., ed. (1985) *The Popular Literature of Medieval England* (*Tennessee Studies in Literature*, 28) (Knoxville).

Heffernan, T. T. (1990) 'Aspects of the Chaucerian apocrypha: animadversions on William Thynne's edition of the *Plowman's Tale*', in Morse and Windeatt (1990).

Henry, A., ed. (1985) *The Pilgrimage of the Lyfe of the Manhode*, vol. I (EETS, 288).

Hieatt, C. B. (1970) 'The moral of the Nun's Priest's Tale', *Studia Neophilologische*, 42.

Hill, J. M. (1991) *Chaucerian Belief: the Poetics of Reverence and Delight* (New Haven).

Hilton, R. H. (1977) *Bond Men Made Free* (London).

Hilton, R. H., ed. (1981) *Peasants, Knights and Heretics* (Cambridge).

Hilton, R. H. (1985) *Class Conflict and the Crisis of Feudalism* (London).

Hilton, R. H. (1992) *English and French Towns in Feudal Society* (Cambridge).

Hilton, R. H. and Aston, T. S., eds (1984) *The English Rising of 1381* (Cambridge).

Hines, J. (1993) *The Fabliau in English* (London).

Hirsch, E. D. (1976) *The Aims of Interpretation* (Chicago).

Hirschkop, K. (1989) 'Introduction: Bakhtin and cultural theory', in Hirschkop and Shepherd (1989).

Hirschkop, K. and Shepherd, D., eds (1989) *Bakhtin and Cultural Theory* (Manchester).

Holquist, M. (1990) *Bakhtin and his World* (London).

Horrell, J. (1939) 'Chaucer's symbolic plowman', in Schoeck and Taylor (1960).

Hotson, J. Leslie (1924) 'Colfox vs Chauntecleer', in Wagenknecht (1959).

Howard, D. R. (1966) *The Three Temptations: Medieval Man in Search of the World* (Princeton).

Howard, D. R. (1972) 'Medieval poems and medieval society', *Medievalia et Humanistica*, 3.

Howard, D. R. (1976) *The Idea of the Canterbury Tales* (Berkeley).

Howard, D. R. (1987) *Chaucer and the Medieval World* (London).

Hudson, A. (1988) *The Premature Reformation* (Oxford).

Huizinga, J. (1970) *Homo Ludens: a Study of the Play Element in Culture* (London).

Humm, M. (1994) *A Reader's Guide to Contemporary Feminist Literary Criticism* (Hemel Hempstead).

Huppé, B. F. (1959) *Doctrine and Poetry: Augustine's Influence on Old English Poetry* (New York).

Huppé, B. F. (1967) *A Reading of the Canterbury Tales* (New York).

Huppé, B. F. and Robertson, D. W. (1963) *Fruyt and Chaf: Studies in Chaucer's Allegories* (Princeton).

Hussey, M., Spearing, A. C. and Winny, J. (1968) *An Introduction to Chaucer* (Cambridge).

Hussey, M., ed. (1965) *The Nun's Priest's Prologue and Tale* (Cambridge).

Innes, M., trans. (1973) *Ovid: Metamorphoses* (Harmondsworth).

Jacobs, E. C. (1980) 'Further Biblical allusions for Chaucer's Prioress', *Chaucer Review*, 15.

James, M. K. (1955-6) 'A London merchant of the fourteenth century', *Economic History Review*, second series, 8.

Jauss, H. R. (1978-9) 'The alterity and modernity of medieval literature', *New Literary History*, 10.

Jefferson, A. and Robey, D., eds (1986) *Modern Literary Theory: a Comparative Introduction* (London).

Jefferson, B. L. (1917) *Chaucer and the Consolation of Philosophy* (Princeton).

Jeffrey, D. L., ed. (1984a) *Chaucer and Scriptural Tradition* (Ottawa).

Jeffrey, D. L. (1984b) 'Introduction' to Jeffrey (1984a).

Jeffrey, D. L. (1984c) 'Chaucer and Wyclif: Biblical hermeneutic and literary theory in the XIV century', in Jeffrey (1984a).

Johnson, L. (1994) 'Reincarnations of Griselda: contexts for the Clerk's Tale', in Evans and Johnson (1994a).

Jones, G. F. (1955) 'Chaucer and the medieval miller', *Modern Language Quarterly*, 16.

Jones, T. (1980) *Chaucer's Knight: the Portrait of a Medieval Mercenary* (London).

Jordan, R. M. (1967) *Chaucer and the Shape of Creation* (Cambridge, Mass.).

Jordan, R. M. (1987) *Chaucer's Poetics and the Modern Reader* (Berkeley).

Joseph, G. (1970) 'Chaucerian "game" – "earnest" and the "argument of herberage" in the Canterbury Tales', *Chaucer Review*, 5.

Josipovici, G. (1979) *The World and the Book* (Princeton).

Justman, S. (1976) 'Medieval monism and abuse of authority in Chaucer', *Chaucer Review*, 11.

Kane, G. (1982) 'Chaucer, love poetry and romantic love', in Carruthers and Kirk (1982).

Karras, R. M. (1992) 'Gendered sin and misogyny in John of Bromyard's *Summa Predicantium*', *Traditio*, 47.

Kaske, R. E. (1959) 'The Summoner's garleek, onyons and eek lekes', *Modern Language Notes*, 74.

Kaske, R. E. (1962) 'The *Canticum Canticorum* in the Miller's Tale', *Studies in Philology*, 59.

Kaske, R. E. (1963) 'Chaucer and medieval allegory', *E.L.H.: a Journal of English Literary History*, 30.

Kaske, R. E. (1965) 'Patristic exegesis in the criticism of medieval literature: the defence', in Betherum (1965).

Kaske, R. E. (1989) *Medieval Christian Literary Imagery* (Toronto).

Kean, P. M. (1972) *Chaucer and the Making of English Poetry*, vol. II (London).

Keen, M. (1965) *The Laws of War in the Late Middle Ages* (London).

Keen, M. (1990) *English Society in the Later Middle Ages* (Harmondsworth).

Keen, M. 'Chaucer's Knight, the English aristocracy and the crusade', in Scattergood and Sherborne (1983).

Kendrick, L. (1988) *Chaucerian Play: Comedy and Control in the Canterbury Tales* (Berkeley).

Kirkpatrick, R. (1985) 'The wake of the *Commedia*: Chaucer's Canterbury Tales and Boccaccio's *Decameron*', in Boitani (1985b).

Kirshner, J. and Wemple, S. F., eds (1985) *Women of the Medieval World: Essays in Honour of J. H. Mundy* (Oxford).

Kiser, L. J. (1991) *Truth and Textuality in Chaucer's Poetry* (Hanover).

Kittredge, G. L. (1911-12) 'Chaucer's discussion of marriage', in Schoek and Taylor (1960).

Kittredge, G. L. (1915) *Chaucer and his Poetry* (Cambridge, Mass.).

Knapp, P. (1989) 'Alisoun of Bath and the reappropriation of tradition', *Chaucer Review*, 24.

Knapp, P. (1990) *Chaucer and the Social Contest* (New York).

Knight, S. (1973) *Ryming Craftily: Meaning in Chaucer's Poetry* (Sydney)

Knight, S. (1986) *Geoffrey Chaucer* (Oxford).

Knoepflmacher, V. C. (1970) 'Irony through scriptural allision: a note on Chaucer's Prioress', *Chaucer Review*, 4.

Knowles, D., ed. (1972) *Augustine: Concerning the City of God Against the Pagans* (Harmondsworth) (translated by H. Bettenson).

Koff, L. M. (1988) *Chaucer and the Art of Storytelling* (Berkeley).

Kolakowski, L. (1971) *Marxism and Beyond* (London).

Kolve, V. A. (1974) 'Chaucer and the visual arts', in Brewer (1990).

Kolve, V. A. (1984) *Chaucer and the Imagery of Narrative: the First Five Canterbury Tales* (Stanford).

Kristeva, J. (1969) 'Word, dialogue and novel', in Moi (1986).

Krueger, R. L. (1993) *Women Readers and the Ideology of Gender in Old French Verse Romance* (Cambridge).

Ladurie, E. Le Roy (1980) *Carnival: a People's Uprising at Romans, 1579-1580* (London).

Lanham, R. A. (1967) 'Game, play and high seriousness in Chaucer's poetry', *English Studies*, 48.

Lapsley, R. and Westlake, M. (1988) *Film Theory: an Introduction* (Manchester).

Larrain, J. (1979) *The Concept of Ideology* (London).

Lawler, T. (1980) *The One and the Many in the Canterbury Tales* (Hamden).

Lawson, S., trans. (1985) *Christine de Pisan: The Treasure of the City of Ladies, or The Book of the Three Virtues* (Harmondsworth).

Lawton, D. (1985) *Chaucer's Narrators* (Chaucer Studies, XIII; Cambridge).

Leicester, H. Marshall (1982) '"Synne horrible": the Pardoner's exegesis of his tale and

Chaucer's', in Carruthers and Kirk (1982).

Leicester, H. Marshall, (1990) *The Disenchanted Self* (Berkeley).

Lenaghan, R. T. (1963) 'The Nun's Priest's fable', *Publications of the Modern Language Association of America*, 78.

Lentricchia, F. (1989) 'Foucault's legacy – a new historicism?', in Veeser (1989a).

Lévi-Strauss, C. (1972) *Structural Anthropology* (Harmondsworth).

Levy, B. S. and Adams, G. R. (1967) 'Chauntecleer's paradise lost and regained', *Mediaeval Studies*, 29.

Lewis, C. S. (1971) *The Discarded Image* (Cambridge).

Lewis, C. S. (1977) *The Allegory of Love: a Study in Medieval Tradition* (Oxford). First published in 1936.

Lewis, R. E., ed. (1978) *De Miseria Condicionis Humane* (Athens, Gao).

Lodge, D., ed. (1988) *Modern Theory and Criticism: a Reader* (London).

Lodge, D. (1990) *After Bakhtin: Essays on Fiction and Criticism* (London).

Loomis, R. S. (1940) 'Was Chaucer a Laodicean?', in Schoek and Taylor (1960).

Loomis. R. S. (1965) *A Mirror of Chaucer's World* (Princeton).

Lord, M. L. (1992) 'Virgil's *Eclogues*, Nicholas Trevet and the harmony of the spheres', *Mediaeval Studies*, 54.

Lowes, G. L. (1934) *Geoffrey Chaucer* (Oxford).

Lubac, H. (1959a/1959b/1961/1964) *Exégèse Mèdièvale: Les Quatre Sens de L'Ecriture*, 4 parts in 2 vols (Paris).

Lumiansky, R. M. (1980) *Of Sondry Folk: the Dramatic Principle in the Canterbury Tales* (Austin).

Luxton, T. H. (1987) '"Sentence" and "solaas": proverbs and consolation in the Knight's Tale', *Chaucer Review*, 22.

MacCracken, H. M., ed. (1934) *The Minor Poems of John Lydgate*, vol. II (EETS, 192).

Macherey, P. (1978) *A Theory of Literary Production* (London).

Mackenzie, N. (1987) 'Boy into bishop: a festive role reversal', *History Today*, 37/12.

Maclean, I. (1980) *The Renaissance Notion of Woman* (Cambridge).

Maddox, D. and Sturm-Maddox, S., eds (1994) *Literary Aspects of Court Culture: Selected Papers from the Seventh Triennial Congress of the International Courtly Literature Society* (Cambridge).

Makarewicz, M. R. (1953) *The Patristic Influence on Chaucer* (Washington).

Mâle, E. (1972) *The Gothic Image* (New York).

Malone, K. (1951) *Chapters on Chaucer* (Baltimore).

Mandel, J. (1985) 'Courtly love in the Canterbury Tales', *Chaucer Review*, 19.

Manly, J. M. (1907) 'A knight ther was', in Wagenknecht (1959).

Manly, J. M. (1926a) 'Chaucer and the rhetoricians', in Schoeck and Taylor (1960).

Manly, J. M. (1926b) *Some New Light on Chaucer* (New York).

Manly, J. M. and Rickert, E. (1940) *The Text of the Canterbury Tales*, 8 vols (Chicago).

Mann, J. (1973) *Chaucer and Medieval Estates Satire* (Cambridge).

Mann, J. (1975) 'The *Speculum Stultorum* and the *Nun's Priest's Tale*', *Chaucer Review*, 9.

Mann, J. (1986) 'Chance and destiny in Troilus and Criseyde and the Knight's Tale', in Boitani and Mann (1986).

Mann, J. (1991a) *Geoffrey Chaucer* (London).

Mann, J. (1991b) 'The authority of the audience in Chaucer', in Boitani and Torti (1991).

Manning, S. (1960) 'The Nun's Priest's morality and the medieval attitude towards fables', *Journal of English and Germany Philology*, 59.

Manning, S. (1979) 'Rhetoric, game, morality and Geoffrey Chaucer', in Pearcy (1979).

Marchalonis, S. (1974) 'Medieval symbols and the *Gesta Romanorum*', *Chaucer Review*, 8.

Martin, P. (1990) *Chaucer's Women: Nuns, Wives and Amazons* (Basingstoke).

Matthews, W. (1974) 'The Wife of Bath and all her sect', *Viator*, 5.

McAlindon, T. (1986) 'Cosmology, contrariety and the Knight's Tale', *Medium Aevum*, 55.

McCall, J. P. (1979) *Chaucer Among the Gods: the Poetics of Classical Myth* (University Park).

McCash, J. H. (1990) 'Mutual love as a medieval ideal', in Busby and Kooper (1990).

McCoy, B. M., trans. (1974) *The Book of Theseus: Teseida delle Nozze d'Emilia by Giovanni Boccaccio* (New York).

McDermott, T., ed. (1989) *St Thomas Aquinas: Summa Theologiae. A Concise Translation* (London).

McKisack, M. (1971) *The Fourteenth Century* (Oxford).

McNamara, J. (1973) 'Chaucer's use of the epistle of St James in the Clerk's Tale', *Chaucer Review*, 7.

Meale, C. M., ed. (1993) *Women and Literature in Britain, 1150- 1500* (Cambridge).

Meech, S. B. and Allen, H. E., eds (1940) *The Book of Margery Kempe* (EETS, 212).

Mehl, D. (1986) *Geoffrey Chaucer: an Introduction to his Narrative Poetry* (Cambridge).

Meyer, P. (1877) 'Plaidoyer en faveur des femmes', *Romania*, 6.

Meyer, P. (1886) 'La bonté des femmes', *Romania*, 15.

Millard, E. (1989) 'French feminisms', in Mills *et al.* (1989).

Miller, R. P. (1955) 'Chaucer's Pardoner, the scriptural eunuch and the Pardoner's Tale', in Schoeck and Taylor (1960).

Miller, R. P. (1970) 'The Miller's Tale as complaint', *Chaucer Review*, 5.

Miller, R. P. (1977) *Chaucer: Sources and Backgrounds* (New York).

Miller, R. P. (1979) 'Allegory in the *Canterbury Tales*', in Rowland (1979).

Millett, B. and Wogan-Browne, J., eds (1992) *Medieval Religious Prose for Women* (Oxford).

Mills, S., Pearce, L., Spaull, S. and Millard, E. (1989) *Feminist Readings/Feminist Reading* (Hemel Hempstead).

Minnis, A. J. (1980) 'John Gower, *sapiens* in ethics and politics', in Nicholson (1991).

Minnis, A. J. (1982) *Chaucer and Pagan Antiquity* (Cambridge).

Minnis, A. J. ed. (1983a) *Gower's Confessio Amantis: Responses and Reassessments* (Cambridge).

Minnis, A. J. (1983b) '"Moral" Gower and medieval literary theory', in Minnis (1983a).

Minnis, A. J., ed. (1987a) *The Medieval Boethius: Studies in the Vernacular Translations of De Consolatione Philosophiae* (Woodbridge).

Minnis, A. J. (1987b) '"Glosynge is a glorious thynge": Chaucer at work on the Boece', in Minnis (1987a).

Minnis, A. J. (1988) *Medieval Theory of Authorship* (Aldershot).

Minnis, A., ed. (1989) *Latin and Vernacular: Studies in Late Medieval Texts and Manuscripts* (Cambridge).

Minnis, A. (1991a) 'Theorizing the Rose: commentary tradition in the *Querelle de la Rose*', in Boitani and Torti (1991).

Minnis, A. (1991b) '*De vulgari auctoritate*: Chaucer, Gower and the men of great authority', in Yeager (1991).

Minnis, A., Scott, A. B. and Wallace, D., eds (1988) *Medieval Literary Theory and Criticism, c. 100-1375: the Commentary Tradition* (Oxford).

Moffat, D. M., ed. (1908) *The Complaint of Nature by Alain de Lille* (New York).

Mohl, R. (1933) *The Three Estates in Medieval and Renaissance Literature* (Columbia).

Moi, T. (1985) *Sexual/Textual Politics: Feminist Literary Theory* (London).

Moi, T., ed. (1986) *The Kristeva Reader* (Oxford).

Montrose, L. A. (1989) 'Professing the Renaissance: the poetics and politics of culture', in Veeser (1989a).

Morgan, J. J. (1970) 'Chaucer and the *bona matrimonii*', *Chaucer Review*, 4.

Morse, R. and Windeatt, B., eds (1990) *Chaucer Traditions: Studies in Honour of Derek Brewer* (Cambridge).

Morson, G. S., ed. (1986a) *Bakhtin: Essays and Dialogues on his Work* (Chicago)

Morson, G. S. (1986b) 'Preface: perhaps Bakhtin', in Morson (1986a).

Morson, G. S. (1986c) 'Dialogue, monologue and the social: a reply to Ken Hirschkop', in Morson (1986a).

Mousnier, R. (1973) *Social Hierarchies: 1450 to the Present* (London).

Muscatine, C. (1957) *Chaucer and the French Tradition* (Berkeley). Muscatine, C. (1972) *Poetry and Crisis in the Age of Chaucer* (Notre Dame).

Muscatine, C. (1986) *The Old French Fabliaux* (New Haven).

Myles, R. (1994) *Chaucerian Realism* (Cambridge).

Neuse, R. (1962) 'The Knight: the first mover in Chaucer's human comedy', in Burrow (1969).

Neuse, R. (1991) *Chaucer's Dante: Allegory and Epic Theater in the Canterbury Tales* (Berkeley).

Newlyn, E. S. (1989) 'Between the pit and the pedestal: images of Eve and Mary in medieval Cornish drama', in DuBruck (1989).

Newton, J. L. (1989) 'History as usual? Feminism and the "New Historicism"', in Veeser (1989a).

Nicholson, P., ed. (1991) *Gower's Confessio Amantis: a Critical Anthology* (Cambridge).

Nicholson, R. H. (1988) 'Theseus's "ordinaunce": justice and ceremony in the Knight's Tale', *Chaucer Review*, 22.

Nolan, B. (1986) '"A poet ther was": Chaucer's voices in the General Prologue to the Canterbury Tales', *Publications of the Modern Language Association of America*, 101.

Nolan, B. (1992) *Chaucer and the Tradition of the Roman Antique* (Cambridge).

North, J. D. (1988) *Chaucer's Universe* (Oxford).

Norton-Smith, J. (1974) *Geoffrey Chaucer* (London).

Nykrog, P. (1957) *Les Fabliaux* (Copenhagen).

Oberembt, K. J. (1976) 'Chaucer's anti-misogynist Wife of Bath', *Chaucer Review*, 10.

O'Donoghue, B., ed. (1982) *The Courtly Love Tradition* (Manchester).

Oerlemans, O. (1992) 'The seriousness of the Nun''s Priest's Tale', *Chaucer Review*, 26.

Olson, G. (1982) *Literature as Recreation in the Later Middle Ages* (Ithaca).

Olson, P. A. (1986) *The Canterbury Tales and the Good Society* (Princeton).

Olsson, K. (1982) 'Natural law and John Gower's Confessio Amantis', in Nicholson (1991).

Olsson, K. (1992) *John Gower and the Structures of Conversion* (Cambridge).

Owen, C. A. (1973) 'The Tale of Melibee', *Chaucer Review*, 7.

Owen, C. A. (1977) *Pilgrimage and Storytelling in the Canterbury Tales: the Dialectic of 'Ernest' and 'Game'* (Norman).

Owen, C. A. (1991) 'Fictions living fictions: the poetics of voice and genre in Fragment D of the Canterbury Tales', in Boitani and Torti (1991).

Owen, D. D. R., ed. (1994) *The Romance of Reynard the Fox* (Oxford).

Owst, G. R. (1966) *Literature and Pulpit in Medieval England* (Oxford).

Painter, S. (1964) *French Chivalry* (Ithaca).

Palmer, J. N. (1974) 'The historical context of the Book of the Duchess: a revision', *Chaucer Review*, 8.

Parker, D. (1970) 'Can we trust the Wife of Bath?', *Chaucer Review*, 4.

Patterson, L. (1978) 'The Parson's Tale and the quitting of the Canterbury Tales', *Traditio*, 34.

Patterson, L. (1983) '"For the wyves love of Bathe": feminine rhetoric and poetic resolution in the Roman de la Rose and the Canterbury Tales', *Speculum*, 58.

Patterson, L. (1987) *Negotiating the Past: the Historical Understanding of Medieval Literature* (Madison).

Patterson, L. (1991) *Chaucer and the Subject of History* (London).

Payne, F. Anne (1981) *Chaucer and Menippean Satire* (Madison).

Payne, R. O. (1973) *The Key of Remembrance: a Study of Chaucer's Poetics* (Westport).

Pearcy, R. J. (1968) 'The Epilogue of the Nun's Priest's Tale', *Notes and Queries*, 213.

Pearcy, R. J., ed. (1979) *Studies in the Age of Chaucer*, vol. 1 (Norman).

Pearsall, D., ed. (1984) *The Nun's Priest's Tale* (Norman).

Pearsall, D. (1985) *The Canterbury Tales* (London).

Pearsall, D. (1986) 'Chaucer's poetry and its modern commentators: the necessity of history', in Aers (1986b).

Pearsall, D. (1987) 'Versions of comedy in Chaucer's Canterbury Tales', in Fichte (1987).

Pearsall, D. (1992) *The Life of Geoffrey Chaucer* (Oxford).

Peck, R. A. (1967) 'Number symbolism in the Prologue to Chaucer's Parson's Tale', *English Studies*, 48.

Peck, R. A. (1978) *Kingship and Common Profit in Gower's Confessio Amantis* (Carbondale).

Peck, R. A. (1984) 'Biblical interpretation: St Paul and the Canterbury Tales', in Jeffrey (1984a)

Pecora, V. P. (1989) 'The limits of local knowledge', in Veeser (1989a).

Phillips, H. (1993) 'Chaucer and Deguileville: the *ABC* in context', *Medium Aevum*, 62.

Popper, K. R. (1989) *Conjectures and Refutations* (London).

Porter, E. (1983a) 'Gower's ethical microcosm and political macrocosm', in Minnis (1983a).

Porter, E. (1983b) 'Chaucer's Knight, the alliterative *Morte Arthur* and the medieval laws of war: a reconsideration', *Nottingham Mediaeval Studies*, 27.

Power, E. (1922) *Medieval English Nunneries* (Cambridge).

Power, E., ed. (1928) *The Goodman of Paris (Le Ménagier de Paris)* (London).

Power, E. (1975) *Medieval Women* (Cambridge).

Pratt, J., ed. (n.d.) *The Acts and Monuments of John Foxe*, 4th edition (London).

Pratt, J. H. (1987) 'Was Chaucer's Knight really a mercenary?', *Chaucer Review*, 22.

Pratt, K. (1994) 'Analogy or logic; authority or experience? Rhetorical strategies for and against women', in Maddox and Sturm-Maddox (1994).

Pratt, R. A. (1966) 'Chaucer and the hand that fed him', *Speculum*, 41.

Prince, S. (1991) *The Warrior's Cinema: the Films of Akira Kurosawa* (Princeton).

Radice, B., trans. (1974) *The Letters of Abelard and Heloise* (Harmondsworth).

Rawski, C. H., ed. (1991) *Petrarch's Remedies for Fortune Fair and Foul*, 5 vols (Bloomington).

Razi, Z. (1979) 'The Toronto School's reconstitution of medieval peasant society: a critical view', *Past and Present*, 85.

Razi, Z. (1983) 'The struggles between the abbots of Halesowen and their tenants in the thirteenth and fourteenth centuries', in Aston *et al.* (1983).

Reid, D. S. (1970) 'Crocodilian humour: a discussion of Chaucer's Wife of Bath', *Chaucer Review*, 4.

Reiss, E. (1979) 'Chaucer and medieval irony', in Pearcy (1979).

Reiss, E. (1980) 'Chaucer and his audience', *Chaucer Review*, 14.

Reiss, E. (1984) 'Biblical parody: Chaucer's "distortions" of Scripture', in Jeffrey (1984a).

Richards, E. J., trans. (1983) *Christine de Pizan: The Book of the City of Ladies* (London).

Rickert, E. (1926-7) 'Extracts from a fourteenth-century account book', *Modern Philology*, 24.

Riddy, F. (1993) '"Women talking about the things of God": a late medieval subculture', in Meale (1993).

Rigby, S. H. (1983) 'Boston and Grimsby in the Middle Ages' (University of London Ph.D. thesis).

Rigby, S. H. (1987) *Marxism and History: a Critical Introduction* (Manchester).

Rigby, S. H. (1992) *Engels and the Formation of Marxism* (Manchester).

Rigby, S. H. (1995) *English Society in the Later Middle Ages: Class, Status and Gender* (Basingstoke).

Rimbault, E. F. (1875) 'An account of the festival of the boy-bishop in England', *Camden Miscellany* (Camden Society, n.s. 14).

Roberts, P. B. (1985) 'Stephen Langton's *Sermo de Virginibus*', in Kirshner and Wemple (1985).

Robertson, D. W. (1968) *Chaucer's London* (New York).

Robertson, D. W. (1969) *A Preface to Chaucer* (Princeton). First published in 1962.

Robertson, D. W. (1970) *Essays in Medieval Culture* (Princeton).

Robertson, D. W. (1974) 'Some observations on method in literary studies', in Cohen (1974).

Robertson, D. W. (1980) '"And for my land thus hastow mordred me?"': land tenure, the cloth industry and the Wife of Bath', *Chaucer Review*, 14.

Robertson, D. W. (1984) 'Chaucer and Christian tradition', in Jeffrey (1984a).

Robertson, D. W. (1985) 'Who were "the people"?', in Heffernan (1985).

Robey, D. (1986) 'Anglo-American New Criticism', in Jefferson and Robey (1986).

Rogers, W. E. (1980) 'The raven and the writing desk: the theoretical limits of patristic criticism', *Chaucer Review*, 14.

Rogers, W. E. (1986) *Upon the Ways: the Structure of the Canterbury Tales* (English Literary Studies, 36; University of Victoria, Canada).

Rooney, A. (1989) *Geoffrey Chaucer: a Guide Through the Critical Maze* (Bristol).

Root, J. (1994) '"Space to speke": the Wife of Bath and the discourse of confession', *Chaucer Review*, 28.

Rosenberg, B. A. (1980) 'The Bari widow and the Franklin's Tale', *Chaucer Review*, 14.

Ross, W. O., ed. (1940) *Middle English Sermons* (EETS, 209).

Rowland, B. (1970) 'The play of the Miller's Tale', *Chaucer Review*, 5.

Rowland, B. (1971) *Blind Beasts: Chaucer's Animal World* (Kent, Ohio).

Rowland, B., ed. (1979) *Companion to Chaucer Studies* (New York).

Rowland, B., ed. (1981) *Medieval Woman's Guide to Health* (London).

Rowland, B. (1985) 'Seven kinds of irony', in Birney (1985).

Rowland, B. (1986) 'Chaucer's working wyf: the unraveling of a yarn-spinner', in Wasserman and Blanch (1986).

Ruggiers, P. G. (1967) *The Art of the Canterbury Tales* (Madison).

Ryan, C., ed. (1989) *Dante: the Banquet* (Saratoga).

Ryan, K. (1989) *Shakespeare* (Hemel Hempstead).

Salter, E. (1983) *Fourteenth-Century English Poetry: Contexts and Readings* (Oxford).

Salu, M. B., trans. (1990) *The Ancrene Riwle* (Exeter).

Sanderlin, S. (1988) 'Chaucer and Ricardian politics', *Chaucer Review*, 22.

Sarup, M. (1988) *An Introductory Guide to Post-Structuralism and Postmodernism* (Hemel Hempstead).

Scase, W. (1989) *Piers Plowman and the New Anti-Clericalism* (Cambridge).

Scattergood, V. J. (1975) *The Works of Sir John Clanvowe* (Cambridge).

Scattergood, V. J. (1991) 'George Ashby's Prison Reflections and the virtue of patience', *Nottingham Medieval Studies*, 37.

Scattergood, V. J. and Sherborne, J. W., eds (1983) *English Court Culture in the Later Middle Ages* (London).

Scheps, W. (1970) 'Chaucer's anti-fable: *reductio ad absurdam* in the Nun's Priests's Tale', *Leeds Studies in English*, n.s. 4.

Schibanoff, S. (1986) '"Taking the gold out of Egypt": the art of reading as a woman', in Evans and Johnson (1994a).

Schoek, R. and Taylor, J., eds (1960) *Chaucer Criticism, volume I: The Canterbury Tales* (Notre Dame).

Sebeok, T. A. and Erickson, M. E., eds (1984) *Carnival!* (Approaches to Semiotics, 64) (Berlin).

Seymour, M. C., ed. (1975) *On the Properties of Things*, 2 vols (Oxford).

Seymour, M. C., ed. (1981) *Selections from Hoccleve* (Oxford).

Shahar, S. (1983) *The Fourth Estate: a History of Women in the Middle Ages* (London).

Shahar, S. (1992) *Childhood in the Middle Ages* (London).

Shallers, A. Paul (1975) 'The Nun's Priest's Tale: an ironic *exemplum*', *E.L.H.: a Journal of English Literary History*, 42.

Sheils, W. J. and Wood, D., eds (1990) *Women in the Church* (Studies in Church History, 27).

Shelley, P. van Dyke (1968) *The Living Chaucer* (New York).

Shoaf, R. A. (1983) *Dante, Chaucer and the Currency of the Word* (Norman).

Shumaker, W. (1951) 'Alisoun in wander-land: a study in Chaucer's mind and literary method', *E.L.H.: a Journal of English Literary History*, 18.

Sisam, K., ed. (1962) *Fourteenth Century Verse and Prose* (Oxford).

Sklute, L. (1984) *Virtue of Necessity: Inconclusiveness and Narrative Form in Chaucer's Poetry* (Columbus).

Smalley, B. (1960) *English Friars and Antiquity in the Early Fourteenth Century* (Oxford).

Smalley, B. (1964) *The Study of the Bible in the Middle Ages* (Notre Dame).

Smalley, B. (1981) *Studies in Medieval Thought and Learning: From Abelard to Wyclif* (London).

Smith, B. H. (1966) *Traditional Imagery of Charity in Piers Plowman* (The Hague).

Smith, N. B. and Snow, J. T., eds (1980) *The Expansion and Transformation of Courtly Literature* (Athens, Gao).

Smith, S. L. (1990) 'The power of women *topos* on a fourteenth-century embroidery', *Viator*, 21.

Spearing, A. C., ed. (1966) *The Knight's Tale* (Cambridge).

Specht, H. (1981) *Chaucer's Franklin in the Canterbury Tales* (Copenhagen).

Speirs, J. (1951) *Chaucer the Maker* (London).

Spencer, W. (1970) 'Are Chaucer's pilgrims keyed to the signs of the zodiac?', *Chaucer Review*, 4.

Spiegel, H., ed. (1987) *Marie de France: Fables* (Toronto).

Spisak, J. (1980) 'Anti-feminism unbridled: two rhetorical contexts', *Neuphilologische Mitteilungen*, 81.

Steele, R. (1898) *The Prose Versions of the Secreta Secretorum*, vol. I (EETS, extra series, 74).

Stephens, D. (1989) 'History at the margins: bagpipes in medieval manuscripts', *History Today*, 39/8.

Strohm. P. (1979) 'Form and social statement in Confessio Amantis and the Canterbury Tales', in Pearcy (1979).

Strohm, P. (1989) *Social Chaucer* (Cambridge, Mass.).

Strohm, P. (1992) *Hochon's Arrow: the Social Imagination of Fourteenth-Century Texts* (Princeton).

Swanson, J. (1989) *John of Wales: a Study of the Works and Ideas of a Thirteenth-Century Friar* (Cambridge).

Swanton, M. (1987) *English Literature Before Chaucer* (London).

Szittya, P. R. (1977) 'The antifraternal tradition in Middle English literature', *Speculum*, 52.

Szittya, P. R. (1986) *The Antifraternal Tradition in Medieval Literature* (Princeton).

Tachau, K. H. (1991) 'Looking gravely at Dominican puns: the "Sermons" of Robert Holcot and Ralph Friseby', *Traditio*, 46.

Taitt, P. S. (1975) *Incubus and Ideal: Ecclesiastical Figures in Chaucer and Langland* (Salzburg: Elizabethan and Renaissance Studies, 44).

Taylor, F. and Roskell, J. S., eds (1975) *Gesta Henrici Quinti* (Oxford).

Thundy, Z. P. (1979) 'Matheolus, Chaucer and the Wife of Bath', in Vasta and Thundy (1979).

Todorov, T. (1984) *Mikhail Bakhtin: the Dialogical Principle* (Manchester).

Tuck, A. (1973) *Richard II and the English Nobility* (London).

Tuck, A. (1985) *Crown and Nobility, 1272-1461* (Oxford).

Tyerman, C. (1988) *England and the Crusades, 1095-1588* (Cambridge).

Underwood, D. (1959) 'The first of the Canterbury Tales', *E.L.H.: a Journal of English Literary History*, 26.

Utley, F. L. (1965) 'Robertsonianism redivivus', *Romance Philology*, 19.

Utley, F. L. (1972) 'Five genres in the Clerk's Tale', *Chaucer Review*, 6.

Van, T. A. (1994) 'False texts and disappearing women in the Wife of Bath's Prologue and Tale', *Chaucer Review*, 29.

Van Hamel, A. G., ed. (1892, 1905) *Les Lamentations de Matheolus et le Livre de Leesce de Jehan de Fèvre de Resson* (Paris, 2 vols).

Varty, K. (1967) *Reynard the Fox: a Study of the Fox in Medieval English Art* (Leicester).

Vasta, E., ed. (1965) *Middle English Survey* (Notre Dame).

Vasta, E. and Thundy, Z. P., eds (1979) *Chaucerian Problems and Perspectives: Essays Presented to Paul E. Beichner* (Notre Dame).

Veeser, H. Aram, ed. (1989a) *The New Historicism* (New York).

Veeser, H. Aram (1989b) 'Introduction' to Veeser (1989a).

Volosinov, V. N. (1986) *Marxism and the Philosophy of Language* (Cambridge, Mass.).

Voltaire, F. M. A. (1972) *Candide* (Harmondsworth). Translated by J. Butt.

Wagenknecht, E., ed. (1959) *Chaucer: Modern Essays in Criticism* (New York).

Walker, C. Bynum (1992) *Fragmentation and Redemption: Essays on Gender and the Human Body in Medieval Religion* (New York).

Walker, D. (1985) 'The psychological realism of fictional characters: another perspective', *Neuphilologische Mitteilungen*, 86.

Warner, M. (1985) *Alone of All Her Sex* (London).

Wasserman, J. N. and Blanch, R. J., eds (1986) *Chaucer in the Eighties* (Syracuse).

Watson, C. S. (1964) 'The relationship of the Monk's Tale to the Nun's Priest's Tale', *Studies in Short Fiction*, 1.

Waugh, S. L. (1991) *England in the Reign of Edward III* (Cambridge).

Webb, H. J. (1947) 'A reinterpretation of Chaucer's Theseus', *Review of English Studies*, 23.

Weissman, H. P. (1980) 'Why Chaucer's Wife is from Bath', *Chaucer Review*, 15.

Wenzel, S. (1967) 'The three enemies of man', *Mediaeval Studies*, 29.

Wenzel, S. (1973) 'The pilgrimage of life as a late medieval genre', *Mediaeval Studies*, 35.

Wenzel, S., ed. (1989) *Fasciculus Morum: a Fourteenth-Century Preacher's Handbook* (University Park).

Wetherbee, W. (1991) 'Latin structure and the vernacular space: Gower, Chaucer and the Boethian tradition', in Yeager (1991).

Whittock, T. (1968) *A Reading of the Canterbury Tales* (Cambridge).

Wickert, M. (1981) *Studies in John Gower* (Washington).

Wilcockson, C. (1992) 'A note on Chaucer's Prioress and her literary relationship with the Wife of Bath', *Medium Aevum*, 60.

Williams, A. (1953) 'Chaucer and the friars', *Speculum*, 28.

Williams, A. (1956-7) 'Two notes on Chaucer's friars', *Modern Philology*, 54.

Williams, G. (1965) *A New View of Chaucer* (Durham, N.C.).

Wilson, K. M. (1985) 'Chaucer and St Jerome: the use of "barley" in the Wife of Bath's Prologue', *Chaucer Review*, 19.

Wilson, K. M. and Makowski, E. M. (1990) *Wykked Wyves and the Woes of Marriage: Misogamous Literature from Juvenal to Chaucer* (Albany).

Winny, J. (1968) 'Chaucer's science', in Hussey, Spearing and Winny (1968).

Wirtjes, H., ed. (1991) *The Middle English Physiologus* (EETS, 299).

Wood, C. (1970) *Chaucer and the Country of the Stars* (Princeton).

Wood, C. (1971) 'The source of Chaucer's Summoner's "Garleek, oynons and eek lekes"', *Chaucer Review*, 5.

Wood, C. (1984) 'Artistic intention and Chaucer's use of scriptural allusion', in Jeffrey (1984a).

Wood, C. (1991) 'Chaucer's most "Gowerian" tale', in Yeager (1991).

Wood, C. T. (1981) 'The doctor's dilemma: sin, salvation and the menstrual cycle in medieval thought', *Speculum*, 54.

Wood, J. (1995) 'Blooming great' (review of H. Bloom's *The Western Canon*), *The Guardian*, 7 February 1995.

Wright, T., ed. (1839) *The Political Songs of England, from the Reign of John to that of Edward II* (Camden Society, 6).

Wright, T., ed. (1859) *Political Poems and Songs Relating to English History*, I (London: Rolls Series).

Wright, T., ed. (1872) *The Anglo-Latin Satirical Poets and Epigrammatists of the Twelfth Century*, vol. I (London: Rolls Series).

Wurtele, D. (1984) 'Chaucer's Canterbury Tales and Nicholas of Lyre's *Postillae litteralis et moralis super totam Bibliam*', in Jeffrey (1984a).

Yates, D. (1983) 'Chanticleer's latin ancestors', *Chaucer Review*, 18.

Yeager, R. F. (1990) *John Gower's Poetic: the Search for a New Arion* (Cambridge).

Yeager, R. F., ed. (1991) *Chaucer and Gower: Difference, Mutuality and Exchange* (Victoria).

Zatta, J. D. (1994) 'Chaucer's Monk: a mighty hunter before the lord', *Chaucer Review*, 29.

Zumthor, P. (1972) *Essai de Poétique Médiévale* (Paris).

Zumthor, P. (1979) 'Comments on H. R. Jauss's article', *New Literary History*, 10.

Zupitza, J., ed. (1883) *The Romance of Guy of Warwick, part I* (EETS, Extra Series, 42).

INDEX